Toni Schindler Zimmerman, PhD
Editor

Balancing Family and Work: Special Considerations in Feminist Therapy

Balancing Family and Work: Special Considerations in Feminist Therapy has been co-published simultaneously as *Journal of Feminist Family Therapy*, Volume 13, Numbers 2/3 2001.

The Haworth Press, Inc.
New York

Balancing Family and Work:
Special Considerations
in Feminist Therapy

Balancing Family and Work: Special Considerations in Feminist Therapy has been co-published simultaneously as *Journal of Feminist Family Therapy*, Volume 13, Numbers 2/3 2001.

The *Journal of Feminist Family Therapy (An International Forum)* Monographic "Separates"

Below is a list of "separates," which in serials librarianship means a special issue simultaneously published as a special journal issue or double-issue *and* as a "separate" hardbound monograph. (This is a format which we also call a "DocuSerial.")

"Separates" are published because specialized libraries or professionals may wish to purchase a specific thematic issue by itself in a format which can be separately cataloged and shelved, as opposed to purchasing the journal on an on-going basis. Faculty members may also more easily consider a "separate" for classroom adoption.

"Separates" are carefully classified separately with the major book jobbers so that the journal tie-in can be noted on new book order slips to avoid duplicate purchasing.

You may wish to visit Haworth's Website at . . .

http://www.HaworthPress.com

. . . to search our online catalog for complete tables of contents of these separates and related publications.

You may also call 1-800-HAWORTH (outside US/Canada: 607-722-5857), or Fax 1-800-895-0582 (outside US/Canada: 607-771-0012), or e-mail at:

getinfo@haworthpressinc.com

Balancing Family and Work: Special Considerations in Feminist Therapy, edited by Toni Schindler Zimmerman, PhD (Vol. 13, No. 2/3, 2001). *"A MUST FOR MANY CLASSROOMS . . . Relevant for family studies courses as well as clinical courses. This book covers a lot of ground. It's personal, political, conceptual, and clinical. It tells personal stories, discusses these people's struggles, and reports important research . . . An excellent introduction to the issues." (Volker, Thomas, PhD, Associate Professor and Director, Marriage and Family Therapy Program, Purdue University, West Lafayette, IN)*

Integrating Gender and Culture in Family Therapy Training, edited by Toni Schindler Zimmerman, PhD (Vol. 12, No. 2/3 and 4, 2001). *"ENGAGING . . . . THE PREDOMINANT THEME IS INFUSION, NOT JUST INCLUSION. In a time when trainers, supervisors, trainees, supervisees, and clients are increasingly likely to come from diverse cultural backgrounds, this book will serve to keep us engaged in dialogue that addresses our own sexism, racism, and homophobia, and broadens our own cultural and gender lenses." (Janie Long, PhD, MFT Faculty, Purdue University, Indiana)*

Feminism, Community, and Communication, edited by Mary W. Olson, PhD, LICSW (Vol. 11, No. 4, 2000). *This important book rethinks therapy, research, teaching, and community work with a renewed emphasis on collaboration, intersubjectivity, and the process of communications as a world-making and identity-making activity. The issues of gender, culture, religion, race, and class figure prominently in this valuable book.*

Transformations of Gender and Race: Family and Developmental Perspectives, edited by Rhea V. Almeida, LCSW, DVS (Vol. 10, No. 1, 1998/99). *Offers superb contemporary thinking in cultural studies, post-colonial theory, gender theory, queer theory, and clinical and research work with numerous populations who have been overlooked and undertheorized.*

Reflections on Feminist Family Therapy Training, edited by Kathy Weingarten, PhD, and Michele Bograd, PhD (Vol. 8, No. 2, 1996). *"Those new to a feminist perspective on family therapy will find their eyes widened; experienced trainers will become immersed in the subjective dialogue." (Kathleen McGuire, PhD, Center for the Study of Women in Society, University of Oregon)*

Cultural Resistance: Challenging Beliefs About Men, Women, and Therapy, edited by Kathy Weingarten, PhD (Vol. 7, No. 1/2, 1995). *"It explores the possibilities for therapy to act in resistance to culturally contructed and dominant narratives that constrain therapists and our clients." (Australian New Zealand Journal of Family Therapy)*

Ethical Issues in Feminist Family Therapy, edited by Maryhelen Snyder, PhD (Vol. 6, No. 3, 1995). *"These deeply felt and tightly reasoned chapters . . . illuminate therapist positions that are more likely to foster just relations." (Kathy Weingarten, PhD, Co-Director, Program in Narrative Therapies, Family Institute of Cambridge, MA)*

Expansions of Feminist Family Theory Through Diversity, edited by Rhea V. Almeida, LCSW, DVS (Vol. 5, No. 3/4, 1994). *"Represents an important turning point in the history of family therapy. The authors explicitly address fundamental power differentials–based on race, gender, social class, and sexual orientation–that organize life for all families in America." (Robert-Jay Green, PhD, Professor and Coordinator of Family/Child Psychology Training, California School of Professional Psychology, Berkeley)*

Feminism and Addiction, edited by Claudia Bepko, MSW (Vol. 3, No. 3/4, 1992). *"Provides valuable clinical information for therapists working with alcohol- and drug-addicted women. It describes methods of therapeutic training and intervention based on an integration of feminist theory and other major theories that expand the boundaries of treatment for addicted women." (Contemporary Psychology)*

Feminist Approaches for Men in Family Therapy, edited by Michele Bograd, PhD (Vol. 2, No. 3/4, 1991). *"A new offering that marriage and family therapists will find to be a valuable addition and resource." (Journal of Family Psychotherapy)*

Balancing Family and Work: Special Considerations in Feminist Therapy

Toni Schindler Zimmerman
Editor

Balancing Family and Work: Special Considerations in Feminist Therapy has been co-published simultaneously as *Journal of Feminist Family Therapy*, Volume 13, Numbers 2/3 2001.

The Haworth Press, Inc.
New York • London • Oxford

Balancing Family and Work: Special Considerations in Feminist Therapy has been co-published simultaneously as *Journal of Feminist Family Therapy*™, Volume 13, Numbers 2/3 2001.

Cover design by Thomas J. Mayshock Jr.

Library of Congress Cataloging-in-Publication Data

Balancing family and work : special considerations in feminist therapy /
    Toni Schindler Zimmerman, editor.
      p. cm.
    "Co-published simultaneously as Journal of feminist family therapy, volume 13, numbers 2/3 2001."
    Includes bibliographical references and index.
    ISBN 0-7890-1734-2 (alk. paper) – ISBN 0-7890-1735-0 (pbk. : alk. paper)
    1. Family psychotherapy. 2. Feminist therapy. I. Zimmerman, Toni Schindler.
RC488.5 .B325 2002
616.89'156–dc21
                                       2002004063

Indexing, Abstracting & Website/Internet Coverage

This section provides you with a list of major indexing & abstracting services. That is to say, each service began covering this periodical during the year noted in the right column. Most Websites which are listed below have indicated that they will either post, disseminate, compile, archive, cite or alert their own Website users with research-based content from this work. (This list is as current as the copyright date of this publication.)

Abstracting, Website/Indexing Coverage . . . . Year When Coverage Began

- *Alternative Press Index (print, online, & CD-ROM from NISC) <www.altpress.org>* **1995**
- *Applied Social Sciences Index & Abstracts (ASSIA) (Online: ASSI via Data-Star) (CD-ROM ASSIA Plus) <www.csa.com>* **1996**
- *CNPIEC Reference Guide: Chinese National Directory of Foreign Periodicals* **1995**
- *Contemporary Women's Issues* **1998**
- *e-psyche, LLC <www.e-psyche.net>* **2001**
- *Family Index Database <www.familyscholar.com>* **2001**
- *Family & Society Studies Worldwide <www.nisc.com>* **1996**
- *Family Violence & Sexual Assault Bulletin* **1992**
- *Feminist Periodicals: A Current Listing of Contents* **1992**
- *FINDEX <www.publist.com>* **1999**
- *Gay & Lesbian Abstracts <www.nisc.com>* **1997**
- *GenderWatch <www.slinfo.com>* **1998**
- *IBZ International Bibliography of Periodical Literature <www.saur.de>* **1996**

(continued)

Special Bibliographic Notes related to special journal issues (separates) and indexing/abstracting:

- indexing/abstracting services in this list will also cover material in any "separate" that is co-published simultaneously with Haworth's special thematic journal issue or DocuSerial. Indexing/abstracting usually covers material at the article/chapter level.
- monographic co-editions are intended for either non-subscribers or libraries which intend to purchase a second copy for their circulating collections.
- monographic co-editions are reported to all jobbers/wholesalers/approval plans. The source journal is listed as the "series" to assist the prevention of duplicate purchasing in the same manner utilized for books-in-series.
- to facilitate user/access services all indexing/abstracting services are encouraged to utilize the co-indexing entry note indicated at the bottom of the first page of each article/chapter/contribution.
- this is intended to assist a library user of any reference tool (whether print, electronic, online, or CD-ROM) to locate the monographic version if the library has purchased this version but not a subscription to the source journal.
- individual articles/chapters in any Haworth publication are also available through the Haworth Document Delivery Service (HDDS).

Balancing Family and Work: Special Considerations in Feminist Therapy

CONTENTS

ABOUT THE EDITOR

Toni Schindler Zimmerman, PhD, is Associate Professor at Colorado State University. She has been the Director of the Marriage and Family Therapy Program at CSU for ten years. This program is strong in both research training and clinical skill training. The CSU MFT Program has been widely recognized for its tremendous efforts for integrating gender and culture in family therapy training. Toni Schindler Zimmerman has been a leader in gender and family therapy integration. In 1999, the MFT Program that she directs was given the AAMFT National Training Award. In 1997, she was awarded the Ruth Strang Research Award by the National Association for Women in Education. Also, in 1997, she was honored as the Colorado Marriage and Family Therapist of the Year by the CAMFT. Currently, she is editor for *Journal of Feminist Family Therapy* and has over 50 publications in the area of Marriage and Family Therapy. Her research, teaching, and outreach efforts are in the areas of gender and culture integration in marriage and family therapy, work and family balance issues in family therapy, and gender and parenting. She recently completed a major research project funded by the Alfred P. Sloan Foundation entitled, "Studying the successful balance of work and family." She is considered an outstanding teacher and trainer by her students and colleagues. Toni lives in Fort Collins, Colorado, with her best friend and husband, Craig, and her two fabulous daughters, Misha and Sage.

Introduction:
Barriers to and Possibilities
in Balancing Family and Work

Toni Schindler Zimmerman

One of the most dominant cultural stories in the United States today, particularly for women, is that balancing family and work is "impossible." This story is laden with images of exhausted women, neglected children, and uninvolved fathers who are raised to hero status for missing an occasional work meeting for a family obligation. These images may reflect reality for some families who face multiple barriers to the successful balance of family and work, such as inflexible, unsupportive work environments structured as if every worker has a "wife" at home, lack of affordable and quality childcare, and inequality in their intimate relationships. In addition to these common barriers, all families face the challenge of balancing family and work in a culture of workaholism, which is reflected by the fact that average work hours in the United States are higher than in any other industrialized country and in a culture with biases against maternal employment. These barriers are often heightened for those marginalized by gender, race, class, and sexual orientation. Clearly, social change must occur on a variety of levels in order to shift from a story of "impossibility" to one of "possibilities" for all dual earners.

Toni Schindler Zimmerman, PhD, is affiliated with Colorado State University, Department of Human Development and Family Studies; Director, Marriage and Family Therapy Program; and Editor, *Journal of Feminist Family Therapy*.

[Haworth co-indexing entry note]: "Introduction: Barriers to and Possibilities in Balancing Family and Work." Zimmerman, Toni Schindler. Co-published simultaneously in *Journal of Feminist Family Therapy* (The Haworth Press, Inc.) Vol. 13, No. 2/3, 2001, pp. 1-3; and: *Balancing Family and Work: Special Considerations in Feminist Therapy* (ed: Toni Schindler Zimmerman) The Haworth Press, Inc., 2001, pp. 1-3. Single or multiple copies of this article are available for a fee from The Haworth Document Delivery Service [1-800-HAWORTH, 9:00 a.m. - 5:00 p.m. (EST). E-mail address: getinfo@haworthpressinc.com].

1

However, this "impossible" story does not reflect all dual-earner families–many are able to balance family and work well. But because lives that reflect balance often are not highlighted in the media or in public or private conversations, we come to believe that the "possible" story is rare or does not exist. Spotlighting these "possible" stories can instill hope for dual-earner families and motivate us to creatively confront the barriers to work-life balance in our own lives and in the larger social context. A belief that something is "possible" is fundamental to the ability to request, fight for, and demand change at an individual, dyadic, and societal level. History is fraught with "impossible" stories gone "possible" once expectations change–stories, for example, of Rosa Parks moving to the front of the bus, women demanding the right to vote, men demonstrating their ability to express emotions and be involved fathers. These all became "possible" stories once expectations changed.

As the director of a family therapy training program, I have come to realize that one of my most important contributions to my students and clients has been to serve as an example of "possibility"–someone who successfully balances family and work. Over the years, I have been asked many times, "How do you do it?"–as if it were an oddity or impossibility that I could be a serious scholar and a playful mother. This repeated question led me to reflect on my life and recognize the factors that support me in successfully balancing family and work, such as my prioritization of fun and recreation; my complete love and affection for my children with whom I adore spending time; my intimate partnership and deep friendship with my wonderful husband who equally shares in all of life's responsibilities and gifts; the meaning and pleasure I derive from my work; my supportive and flexible work environment with an on-site preschool; my ability to focus and get a lot of work done in a short time; my commitment to work to "time" and not "task"; and my ability to build teams of students to work with me while advancing their careers. Even our elementary school is just one mile from campus, making it convenient to volunteer weekly, meet the kids for lunch, or drive to field trips. I literally feel surrounded by structures and relationships that support balance. Yet, an additional factor that contributes to balance is my belief that successful balancing of work and family is "possible" and within my reach. Not everyone has the support that I enjoy, and, for all families, we must continue to lobby for serious structural, institutional, and societal change to correct this. Yet, without a belief that balance is "possible," even with similar support systems to mine, families may live the "impossibility" story because disbelief (based on negative media images) has become a major barrier to balance.

The pressing nature of the question, "How do you do it?"–repeated by students, clients, and colleagues–required more than personal reflection. It motivated me and my colleague to conduct a two-year grant-funded study where we asked, "How do you do it?" of couples successfully balancing family and work. In addition to this study, I am excited to devote this special volume to the important topic of balancing family and work. As therapists we need to continue to dialogue about family and work issues with each other, with our clients, and at political levels in order to create change. The change that I hope we will see in the future will be a society filled with "possible" stories that are not unique outcomes, but rather routine for all families.

Is Balancing Family and Work a Sustainable Metaphor?

Gonzalo Bacigalupe

SUMMARY. Using personal, clinical, and research experiences, the author explores various challenges families and therapists face in the information society and how new dominant metaphors about personhood and family have the potential of entrapping families and individuals. The author reflects on how to frame therapeutic work with couples and families as they attempt to navigate through a new economic order and its predominant discourses in post-industrialized societies such as the United States. As a political activist in South America and, later, a clinically minded systems clinician, the author's awareness of social ecologies as framing our experiences and agency informs these reflections. This article developed out of an earlier presentation at a meeting of the Council on Contemporary Families Annual Meeting in 1999[1] and was formulated as a response to the question: What Works for Families? *[Article copies available for a fee from The Haworth Document Delivery Service: 1-800-HAWORTH. E-mail ad-*

Gonzalo Bacigalupe, EdD, is Assistant Professor and Director, Family Therapy Program, Graduate College of Education, University of Massachusetts Boston.

The author is grateful to innumerous individuals, couples, and families with whom we have exchanged some of the ideas explored in this article. My colleague and friend Jodie Kliman's editorial feedback was invaluable, critical, and supportive. My family has always been a source of ideas, support, and challenges, one of which was the writing of this article. Thanks for your patience!

Address correspondence to: Gonzalo Bacigalupe, UMB, Graduate College of Education, 100 Morrissey Blvd., Boston, MA 02125-3393 (E-mail: *gonzalo.bacigalupe@ umb.edu*).

[Haworth co-indexing entry note]: "Is Balancing Family and Work a Sustainable Metaphor?" Bacigalupe, Gonzalo. Co-published simultaneously in *Journal of Feminist Family Therapy* (The Haworth Press, Inc.) Vol. 13, No. 2/3, 2001, pp. 5-20; and: *Balancing Family and Work: Special Considerations in Feminist Therapy* (ed: Toni Schindler Zimmerman) The Haworth Press, Inc., 2001, pp. 5-20. Single or multiple copies of this article are available for a fee from The Haworth Document Delivery Service [1-800-HAWORTH, 9:00 a.m. - 5:00 p.m. (EST). E-mail address: getinfo@haworthpressinc.com].

KEYWORDS. Work-family balance, metaphors, therapeutic work

Forms of practice and forms of knowledge, although distinct, often converge in their consequences. Practices codify actions and prescribe how to deal with individuals, groups, families, and communities. Knowledge produces formulations of "truth." We come to "see" things in particular ways through the concepts and theories we develop about them: how we name, characterize, explain, and predict. Understanding is imposing a view upon reality. (Chambon, 1999, p. 17)

We forget that we are history. . . . We are not used to associating our private lives with public events. Yet the histories of families cannot be separated from the history of nations. (Griffin, 1992, p. 4)

Like many readers of *Journal of Feminist Family Therapy*, my work as a clinician, consultant, and scholar includes consulting with individuals, couples, families, and systems to find resolution to family life and organizational problems or to navigate various life challenges. Zimmerman and Haddock (2000) have suggested, "it is important for therapists to analyze societal messages and their own stereotypes about the dual-earner arrangement and working mothers" (p. 4; Haddock, Zimmerman, Ziemba, & Current [in press]). Similarly, Strober (1988) concluded, "we are moving toward a world where men and women are more equal, both at home and at the workplace. Despite the wishes of some, it seems unlikely that public policy can reverse the trend. The sensible role for public policy is to facilitate the transition" (p. 185). The study of this issue has focused on role strain and how fathers and mothers differently experience combining work and family activities. Attention has been given to these difficulties as they relate not only to the care of young children, but also of disabled relatives and elderly parents. Juggling work and family has also been addressed as it impacts and is affected by employers and workplace environments. In this article, I explore how the discourse[2] of balancing work and family affects both therapists and families. Its focus on resolutions that are solely based on individual and family interventions rather than in a larger critique of new societal trends that organize our lives is problematic.

The discourse of balancing work and family creates stressful demands in an accelerating quest for productivity in the remunerated working environments and the intimate spaces that are not income producing. From a therapeutic perspective, Fraenkel and Wilson (2000) have suggested that the myths of "spontaneity," "infinite perfectibility," and "total control" trap couples in the notion that it is possible to resolve privately what I call the dilemmas of parental "multitasking" in the new economy. Levner (2000) has proposed to redefine dual earners as families with "three-careers": one partner's, the other partner's, plus their family's career. These authors address the limits to how much couples can actually accomplish in a finite amount of time—myths that there are no limits are conveniently fed by notions of balancing work and family. Social policy and market demands do not necessarily facilitate couples' healthy resolution of these demands, not just because we have to work more hours to sustain a certain kind of lifestyle, but also because dominant discourse assumes that it is possible to achieve such a balance.

Some people who come to therapy have "unsuccessfully negotiated" this social and political dilemma in their relationships. The dilemma is not personal, however, but rather a systemic difficulty that has more to do with available moral discourses about how work and family relate. Like many of my clinical colleagues, my own family's struggles often seem to parallel those of the clients and professionals with whom I consult. Their stories, like ours, are often part of a larger problem-saturated scenario gone berserk by institutional oppression. A brief description of my own family life, nonetheless, may suggest otherwise.

As a "successful" immigrant, I have achieved what predominant hegemonic discourses suggest is constitutive of the "American dream." My wife and I are married, own a single detached house (and a large mortgage) in a beautiful neighborhood; we have a bright adolescent girl in a prestigious public school system and a shy but energetic toddler who attends a child care facility close by. My employment provides a variety of opportunities as I work towards obtaining a tenured position at an urban university, consult with various public and private organizations, and maintain a small private practice at my home office. My wife works full-time as a director of a nonprofit community organization, is often hired to carry out program evaluations, and sometimes trains professionals about gender and development. Definitely, we represent a success story; the census statisticians are not troubled when they have to categorize our socioeconomic status. What is the problem then? How can I dare to compare our life with the lives of some of my non-wealthy clients and students, and less economically successful clinicians? How can the life of a multi-stressed family served by a family stabilization team compare with the life of the privileged, successful professional?

Financially, however, my life is fairly unstable. Not like venture capitalists, my salary as a professor pays only about two-thirds of the mortgage, and our house is only a few months away from being owned by one of the largest banks in the country. The child care bill is as expensive as the college my daughter may attend in a few years; our au-pair and/or child care costs are so expensive that one of our salaries could be eliminated to compensate for the cost of taking care of our toddler. With no savings, with elderly parents and relatives who will soon need our financial support, and with rising health costs, a small turn of events could quickly bring our upper-middle class status into question. Our son has severe chronic asthma and other allergies that doctors overmedicate or are unable to treat, another source of uncertainty added to medical, psychological, and financial problems. Both cars, bought when we were graduate students, are becoming rusty and unsafe. Counter to research and clinical descriptions of Latino families, since our immigration has not been part of an extended family migration process, we have no local relatives to help us with our children or other emergencies.

Some of these dimensions and challenges are also pervasive among some of my clients, friends, and colleagues. The idea of family as the place where the private is protected from the public space, "a world of our own making" (Gillis, 1996), feeds a mythical discourse about boundaries between work and family, boundaries intended to protect us from the dynamics of the workplace. The family context is, however, a site in which adults, today, transform themselves into multitasking[3] beings. We carry on an innumerable number of tasks familiar to many readers, often several at the same time. We–in alphabetical order–analyze, answer, argue, awake, bargain, bathe, buy, call, clean, contain, cook, cure, deal with, decide, discuss, drive, feed, fix, freeze, gather, give, go, handle, hold, imagine, instruct, junk, listen, lose, love, make, meet, move, negotiate, open, organize, pay, plan, praise, prepare, prioritize, receive, repair, rub, reheat, ritualize, run, say, scrub, shop, sign, stay, talk, throw away, treat, wash, watch, work, worry, write, zip, on and on. Purposely, I have not organized this list in any special order, since, for the most part, they are tightly and unexpectedly linked in an unrelenting pattern in which we respond to the demands of "balancing work and family"–all while we do other things.

We are immersed, without relief, in a continuous multitasking environment while we attempt to create a sense of intimacy and "spontaneous flow."

We also try to stay attuned to the needs of each other as a couple, as parents, as friends, etc. Furthermore, many of us (and not as an afterthought) attempt to do this while we claim some form of feminist sensibility. For couples therapy, that includes a feminist agenda which questions a patriarchal order in their relationship changes and introduces expectations of equality that are not supported by the larger system. The balancing of family and work is not only about one member taking the burden for finding this balance, as the media often suggests. In parallel, caring in a multitasking context, immigrants have an additional set of demands. We have to bear, confront, critique, and deconstruct subtle forms of racism, the burden of continuous translation, and the silent task of keeping multiple identities alive (see, for example, Arthur & Shapiro, 1996; Thompson & Tyagi, 1996). In our own and many of my immigrant clients' experiences, for instance, calling and setting up an appointment with the pediatrician are stressful activities that are full of potential misunderstandings. The telephone operator may be confused by the foreign accent. The day of the appointment, the receptionist may react impatiently with the immigrant family's lack of knowledge about written forms as well as the rules that govern "good patient but assertive client" behaviors. Furthermore, subtle forms of racism may foster a climate of distrust and confusion towards the medical and paramedic personnel.

While carrying on, my partner and I both attempt to work at empowering others, often in very impoverished community, educational, and organizational contexts. Both of us are inclined to define our professional work as political endeavors: our assumptions tell us that we are agents of change. Our positions place us in contact with people who are mostly poor, of color, immigrants, survivors of psychological or social trauma and violence, or some combination of any of these dimensions. Besides reflecting upon my own experience as a clinician, educator, and researcher, some of these concerns also reflect the challenges of my students, whose juggling act may be similar but compounded by even fewer resources as they pursue graduate studies and work full-time.

THE CLINICAL PRACTITIONER'S CHALLENGE: WHAT WORKS FOR FAMILIES AND THE PRACTITIONERS THAT WORK WITH THEM?

As Coontz has stated (2000), we must have a political sensibility in the clinical room, bringing our understanding of how the larger context impacts the family's reality and available stories about this dilemma. As a therapist working with human rights violation victims, intimate violence survivors, and child sexual abuse survivors (Bacigalupe, 1990, 2000a, 2000b, in press), I find that an explicitly political mind is not only necessary but also an ethical imperative in therapy. A family benefits from a vision rather than from expert predictions. A clinical stance that emphasizes a prognosis that is attached to psychopathology or interactional dysfunctionality overwhelms families and makes practitioners less accountable.

At the age of seven, our daughter had a traumatic accident at her after-school program. She started to have academic and behavioral problems in the classroom, although she had been a bright and avid learner. Worried about the psychological impact of the accident on her well-being and academic success, we requested help from a school counselor. The counselor's first comment was actually a very firm recommendation about my wife and me attending couples therapy. Although our daughter was presenting serious posttraumatic symptoms a few weeks after the accident, the counselor stated that we needed to deal with our marriage first to be able to help our daughter. Her plausible but inaccurate clinical diagnosis missed our deep sense of isolation and devastation during that period, in which we, recent immigrants, were both studying and working while raising our daughter in a semi-rural community in New England. Her clinical approach was informed by a specific causal theory about children's behaviors, not only a conceptual framework which suggested that our daughter's difficulties were due to couple problems, but a theory that she applied without listening carefully to our needs in a contextually informed stance. We discarded her "expert" assessment and sought other forms of support, including frequent communications with our family abroad and the help of a psychologist who worked with our daughter for a few months and invited us to work with her jointly in an effort to heal her psychological and physical wounds.

Striking a balance between family and work during a stressful period is a tremendous burden. Balancing is somewhat possible when there is some level of optimum fit in various dimensions of families' lives. Families in therapy are often going through a difficult period in their lives. Besides having to adapt to rapid changes of the new economy and to resolve family stresses, they attempt to find solutions within the constraining discourse of balancing work and family. A therapist, under these circumstances, must frame the couple's concerns within the context of family's positioning vis-à-vis the struggle with social inequities. Choosing to individualize these experiences as solely personal and/or familial prevents one questioning a core oppressive element in the changing economy: the idea that people need to resolve their struggles via personal changes rather than through the redesign of friendlier working places, just salaries, and institutionalized forms of solidarity and justice (i.e., access and quality of child care).

To help families succeed requires acknowledging the need for others to support and accompany them; families need validation through discovery, remembering, and affirmation (financial, social, psychological, and cultural). When I ask my family therapy interns, early in their training, about how they plan to work with families to connect with resources, they start by naming what they know are available social services. Yet reimbursable services (to use an administrative perspective) are often unrelated to the actual needs of an individual or family. Many therapists, under these conditions, do not design treatment plans based on what may work better for the people requesting help, but rather according to existing institutional resources. Beginning therapists often neglect to involve families in finding out carefully about their requests and in assessing whether these resources are available outside the formal service system. For example, solutions may exist within the clients' network, but not necessarily on the form of another professional providing services. Clinical practitioners may take for granted the idea that all families find professional resources useful or meaningful to their lives. In the case of poor and minority families who "may not see social services as central to addressing their problems" (Halpern, 1999, p. 13), exploring what professionals can provide evolves into a futile and frustrating task.

Reciprocal collaboration, which includes a "not knowing" stance of respectful curiosity (Anderson, 1997), is a powerful stance since professionals are located within the system rather than being neutral observers. Locating the clients' dilemmas in the larger political and economic context (Kliman, 1994) invites conversations about our own position vis-à-vis the discourses of family and work. Reflecting upon our own struggles with the burdens of multitasking may initiate a more meaningful engagement with the difficulties that families bring forth in the clinical context. Second, in addition to acknowledging the reconstructive power of language in the therapeutic encounter, we need to reach out to families and share our expertise about concrete and symbolic resources (Boyd-Franklin & Bry, 2000; Minuchin, Colapinto, & Minuchin, 1998). And third, besides the clinical encounter, institutions and practitioners must intervene preventively and offer resources before a major crisis. For instance, we should offer supportive and creative spaces for pre-teens and teens before we have to help them replace antisocial or destructive behaviors. Families that are served through institutionalized programs (protective services, welfare, justice system, etc.) encounter service systems that assess their situation based on bureaucratic expectations. Programmatic decisions made on the basis of an assessment of how things may change in an optimum situation construe unrealistic or vague expectations about families (and practitioners). Thus, fear of failure, emergencies, and unsuccessful engagement of families (and clinical practitioners) become the norm. Community mental health clinics, for example, calculate clinicians' productivity as if clinicians were disembodied robotic entities who do not get sick, need a vacation, have children, etc. In this environment, clinicians evaluate their own work based on their capacity to write treatment plans that fulfill insurance regulations, and without a strict regard for the families' welfare. From a policy perspective, the last decade's redesign of the administrative apparatus–managed care–has not necessarily resolved the compounding problems families confront as they attempt to cope with health, financial, educational, and emotional stresses in the new economic order (Sluzki, 2000).

Minority and poor families, in particular, are more impacted than other families by social policies and are less able to protect themselves from social policies that target them (Sugrue, 1999). Policies that target poor families and minorities have done little to integrate them "into the economic and social life of mainstream society" (Lawson & Wilson, 1999, p. 472). Their familial and social networks, like those of immigrants, are more affected and thus under more stress. Lack of supportive policies destabilizes social networks by reducing affordable housing, child care, health, job opportunities, and welfare benefits. These families are then further strained, not just because of a lack of resources but also because that very lack forces others to help and use their own resources. These changes and the related lack of support impact a whole extended network system, rather than only a few individuals. In the case of immigrants who continue to support families in their countries of origin (Hondagneu-Sotelo, 2000), savings by one family unit may be spent to aid another extended family or neighbor. For immigrant families who rely on other families to make ends meet, changes in social policy or drastic economic changes in other countries can have a profound impact on the livelihoods of those who are thriving here but do not necessarily have accumulated resources (i.e., savings). For families to thrive under these conditions and for practitioners to be effective, the art of collaborative networking is paramount: learning about its value, the ways you carry it out, and the tools that are needed.

An extraordinary amount of persistence is needed for families to access resources. They need a listening stance sustained in a deep caring rather than a pro forma application of some bureaucratic procedure (Pakman, 1999; Weingarten, 2000). Immigrant families, for instance, cannot just be asked to respond positively to an offer of help in the form of a list of phone numbers when they are overwhelmed with multiple demands that involve their family and work (Bacigalupe, 2000c). A colorful brochure does not invite these families to engage collaboratively with those who attempt to help them, nor does this approach aid them in resolving the demands of work and family. For low-income families, this balance is compounded by the intervention of protective or social services that insist on their "reformation" through parenting classes or other interventions designed as if the sole focus of parents' attention could be on parent-child boundary making, affective responses, or couples communication (see Dodson, 1999; Garcia Coll, Survey, & Weingarten, 1998). Practitioners and institutions should not simply make resources available for families; they should make sure mutual caring is embedded in the process, which, when lacking, is emotionally, socially, and financially straining for family members within networks. Families are sustained by relationships of reciprocity even in the context of evolving boundaries (as in the case of continuous immigration) (Falicov, 1998). Searching for what works can elicit partnerships and communities that can effectively overcome the tremendous social disparities that go unvoiced when professionals individualize social inequities and mythical discourses into personal and familial experiences.

Practitioners working with families need to recognize cultural difference and its challenge to power and authority, depending upon how social class, race, and gender intersect. The power of the intersection of these various markers is compounded by how the social context provides families with the possibility of partnerships, projects, sites of worship, places to construct and dream, vacations, and weekends. The unavailability of these spaces curtails families' capacity to balance work and family tasks, introducing new forms of marginalization and oppression. Trust has qualitatively diverse meanings among groups of communities; recognizing these nuances may make the difference between life and death. Minority families, for instance, are generally suspicious of non-medical professionals and thus their capacity to access resources that would strengthen their capacity to resolve the strains of managing multiple tasks are severely diminished (Bacigalupe & Gorlier, 2000). And, as we have learned well from brief therapy and solution-focused approaches (Berg & Reuss, 1998; Turnell & Edwards, 1999), professionals need to step out in an appropriate and timely manner.

DEPRIVED OF A VACATION (AND MUCH MORE)

María, a 37-year-old immigrant from Ecuador who has lived in Los Angeles for more than a decade, is concerned about the behaviors of her 14-year-old son.[4] She describes her former husband and the father of her four children, who abandoned the family two years ago, as physically abusive and a substance abuser. Like his father, María's older adult child is not attending the consultation; he is also described as a substance abuser and physically abusive. Various therapists have diagnosed María with depression and given her medications. Her family therapist requested a consultation to explore a strength-based approach with María's family after intervening unsuccessfully to try and help her cope with family and individual difficulties. I interviewed María and her three youngest children and reflected with her therapist and a reflecting team. For the purpose of this article, I highlight how one of the most powerful turning points in the session was when the family concluded that María's unrelenting pace has impacted each one of them, including the "rebellious" 14-year-old. At the beginning of this segment, it is not María who is sensitive to the burden of work; rather, it is her adolescent boy and her sister, who clearly voice how work *is* María's life.

The transcript that follows highlights only one important aspect from the whole consultation. Previous to this dialogue with the family, we had explored their immigration and couple history including a clear acknowledgement of how Maria's former husband's violence has been traumatic to her and the children. As a consultant, I mapped their previous efforts at dealing with some of their problems and how they might be able to access other forms of support. Weaving a complex intervention that validates this family's inner pain, as well as the social contexts that constrain their present and future, was initiated through the help of the team watching behind the one-way mirror and the reflecting team that the family listens to.

The conversation with the family gave birth to the "vacation," an idea that is instructive as a metaphoric comment of larger social issues and not necessarily as the solution to this family's ordeal.[5] It is not a coming back to individualistic, family therapy solutions, or simple social policies that reify a specific family structure. It is, however, a reminder for therapists that "details" like this one are powerful metaphors that capture the complexity of this family's and many other families' dilemmas.[6]

> G: *(Consultant): Noel, you are very aware of your mom's needs, you said twice "Calm down, Mom," and you are really concerned about her taking all of the time. Do you have a sense? I know this is a wild guess (laughter) and I don't want you to tell me "I don't know"; just make a wild guess. How much time do you think your mom needs to get rid of that suffering and pain that she has?*
>
> N: *(Teenage Son): She needs a vacation.*
>
> G: *She needs a vacation. Have you ever seen her take a vacation?*
>
> N: *She doesn't have time.*
>
> G: *Does it make you sad that she doesn't take a vacation?*
>
> N: *Very sad. . . .*
>
> G: *She hasn't taken a vacation for a long time. What do you think needs to happen for her to take a vacation?*
>
> N: *I don't know. Could you repeat the question?*
>
> G: *What do you think needs to happen for her to take a vacation?*
>
> N: *Big thing is the money.*
>
> G: *Besides the money, I was saying before that we may win the lottery and things will change, but sometimes that won't happen and we'll be struggling with financial things for a while.*
>
> N: *She is worried about us, she gets up and starts doing things, she doesn't stop, and nothing stops her.*
>
> G: *So she cannot take a nap and forget the world?*
>
> N: *No, I don't think so.*

G: *Do you think that if you leave, then she will be able to take a rest?*

N: *Maybe. I doubt it though.*

G: *So if you have the money you will pay for her to go on a cruise, right?*

N: *Yeah.*

G: *That won't happen?*

N: *You never know.*

G: *There is something else I am going to ask you. I was thinking when I was interviewing the three therapists before (reflecting team) and thinking about this idea of what it means to be a man in this house, in this family. It must be extremely hard to be the last one in the line.*

N: *Yeah, there is still my older brother (he did not attend the session) too though.*

G: *You're the last one who can buy her cruise. It will be as hard, right? Did you have a sense that at some point he might have thought, what you need is a cruise?*

M: *(María): Not really.*

G: *Do you have a sense of what your mom needs too? Your brother thinks that she needs a vacation; I called it a cruise.*

A: *(Youngest Daughter): I think she should go on a vacation....*

G: *So you agree with your brother that she has a hard time to take a nap, to take thirty minutes off.*

V: *(Older Daughter): If we tell her to take a nap, she says, "No, I have to go, I have to sell Avon things."*

G: *So you also sell Tupperware?*

M: *Yes, a little bit.*

GB: *So you say that she doesn't give herself the rest at all.*

N: *She doesn't know when to take a break.*

V: *Always doing something.*

G: *Have you thought about taking a nap when you come to therapy here?*

M: *Yes.*

All: *(Laughter)*

G: *When you're in the waiting room and you want a nap, well, the next therapist can tell you to come half an hour earlier and then you can take a nap in the waiting room, unless you want to sell Avon products to people in the waiting room.*

V: *She's like that, she's taking care of us in the pool and she starts talking.*

GB: *So they call you the little ant, you look like a big ant.*

MA: *Aha. . . . (laughter). Yes, that's what those who know me, call me. . . .*

This consultation segment highlights how an accepted notion of what is a good parent and hard worker has been left untouched in previous conversations between this woman and her family therapists. The children's assessment of their mother's overworked schedule seems like a breakthrough as it reveals not only her efforts and ways of coping but the larger problematic nature of work and parenting for those who are barely making it in this country. María's multiple roles may be a source of serious individual and familial difficulties that are compounded by a history of violence and abuse. What have been available for her and her family, however, have been mostly psychological descriptions that do not support a political and ecological understanding of these difficulties. The vacation conversations are only a step, addressing these concerns is only a first step in acknowledging the need for a larger support. For María, the burden of balancing work and family has intersected with serious difficulties in both realms. In her family, she has been abused and traumatized. At work, she may not be obtaining enough income to sustain four children and herself in a large urban city. A therapist would need to be both attentive to María's concerns (including a history of abuse and trauma) and the trappings of coping with parenting in a social context that does not provide enough concrete social support and/or discursive resources that facilitate making meaning of the problems and potential resolutions. For María, the multitasking metaphor may not have been as useful as it would be for families that are more privileged.

CONCLUSION

We are all positively affected by more accepting and affirmative ways of defining different family forms. Normative models of family can have a pernicious effect on families undergoing drastic changes due to traumatic events and/or dislocation in new lands and may not really capture complex issues like balancing work and family. Families, practitioners, and researchers may be caught in either/or choices (the opposing choices media likes to play out) that restrain our knowledge and our capacity to change the dominant ideas shaping family policy. We are required to search for a *both/and* logic. Like María's family, all families need space and time to carry out their multiple tasks. Since interdependence is sustained on dependency, passion, and desire, multitasking exhausts families. The requirements of relationships involve "non-productive time."

At the time I write the last words of this article, our youngest child's au pair is no longer helping us take care of him. Re-imagining our family routines reminds me again of the struggle to find out how to balance the needs of each of these many routines. Besides the "real" struggle with an enormous amount of tasks, as related earlier in this article, we have to find out how to counter mainstream messages about idealized views of balancing family and work. It demands a collective effort that includes others rather than an individual family effort. It seems that little is available "out there" about the never-ending process of not finding such a balance; it is quite an unbalancing act.

NOTES

1. More information can be found at the CCF website: *http://www.slip.net/~ccf/*

2. Discourses are the linguistic practices which, in particular historical periods, allow certain kinds of social relationships to emerge, while many others are silenced or forgotten. Discourses in therapy, therefore, articulate the prevailing ideologies in therapeutic practices. Discursive structures are essentially expressions of faith and truism that reflect fundamental knowledge structures. They define the practices and conceptual formulations in a particular historical, social, and political context. A discourse provides us with "not just a way of seeing but a way of constructing seeing" (Edwards, 1991, p. 523).

3. Multitasking is synonymous in the computer world with "multi-processing," "multiprogramming," "concurrency," and "process scheduling." It refers to the ability to execute more than one task or program at the same time. It is a technique used in a computer operating system for sharing a single processor between several independent jobs. In multitasking, only one computer processor unit (CPU) is involved, but it switches from one program to another so quickly that it gives the appearance of executing all of the programs at the same time.

4. Names have been changed to protect family's confidentiality.

5. The author thanks the reviewers for emphasizing the need to highlight this dimension.

6. The transcript that follows was translated by the author.

REFERENCES

Anderson, H. (1997). *Conversation, language, and possibilities: a postmodern approach to therapy.* New York: Basic Books.

Arthur, J., & Shapiro, A. (Eds.). (1996). *Color class identity: the new politics of race.* Boulder, CO: Westview Press.

Bacigalupe, G. (1990). Voices under arrest: political violence and a Chilean family. *Family Therapy Case Studies, 5*(2), 31-38.

Bacigalupe, G. (2000a). Family violence in Chile: exploring prevalence and clinical dimensions. *Journal of Family Psychotherapy, 11*(2), 39-57.

Bacigalupe, G. (2000b). Family violence in Chile: political and legal dimensions in a period of democratic transition. *Violence Against Women, 6*(4), 429-450.

Bacigalupe, G. (2000c). *Psychotherapists working with Latino families: unheard discourses and practices.* Paper presented at the American Psychological Association, 108th Annual Conference, Washington, DC.

Bacigalupe, G. (in press). Latina survivors of child sexual abuse. In L. Walker, S. W. Gold & B. A. Lucenko (Eds.), *Handbook on child sexual abuse* (2nd ed.). New York, NY: Springer.

Bacigalupe, G., & Gorlier, J. C. (2000, November). *Latino Medicaid consumers' experiences: obtaining health care and caring for their families' health.* Paper presented at the American Public Health Association, 109th Annual Meeting, Boston, MA.

Berg, I. K., & Reuss, N. H. (1998). *Solutions step by step: a substance abuse treatment manual.* New York, NY: W. W. Norton & Company.

Boyd-Franklin, N., & Bry, B. H. (2000). *Reaching out in family therapy: home-based, school, and community interventions.* New York, NY: The Guilford Press.

Chambon, A. S. (1999). Foucault's approach: making the familiar visible. In A. S. Chambon, A. Irving & L. Epstein (Eds.), *Reading Foucault for social work* (pp. 51-81). New York: Columbia University Press.

Coontz, S. (2000, June 21). *Inventing today's families: an historian's view of the challenge.* Paper presented at the American Family Therapy Academy 22nd Annual Meeting, San Diego, CA.

Dodson, L. (1999). *Don't call us out of name: the untold lives of women and girls in poor America.* Boston: Beacon Press.

Edwards, D. (1991). Categories are for talking: on the cognitive and discursive basis of categorization. *Theory & Society, 1*, 515-542.

Falicov, C. J. (1998). *Latino families in therapy: a guide for multicultural practice.* New York, NY: The Guilford Press.

Fraenkel, P. (2000). Clocks, calendars, and couples: time and the rhythms of relationships. In P. Papp (Ed.), *Couples on the fault line: new directions for therapists* (pp. 63-103). New York, NY: The Guilford Press.

Garcia Coll, C., Survey, J. L., & Weingarten, K. (Eds.). (1998). *Mothering against the odds: diverse voices of contemporary mothers.* New York, NY: The Guilford Press.

Gillis, J. R. (1996). *A world of their own making: myth, ritual, and the quest for family values.* New York, NY: Basic Books.

Griffin, S. (1992). *A chorus of stones: the private life of war.* New York: Doubleday.

Haddock, S. A., Zimmerman, T. S., Ziemba, S. J., & Current, L. R. (in press). Ten philosophies for work and family balance: advice from successful families. *Journal of
Marital and Family Therapy*.

Halpern, R. (1999). *Fragile families, fragile solutions: a history of supportive services
for families in poverty*. New York: Columbia University Press.

Hondagneu-Sotelo, P. (2000). The international division of caring and cleaning work.
In M. H. Myer (Ed.), *Care work: gender, labor and the welfare state* (pp. 149-323).
New York & London: Routledge.

Kliman, J. (1994). The interweaving of gender, class, and race in family therapy. In M.
Pravder-Mirkin (Ed.), *Women in context: towards a feminist reconstruction of psychotherapy* (pp. 25-47). New York, NY: Guilford Press.

Lawson, R., & Wilson, W. J. (1999). Poverty, social rights, and the quality of citizenship. In S. Coontz (Ed.), *American families: a multicultural reader* (pp. 470-477).
New York, NY: Routledge.

Levner, L. (2000). The three-career family. In P. Papp (Ed.), *Couples on the fault line:
new directions for therapists* (pp. 29-47). New York, NY: The Guilford Press.

Minuchin, P., Colapinto, J., & Minuchin, S. (1998). *Working with the families of the
poor*. New York: The Guilford Press.

Pakman, M. (1999). Designing constructive therapies in community mental health:
poetics and micropolitics in and beyond the consulting room. *Journal of Marital
and Family Therapy*, *25*(1), 83-98.

Sluzki, C. E. (2000). Patients, clients, consumers: the politics of words. *Families, Systems & Health*, *18*(3), 347-352.

Strober, M. H. (1988). Two-earner families. In S. M. Dornbusch & M. H. Strober
(Eds.), *Feminism, children and the new families* (pp. 161-190). New York, NY: The
Guilford Press.

Sugrue, T. J. (1999). Poor families in an era of urban transformation: the "underclass"
family in myth and reality. In S. Coontz (Ed.), *American families: a multicultural
reader* (pp. 243-257). New York, NY: Routledge.

Thompson, B., & Tyagi, S. (Eds.). (1996). *Names we call home: autobiography on racial identity*. New York NY: Routledge.

Turnell, A., & Edwards, S. (1999). *Signs of safety: a solution and safety oriented approach to child protection casework*. New York: W.W. Norton & Co.

Weingarten, K. (2000). Witnessing, wonder, and hope. *Family Process*, *39*(4), 389-
402.

Zimmerman, T. S., & Haddock, S. (2000). *Successfully balancing family and work*.
Paper presented at the American Family Therapy Academy Annual Meeting, San
Diego, CA.

Walking the Walk:
Insights from Research on Helping Clients
Navigate Work and Family

Shelley M. MacDermid
Leigh A. Leslie
Lara Bissonnette

SUMMARY. Challenges related to managing multiple life roles, particularly work and family roles, often bring individuals or couples to psychotherapy. While a vast empirical literature exists on issues in managing work and family roles, there is little integration of this research into family therapy practice. The purpose of this article is to offer an initial attempt at such integration by considering the implication of work-family research for clinical interventions. The first section of this article identifies three themes from research on work-family relationships that seem to offer good possibilities for the development of therapeutic interventions. The second section offers suggestions about ways that these themes might fruitfully be used in the therapy room. *[Article copies available for a fee from The Haworth Document Delivery Service: 1-800-HAWORTH. E-mail ad-*

Shelley M. MacDermid, PhD, is affiliated with the Department of Child and Family Studies, Purdue University. Leigh A. Leslie, PhD, is affiliated with the Department of Family Studies, University of Maryland. Lara Bissonnette is affiliated with the Department of Child and Family Studies, Purdue University.

This article is based on a Research Update for Practitioners presented at the annual meeting of the National Council on Family Relations, Minneapolis, MN, November, 2000. We are grateful to Elaine Anderson for the invitation to prepare the research update.

dress: <getinfo@haworthpressinc.com> Website: <http://www.HaworthPress.com>
© 2001 by The Haworth Press, Inc. All rights reserved.]

KEYWORDS. Work, family, balance, work-family relationships, clinical interventions

Virtually every employed adult struggles at times with the management of multiple demands at and away from work–"balance" seems to have become the mantra of the modern age. Work-related troubles frequently bring individuals and couples into treatment, yet work-family issues receive relatively little systematic attention in marital and family therapy literature. To address this gap, the authors of this article have "put their heads together" to merge their expertise in work-family research and in marital and family therapy for the benefit of their practitioner colleagues.[1] We draw from our experiences as researchers, teachers, and practitioners to address the question of how empirical research can inform clinical practice around work and family issues.

The first section of this article identifies three contributions from the research literature that we think offer marital and family therapists good "raw material" for the development of successful intervention techniques related to work and family. We in no way attempt to offer a comprehensive review of work-family research. Instead, our goal is to identify empirical work that we believe can be readily translated to practice and has good potential to empower or energize clients. The themes selected from the work and family research literature are: (1) roles and boundaries; (2) strategies and tactics; and (3) commitment and control.

The second section considers how marital and family therapists might apply these ideas in therapy. We identify how, in our experience, work and family problems often manifest themselves in therapy. We then spell out clinical frames and techniques for addressing these problems that can be culled from the work and family research themes.

THEMES FROM WORK AND FAMILY RESEARCH

Although we sometimes use the phrase "balancing work and family" in our own work, we see it as problematic. The word "balance" usually conjures up a visual image of weight scales, and with that image the suggestion that balance can be achieved as a static property, once and for all. The word also suggests that the route to balance is through equal allocations of time to important life roles. "Balance" is not a systemic word. It pits one role against another, ignoring the complex configuration of roles most people occupy. As a result, adhering to the metaphor of balance can set up a constant feeling of failure.

Daily life is dynamic. Every day is an endless series of decisions about what to do first, what to do next, which experiences to seek out, and which ones to avoid. Ellen Galinsky (1999) prefers the term "navigation" to reflect this dynamic nature of the relationship between work and family. The term "navigation" emphasizes constant movement toward a destination. It emphasizes the complexity and dynamism of each day–and the constant adjustments made to both anticipate and respond to external forces. Like a ship facing a storm, those external forces are sometimes more than can comfortably be dealt with; at other times, forward progress is easily made. Successful navigation is marked not by constantly smooth weather and seas, but by staying one's course despite obstacles. Similarly, the navigation of work and family might be more successful when the focus is on staying the course rather than on whether the final destination of perfect "balance" has been achieved. Thus, throughout this article, we choose the metaphor of navigation, instead of balance, to guide our review of research and our application of research to clinical practice.

Roles and Identities

Almost every adult spends time in activities or roles that are important: some are enjoyable, some fulfilling, and some simply necessary. Researchers have spent a great deal of time studying these multiple roles and their impact in individual and family life. In some ways, the concept of roles is a recent invention. Prior to the industrial revolution, the home was the center of economic production, education, health care, and many other social functions. Work and family were interwoven, occurring in the same space and at the same time. Further, women and men shared responsibility for children and worked side by side as economic providers for the family. With industrialization, large-scale production moved from the home to the factory and the office, taking with it men, children, and unmarried women (Blau & Ferber, 1992), and spawning new research interest in social roles.

Around the middle of the 20th century, scholars, including Goode (1960) and Kahn (1964), asserted that the industrial revolution had resulted in competition among role commitments. The "hydraulic" or "scarcity" model assumed that energy devoted to one role always came at the expense of another, with strain as the inevitable result. With an assumption of fixed resources at its core, the hydraulic model implied that the way to cope with role strain is to pick priorities, reducing the use of resources.

Stephen Marks (1977) questioned the hydraulic model in two ways. First, he reminded us that involvement in roles can generate energy–that "charged up" feeling–or other resources. Several lines of research have supported this "enhancement" hypothesis. Barnett and others (Baruch & Barnett, 1986) have shown that good experiences in one role can compensate for bad experiences in another. Sieber (1974) identified status, privileges, and personal gratification as resources that might transfer across roles, and Crouter (1984) and Kirchmeyer (1992) found positive spillover between roles. Thus, not just the quantity but also the quality of individuals' role experiences determines the degree to which they will feel strain.

Marks and his colleagues also argued that choosing priorities would only work as a coping strategy for individuals who tend to organize their identities in a hierarchical way. They pointed out that most researchers had assumed but never tested the degree to which identity structures are hierarchical (Marks & MacDermid, 1996). In an initial study, Marks and MacDermid (1996) contrasted individuals who reported hierarchical identity structures with individuals who reported a more even attitude of engagement across their role system. "Engagement" was defined as "approaching *every* role with an attitude of attentiveness and care" (p. 421). An attitude of engagement is a characteristic of a person, not any specific role. Some individuals organize their identities hierarchically; others adopt a style of engagement. The sample for the study was made up of very busy people–college students and married employed mothers. In both groups, individuals who reported more even engagement across their role systems reported significantly higher self-esteem, lower feelings of overload, and less depression than individuals who reported more hierarchical identity structures. But they were no less busy, carrying just as many credit or work hours with comparable grade point averages or earnings, and socializing just as much (Marks & MacDermid, 1996).

A subsequent study (Marks, Huston, Johnson, & MacDermid, in press) looked at the correlates of engagement in a sample of heterosexual mothers and fathers. Using regression equations, we statistically predicted levels of engagement using each partner's attitudes, involvement in paid and unpaid work, and parenting and leisure activities. We called variables with significant and positive regression coefficients "assets" for engagement. For wives, assets included longer work hours for themselves and their husbands, greater satisfaction with job and marriage and stronger attachment to the parental role. Wives also reported greater engagement when they spent more leisure time with their husband and relatives, and when their husbands worked more hours on weekends, spent more leisure time alone with the children, and exerted more effort to maintain the quality of the marital relationship. As for wives, assets for husbands included marital satisfaction, parental attachment, and more hours worked on weekends. Husbands also reported more engagement when they had a preschool child, when they spent more leisure time with that child, and when their own incomes were higher.

We labeled variables with negative regression coefficients "threats" to engagement. Wives' engagement appeared to be threatened by financial strain, by more leisure time alone with children, and by working more hours on weekends. Husbands' engagement was threatened by working more hours in general, and by solitary leisure.

One conclusion that emerges from examining these threats and assests is that roles are interconnected not only within but also across individuals. For example, wives' engagement is related not only to their own work hours, but also to their leisure and their *husband's* leisure alone with their children. Conversely, husbands' engagement is related to their own and their wives' work hours. These interrelationships suggest that engagement styles are related not to a single role but to characteristics of the entire role system and even characteristics of the partner's role system. A similar conclusion emerged from Parcel and Menaghan's (1994) extensive study of the joint effects of mothers' and fathers' jobs on their children.

The second conclusion is that the correlates of engagement appear to be highly gendered. In this working class sample, wives' engagement is positively related to opportunities to spend enjoyable time *away* from their children, while their husbands' engagement is related to spending enjoyable time *with* children. Thus, not only do individuals vary in the degree to which their identities are organized by hierarchy or engagement; the conditions that foster their engagement or attentiveness to all their roles also appear to vary.

Strategies and Tactics

Strategic or long-range planning is an important management tool in the corporate world for reaching one's destination. Strategic plans are brought to fruition via day-to-day activities or "tactics." One of the first elements of strategic planning is to identify the vision or "ideal end-state"–what the organization will look like when the plan has been carried out. Once the ideal end-state or destination has been defined, it is possible to select the tactics or the route.

Business leaders know that tactics must be aligned with strategies if end-states are to be achieved. We think the language of strategic planning also can be usefully applied to the personal management of role systems. Three contributions from the research literature support the importance of alignment in navigating work and family life.

According to Hall and Moss (1998), the psychological contract between workers and employers has changed in recent decades. No longer can individuals expect the external rewards of the traditional career–the steady promotions, company car, and corner office. Instead, their careers must now be protean, driven by their own interests and needs, with the satisfaction of developing new skills as one of the primary rewards. In the protean model, career success comes from *aligning* individual needs and organizational rewards.

Women may be especially well-suited for protean careers because they have traditionally been more likely than men to shape their career involvement according to personal and family needs. Empirical support comes from a recent study of women voluntarily working part-time as managers and professionals (MacDermid, Lee, & Buck, in press). When women reporting the most personal benefits were contrasted with women reporting the fewest, the main difference between the groups was women's personal definitions of success. Women who had more internally-oriented definitions of career success, more consistent with the protean model, perceived their part-time work arrangements as far more rewarding than women whose personal definitions were more externally derived and thus poorly aligned with the new employment contract.

Another example of alignment in the research literature is *fit*—the alignment of what is asked of workers and the resources they have to respond. Research conducted from this perspective emphasizes the *match* between individuals' resources and the challenges they face, rather than emphasizing one or the other. Although studies have been conducted for many years on person-environment fit, Pittman (1994) was one of the first to apply the concept to the study of work and family, and Barnett presented an elaborated model in 1998. According to both of these models, work-family conflict must be understood by looking at both job demands and individuals' resources. Because fit is a function of *both* demands and resources, this model reminds us that interventions can be successful by targeting either element. That is, fit can be improved by reducing demands *or* increasing resources.

Finally, a recent study of tradeoffs by Barnett and Gareis (2000) showed that the quality of life of physicians was more strongly related to their comfort with the tradeoffs they had made in choosing to work part-time than with the number of hours they actually worked. These findings illustrate the notion of "adaptive strategies." According to Moen and her colleagues, families develop and pursue strategies for managing work and family across the life course that allow them to achieve goals in both domains (e.g., career success and active parenting) (Becker & Moen, 1999; Moen & Wethington, 1992).

Commitment and Control

Valuing and achieving alignment are two very different things. What does research have to tell us about how control over very complicated lives can be achieved? Research on commitment to marriage offers some clues.

Johnson, Caughlin, and Huston (1999) propose that commitment to marriage comprises three elements. The first is *personal*, or the extent to which the individual desires to remain in the marriage. The parallel for navigating work and family is the extent to which the individual worker really wants to recalibrate, particularly given social rewards for being "busy." *Moral* commitment is the extent to which individuals choose to remain in their marriage for moral reasons. Workers who feel a strong sense of moral responsibility in their jobs may face special challenges in navigating work and family because to cut back on the job would feel immoral. Such jobs might include minister, physician, or teacher. *Structural* commitment refers to the constraints or barriers that prevent exit from a relationship. Regarding work and family, structural commitments are the penalties that workers face for "stepping down"– such as loss of pay, perks, or access to the "fast track."

Empirical results of Johnson et al.'s research showed that for marriage, personal commitment was most consistently related to satisfaction, attitudes about divorce, and respondents' consideration of alternatives to marriage. We think these results suggest an interesting lesson for work-family navigators: while we might believe that change is not possible for moral or structural reasons, it may in fact be personal commitment that is driving our lives. We may have more control than we think.

What are the benefits of control? Early research on control focused on the high levels of stress generated by jobs that presented many demands but offered little control over them (Karasek, 1982). Other research revealed that intellectual flexibility was stunted by heavy constraints on opportunities to make decisions (Kohn & Schooler, 1978; Parcel & Menaghan, 1994). Thomas and Ganster (1995) found relationships between perceptions of control and cholesterol levels, depression, and somatic complaints, mediated through workers' perceptions of work-family conflict. Lachman and Weaver (1998) found that perceptions of control mediated the negative effects of low income–when control was very low, income was more important. When income was low, having control in your job mattered more. With control, the management of role boundaries appears to be easier.

LESSONS FOR INTERVENTION

We turn now to the clinical implications of this research on work and family life. How do we utilize these data to help our clients feel competent and self-directed as they attempt to manage the multiple roles in their lives? Obviously, problems related to managing work and family present themselves in session in a variety of ways. Thus, clinicians have to select their approach based on the manner in which these issues manifest themselves and clients' economic, social, and psychological resources. In the following section we will identify three common ways that problems in managing the interface of work and family life are presented in therapy and the implications of the research for each of these areas, with particular attention given to gender. We acknowledge at the outset that there are many work-family issues that come up in therapy that we are not addressing. As with the review of research, our attempt is not to be comprehensive, but instead to offer applications that we have found useful. Three places we have found that clients often manifest problems managing work and family life are: (1) seeing the big picture, (2) clarifying and adjusting roles, and (3) pragmatics of making it work.

Seeing the Big Picture

An overused but very accurate metaphor that is applicable to the way in which some clients present with work and family problems is that "they can't see the forest for the trees." Women and men sometimes enter therapy focusing on the specific work and family problem or dilemma that is currently causing them concern without a sense of perspective about the larger work and family interface. Clients want answers to a particular issue: "I feel guilty that my kids have to go to an after school program because of my work schedule," "My husband's work schedule is so rigid that I have to manage everything with the kids," or "My boss doesn't understand what it is like to work and raise a family." While the issues are real, clients may first need to back up and take a look at the bigger picture that is the constellation of work and family roles in their family system, whether the family make-up is that of a single parent, of two parents, or a parent and a grandparent. Research would suggest that when clients have a restricted focus on a work/family problem, several interventions might be helpful.

Move clients from a focus on "balance" to "navigating." The lexicon of "balancing work and family" that has been integrated into our public discourse has also been internalized by many adults in ways that limit their perspectives. As described previously, such thinking can limit clients by suggesting a static, here and now solution. While movement to the navigation metaphor is simply a reframe, it is a reframe that may free clients to think more creatively and holistically about their situation. In addition, previous research (Anderson & Leslie, 1991) has shown that reframing is a highly effective strategy in managing work and family stress. Not only can clients be encouraged to adopt the language of navigation, but they can also be encouraged to talk about how the current situation seems different when viewed as a part of an ongoing process of management and movement to a destination instead of a static problem to be solved.

Identify goals and markers. Beyond reframing the challenge of managing work and family demands, the metaphor of navigating opens the door for clinicians to help clients identify their long-term goals relative to the interaction of work and family in their lives. Using the navigation term of "destination," clients can be encouraged to think about how they want to be able to describe their family and work life in 5 or 10 years. Perhaps the goal is to be an emotionally close and financially secure family with adult children who are secure, responsible, and independent. Parents can then be encouraged to identify markers along the way that will help them know they are on course for that destination. Markers may encompass the spectrum of relevant domains from children (e.g., children will be able to complete homework fairly independently) to family life (e.g., we will have a "family fun" outing at least once a month) to career (e.g., I will get positive annual evaluations and periodic promotions) to finances (e.g., I will make monthly contributions, no matter how small, to the children's college fund and my retirement). The important point here is to help parents chart a developmentally appropriate course for how they want to navigate the demands of work and family life. This map can then be referred to periodically to assess their progress and correct the course where necessary.

It should be noted that such discussions can shed light on both incongruency in parents' values concerning goals and markers and gendered assumptions about goals, values, and roles. For example, parents may say, "we want to increase the amount of time a parent is spending with the children." However, examination of the statement may reveal assumptions on the part of at least one if not both parents that the parent to increase time with the children will be the mother. It is not unusual for statements that are made in gender neutral language (parent) to mask gendered thought (mother). While an excellent literature exists examining how to address gendered beliefs (e.g., Gosling & Zangari, 1996; Knudson-Martin, 1994; Mirkin & Geib, 1999–just to name a few), we would like to emphasize that in our experience these gendered assumptions and values are often subtle and frequently beyond the conscious awareness of both spouses. It is not unusual for couples to come into therapy being strongly committed to the importance of each partner finding fulfillment both in the personal and work arenas. Yet these same couples often have internalized societal beliefs about the different "natures" and "abilities" of men and women that would make mothers the better candidate to care for children and make sacrifices at work. At a minimum, therapists should always seek clarification for any gender neutral language that is used in setting goals (e.g., parents will establish themselves professionally, parents will spend more time with children, family will have dinner together) to ascertain if the goals really apply to all or if they are given different weight based on the gender of the parent. If gender inconsistencies are found, the socially constructed sources of these inconsistencies will need to be examined.

Pay attention to alignment of time and resources. Once goals and markers are identified, the degree to which current activities and time allocations are likely to fulfill those goals can be examined. Of course, all of us face non-negotiable or difficult-to-negotiate constraints, and those constraints often vary by gender. For example, in the work setting men are often subtly and not-so-subtly discouraged from staying home with newborn or sick children. Women, on the other hand, are often steered away from particular positions or projects because it is assumed they are less committed to their work. Nonetheless, the secret is to realistically assess which constraints are negotiable and which are not. Far too often, clients list as "non-negotiable," areas where they can make some change, even if it is slight. The dilemma is that making change frequently comes with sacrifices. Yet this is where goals and markers are helpful to both the therapist and clients.

Again, this process may illuminate gender-based assumptions by family members about the importance and demands of work and family roles. Work and family research has indicated that partners, but particularly husbands, underestimate the time that their partners spend in family housework and child care (Coltraine, 1998). A critical part of aligning time and resource may be to have partners learn from each other how much time each spends in family work. Particularly hidden is the organizational oversight that wives often do in heterosexual couples (see Zimmerman et al. on this issue). We have found the technique of daily time use diaries, with modifications, helpful in increasing clients' awareness of their partner's time commitments, and in illuminating inequities in time devoted to family responsibilities. Time use diaries are misleading if they only record behaviors such as washing the dishes or helping kids with homework. To represent family work, diaries must also include the time that each person spends planning, thinking about, or mentally coordinating family tasks and activities. Keeping track of when dentist appointments have to be scheduled or figuring out how to get different kids to a soccer game, a clarinet practice, and a birthday party–all within 30 minutes of each other, is no less family work than vacuuming or mowing. Because the completion of a diary that includes both what one is doing and what one is mentally keeping track of can be a burdensome task, we suggest breaking it up so that partners record physical and mental activities on alternating days. Also, because men are more likely than women to receive assistance with their family chores (Baruch & Barnett, 1986), diaries should indicate whether tasks are done alone or with assistance.

Finally, a critical piece of assisting clients in developing satisfactory alignment relative to work and family needs is to anticipate disruption and course realignment. "Predicting relapse" or identifying predictable setbacks or barriers is a stable part of family therapy. Likewise, recognizing that some days, weeks, and even months will be better than others and that clients will sometimes get off course needs to be part of the therapy. The navigation metaphor allows clients to frame current problems or stress as "storms" that have to be countered in order to stay on course. Expanding the metaphor to tracking and anticipating storms further gives clients a sense of control as they prepare to weather a predicted storm caused by events such as unusually heavy demands at work or competing sports schedules for children.

Clarifying and Adjusting Roles

Perhaps the most common presentation of work and family problems in the clinical arena is the pitting of work and family roles against one another. This role competition can present in many ways, whether it be one person struggling with the roles of parent and worker, partners in conflict because one partner emphasizes the work role while the other feels forced to manage all the family roles, or one partner feeling angry because the role of spouse has been pushed aside by the demands of parent and worker roles. Drawing from the work and family research, several approaches seem beneficial in addressing these role-based problems.

Identify clients' assumptions about roles. Below role struggles or conflicts are often clients' assumptions about how they "should" perform (or their partner should perform) each role. Sometimes the conflict is within one person as the individual has certain assumptions about two roles (e.g., mother, employee) that seem to compete with one another. Other times the conflict is between the two adults (e.g., different assumptions about how the role of mother should be performed). Such situations require that clients examine their own, as well as society's, assumptions or values about the nature of certain roles. This can be particularly important for heterosexual couples in that notions of breadwinner father and nurturing mother have been well-socialized into our collective psyche. (The reader is encouraged to examine Real, 1995; Sheinberg & Penn, 1991; and Weingarten, 1995, for examples of how to challenge and reconstruct these cultural stereotypes.) Further, clients must be helped to examine the rewards and costs of each role, recognizing that roles really do compete sometimes and one may have to forgo some of the rewards of one role to be able to carry out the other role.

Closely aligned with the idea of assumptions about roles is the source of individuals' commitments to their roles. Utilizing the terminology of moral, personal, and structural commitment borrowed from the work and family literature may help clients explore their role assumptions in greater depth and locate the source of their difficulty in changing.

For example, a father may express an interest in spending more time with his child (marker) but maintain that he will have to sacrifice this because supporting the family financially is his most important role. Examining his assumptions, and society's assumptions, about his roles both as father and as employee may help him recognize that part of his hesitancy to work fewer hours, get off the corporate "fast track," or share more of the responsibility for financial support with his wife is the loss of status and prestige he will experience in his career. Likewise, he may acknowledge that he doesn't find care of children as rewarding as landing a big contract. As Pasick (1990) and others have pointed out, work is so socialized into men's self-concept that the costs of scaling down the work role may initially be much more evident to men than the rewards of a more active parenting role. Employing the terminology of commitments, the father may feel a moral commitment to his role as father ("I should spend more time with my child"), but finds the financial (structural commitments) and prestige (personal commitments) rewards of work more appealing. Providing clients with a language to talk about the different ways they are connected to their roles may help them both clarify their assumptions and decide to what extent they are willing to make changes.

While we often think of this type of gender-based struggle occurring in heterosexual couples, it is equally likely that single parents and gay and lesbian couples will likewise have gendered-based assumptions about role performance that may make it difficult to renegotiate the allotment of time to certain roles and tasks. One does not need to have a partner of the opposite sex, or a partner at all, to hold gendered beliefs and role assumptions.

Identify clients' orientation about roles. We are using the concept of role orientation here to refer to the stance one takes towards his or her roles, whether they be family or work roles. The research would suggest two critical aspects of one's role orientation should be explored: (1) the extent to which one approaches roles from a hierarchical perspective and (2) the extent to which one approaches roles from a protean perspective.

In addressing one's hierarchical orientation, therapists need to help clients examine whether they see one role as primary with other roles "interfering" with the performance of that major role, or whether they attempt to be more evenly "engaged" in all roles. While the research mentioned previously suggests the mental health benefits of more even engagement across roles, it is common for both men and women to have been socialized to give prominence to one role, men as providers, women as caretakers, even when each is fulfilling both roles. While this tendency to see one role as primary exists for both men and women, it is our experience that men tend to have more difficulty valuing and working towards even engagement in roles. The strong emphasis on hierarchy and focus of purpose in both men's socialization and current work environments reinforces and constructs gendered ideology about the primacy of certain roles. One useful technique for beginning to shake this tight frame for a man is to have him evaluate his life as a 65- or 70-year-old. If a man is able to step out of the pressures of the moment and engage in anticipatory reflection of what mattered in his life, role orientation can sometimes be altered. It is even more helpful in the process of examining role orientation if he is able to speak with his own father or a respected older male about what mattered in the elder man's life.

One's protean orientation, or the degree to which one's reward system is self-derived versus externally based is likewise important in clarifying the difficulties clients sometimes have in altering their roles. Those with externally driven reward systems may be less inclined than protean oriented clients to try non-traditional, creative solutions for role navigation. This reluctance may stem from their reliance on socially accepted standards of performance and reward. Challenging clients' reliance on external "shoulds" in regards to work and family roles, may help them recognize their personal motivations and rewards in different roles and increase their openness to crafting an integration of roles that is satisfying, even if socially unconventional. Again, the language of personal, moral, and structural commitments to having a role performed a particular way may help clients distinguish between their own beliefs and those that are externally imposed. For example, helping women identify the endless number of ways they are bombarded with messages about what is a "good" mother from TV, books, magazines, movies, as well as friends and family, enables them to better understand sources of their structural commitment to being a particular type of mother. Such an exercise also frees women to examine their own values, desires, and preference about the type of mother they strive to be separate from the social mandates they encounter.

Think systemically. Just as it is common for families to identify a particular member as the problem, individuals or couples sometimes identify a particular role–usually the work role–as the "problem." And just as in therapy, the identified "problem" is usually only the most visible element of a complex set of connections. The lesson is that opportunities for change should be sought widely, not just within the most obvious role. Just as successful coping does not always mean choosing one role over another, it does not mean problematizing and "fixing" one role. Instead, solutions need to be worked out in the entire family system of roles, possibly including children and extended family and friends.

Developing Behavioral Strategies

Clients may have a sense of their goals and markers in navigating their work and family life, may have examined, clarified, and chosen their role orientation and assumptions, and yet still feel a since of inadequacy in structuring work and family life in a satisfactory way. Ultimately, the realization of their goals may come down to basic behavioral strategies that help them organize and manage their various roles. The following guidelines, while not comprehensive, are drawn from the empirical literature and provide a good starting point in helping clients develop viable strategies.

Manipulate the boundaries between roles. In some cases, it is effective to strengthen the boundaries between roles, and using basic problem solving approaches towards this end may be beneficial. For example, many women in the study of part-time managers and professionals mentioned earlier reported that it was easier to leave work when they were obligated to pick up children at child care. Some had intentionally arranged this obligation in an effort to firm up the boundary between work and family life and help to ensure that they would work less. Another kind of structural manipulation occurs when individuals take on additional commitments. For example, it may be more effective for couples to commit to attending an exercise or hobby class together in the evening than to simply promise one another to spend more time together at home. Making positive commitments that actively compete with work for attention is likely to be more effective than simply promising to work less.

In other circumstances, it might be useful to weaken the boundaries between roles. Time allocated to one role is not necessarily unavailable to another. Again, problem solving with clients to identify when time devoted to one role is still available to another may help relieve their perceived time crunch. Sometimes it is possible to participate in two rewarding productive activities at once. We know an academic dean, for example, whose job requires him to attend many social and sporting events. Feeling deeply the separation from his family during evenings and weekends, he developed a strategy of selecting or shaping events that his wife and children might be likely to enjoy, and then using those events as opportunities to spend time with one or more members of his family.

It is important to note, as our examples demonstrate, that the process of managing boundaries between roles is often a different experience for women and men. Juggling and integrating multiple roles is something many women do, so the challenge for them is to learn to set and maintain clear boundaries between roles. Men, on the other hand, often have to work to learn to blend roles instead of compartmentalizing them.

Observe personal experiences of high and low control. Research shows us that the experience of low control is both stressful and potentially harmful to physical and mental health. Helping clients identify their degree of control in each of their roles is the first step in increasing personal control. Reflections about when experiences are perceived as energizing versus draining offer important clues. Often, feeling drained, guilty, or "put upon" signals a lack of control over life demands. Once the circumstances and consequences of low control are recognized, coping strategies can be more easily developed. This may include identification of resources one has to bring to a role, areas of flexibility in the role system, or pairing times of low control with times of high control. For example, a mother may find that the two hours after she leaves work, when she picks up the kids and goes home, is the worst time of the day. She is tired, the kids are tired, dinner must be prepared, and homework must be done. While she may see this as a time to be endured, examining her degree of control in the situation may provide clues to possible changes. If she finds that the feeling of lack of control comes from frequently having her efforts to cook dinner interrupted with kids who want help with homework, she may realize that the solution lies not in constantly telling the kids they can do it themselves, but in separating the times when dinner is prepared and homework is done. In one family we worked with, the parents agreed that three things had to be done every weekday evening: dinner had to be prepared, the kitchen had to be cleaned, and homework had to be finished. Since they truly had no control over when they got off work, the mother had to be the one to pick up the kids and begin dinner. While this was a low control situation because of the inflexibility of time schedules, control was added by deciding with the children that nothing else was allowed to interfere with dinner preparation. Children were free to do their homework but only to the extent that it could be done without assistance. The mother then felt some degree of control and predictability in the kitchen as she cooked dinner. After dinner, the two tasks of clean-up and homework had to be done, and since the mother had prepared dinner, she got to choose each evening which one of the two tasks she would like to oversee that night and the father would do the other. What the parents gave up was having the kids help with the clean-up. However, for the mother it was a sacrifice she was willing to make because it gave her a sense of some control both over dinner and in the activities after dinner. True, it was not the control of choosing to sit down and read a good book, but it was enough of an increase in predictability to make a qualitative difference in her experience of the weekday evening hours with her family.

CONCLUSIONS

The vast majority of families entering therapy today are juggling many demands and roles in both the employment and family domains.

Furthermore, these are domains that are typically the most important in their lives. Unfortunately, while an extensive research literature has been compiled over the last several decades on how families are affected by and manage the intersection of these domains, little of this work has been used to inform clinical practices. While the work presented here is far from comprehensive, it is an initial attempt to identify potential therapeutic implications of this burgeoning body of empirical work. It is our belief that families will benefit when researchers and practitioners, be they therapists or family life educators, are able to share and utilize each other's knowledge and expertise. Toward that end, we hope that additional teams of researchers and clinicians will continue to examine the way in which research can inform practice and, additionally, practice can inform research.

NOTE

1. Both the first and second author have extensive experience as work-family researchers with an applied focus. Dr. MacDermid works extensively with corporations, including directing the Midwestern Work-Family Association, a membership organization for employers interested in family issues. Dr. Leslie is a marriage and family therapist and therapist educator and supervisor, who focuses not only on work and family stress, but the gendered nature of much of this stress.

REFERENCES

Anderson, E. A. & Leslie, L. A. (1991). Coping with employment and family stress: Employment arrangement and gender differences. *Sex Roles, 24,* 223-237.

Barnett, R. C. (1998). Toward a review and reconceptualization of the work/family literature. *Genetic, Social, and General Psychology Monographs, 124,* 125-182.

Barnett, R. C. & Gareis, K. C. (2000). Reduced-hours employment: The relationship between difficulty of tradeoffs and quality of life. *Work and Occupations, 27,* 168-187.

Baruch, G. K. & Barnett, R. C. (1986). Role quality, multiple role involvement, and psychological well-being in midlife women. *Journal of Personality and Social Psychology, 51,* 578-585.

Becker, P. E. & Moen, P. (1999). Scaling back: Dual-earner couples' work-family strategies. *Journal of Marriage and the Family, 61,* 995-1007.

Blau, F. & Ferber, M. A. (1992). Women and men: Changing roles in a changing economy. In F. Blau & M. A. Ferber, *The economics of women, men, and work* (pp. 13-33). Englewood Cliffs, NJ: Prentice-Hall.

Crouter, A. C. (1984). Spillover from family to work: The neglected side of the work-family interface. *Human Relations, 37*, 425-442.

Galinsky, E. (1999). *Ask the children.* New York, NY: William Morrow and Company.

Goode, W. J. (1960). A theory of role strain. *American Sociological Review, 25*, 483-496.

Hall, D. T. & Moss, J. E. (1998). The new protean career contract: Helping organizations and employees adapt. *Organizational Dynamics, 26*, 22-37.

Johnson, M. P., Caughlin, J. P., & Huston, T. L. (1999). The tripartite nature of marital commitment: Personal, moral, and structural reasons to stay married. *Journal of Marriage and the Family, 61*, 160-177.

Kahn, R. L., Wolfe, D. M., Quinn, R. P., & Snoek, J. D. (1964). *Organizational stress: Studies in role conflict and ambiguity.* New York: John Wiley & Sons.

Karasek, R. A., Schwartz, J., Theorell, T., Pieper, C., Russell, B. S., & Michela, J. (1982). *Final report: Job characteristics, occupation and coronary heart disease.* New York: Columbia University, Department of Industrial Engineering and Operations Research.

Kirchmeyer, C. (1992). Perceptions of nonwork-to-work spillover: Challenging the common view of conflict-ridden domain relationships. *Basic and Applied Social Psychology, 13*, 231-249.

Knudson-Martin, C. (1997). The politics of gender in family therapy. *Journal of Marital and Family Therapy, 23*, 421-437.

Kohn, M. L. & Schooler, C. (1978). The reciprocal effects of the substantive complexity of work and intellectual flexibility: A longitudinal assessment. *American Journal of Sociology, 84*, 24-52.

Lachman, M. E. & Weaver, S. L. (1998). The sense of control as a moderator of social class differences in health and well-being. *Journal of Personality and Social Psychology, 74*, 763-773.

MacDermid, S. M., Lee, M. D., & Buck, M. (in press). Women professionals and managers in alternative work arrangements: Rethinking the meanings and manifestations of career development and success. Invited submission, *Journal of Management Development.* Special issue edited by Ron Burke.

Marks, S. R. (1977). Multiple roles and role strain: Some notes on human energy, time and commitment. *American Sociological Review, 42*, 921-936.

Marks, S. R., Huston, T. L., Johnson, E. M., & MacDermid, S. M. (in press). Role balance among white married couples. Accepted for publication in *Journal of Marriage and the Family.*

Marks, S. R. & MacDermid, S. M. (1996). Multiple roles and the self: A theory of role balance. *Journal of Marriage and the Family, 58*, 417-432.

Mirkin, M. P. & Geib, P. (1999). Consciousness of context in relational couples therapy. *Journal of Feminist Family Therapy, 11*, 31-51.

Moen, P. & Wethington, E. (1992). The concept of family adaptive strategies. *Annual Review of Sociology, 18*, 233-251.

Parcel, T. L. & Menaghan, E. G. (1994). *Parents' jobs and children's lives.* New York: Aldine de Gruyter.

Pasick, R. S. (1990). Raised to work. In R.L. Meth & R. S. Pasick (Eds.), *Men in therapy: The challenge of change* (pp. 35-54). New York: Guilford.

Pittman, J. F. (1994). Work/family fit as a mediator of work factors on marital tension: Evidence from the interface of greedy institutions. *Human Relations, 47*, 183-209.

Real, T. (1995). Fathering our sons: Refathering ourselves: Some thought on transforming masculine legacies. *Journal of Feminist Family Therapy, 7,* 27-43.

Salter, C. (1999). Enough is enough. *Fast Company, 26,* 120-136.

Sheinberg, M. & Penn, P. (1991). Gender dilemmas, gender questions, and the gender mantra. *Journal of Marital and Family Therapy, 17,* 33-44.

Sieber, S. D. (1974). Toward a theory of role accumulation. *American Sociological Review, 39,* 567-578.

Thomas, L. T. & Ganster, D. C. (1995). Impact of family-supportive work variables on work-family conflict and strain: A control perspective. *Journal of Applied Psychology, 80,* 6-15.

Weingarten, K. (1995). Radical listening: Challenging cultural beliefs for and about mothers. *Journal of Feminist Family Therapy, 7,* 7-22.

Effects of Accommodations
Made at Home and at Work on Wives'
and Husbands' Family and Job Satisfaction

Krista J. Brockwood
Leslie B. Hammer
Margaret B. Neal
Cari L. Colton

SUMMARY. As part of a larger national study of 309 dual-earner couples caring both for children and aging parents, participants were surveyed about the behavioral accommodations they made at home (e.g., limiting time spent with family) and at work (e.g., changing work schedules), and about their satisfaction levels in both domains. Results indicated that wives made more frequent accommodations than did husbands, both at

Krista J. Brockwood, MS, is affiliated with the Department of Psychology, Portland State University. Leslie B. Hammer, PhD, is Associate Professor, Department of Psychology, Portland State University. Margaret B. Neal, PhD, is Professor, Community Health and Institute on Aging, Portland State University. Cari L. Colton, MS, is affiliated with the Department of Psychology, Portland State University.

This study was funded by the Alfred P. Sloan Foundation (grant # 96-10-20). An earlier version of this article was presented at the conference for Work and Family: Expanding the Horizons, sponsored by the Business and Professional Women's Foundation, The Center for Working Families at UC Berkeley, and the Alfred P. Sloan Foundation in March, 1999, San Francisco, CA.
Address correspondence to: Leslie B. Hammer, Department of Psychology, Portland State University, Portland, OR 97207-0751 (E-mail: *hammerl@pdx.edu*).

[Haworth co-indexing entry note]: "Effects of Accommodations Made at Home and at Work on Wives' and Husbands' Family and Job Satisfaction." Brockwood et al. Co-published simultaneously in *Journal of Feminist Family Therapy* (The Haworth Press, Inc.) Vol. 13, No. 2/3, 2001, pp. 41-64; and: *Balancing Family and Work: Special Considerations in Feminist Therapy* (ed: Toni Schindler Zimmerman) The Haworth Press, Inc., 2001, pp. 41-64. Single or multiple copies of this article are available for a fee from The Haworth Document Delivery Service [1-800-HAWORTH, 9:00 a.m. - 5:00 p.m. (EST). E-mail address: getinfo@haworthpressinc.com].

41

work and at home. Accommodations made were related to satisfaction in a number of ways. For both husbands and wives, the extent to which a spouse made accommodations at home was negatively related to their own family satisfaction. *[Article copies available for a fee from The Haworth Document Delivery Service: 1-800-HAWORTH. E-mail address: <getinfo@ haworthpressinc.com> Website: <http://www.HaworthPress.com> © 2001 by The Haworth Press, Inc. All rights reserved.]*

KEYWORDS. Work and family, gender issues, marriage and family, sandwiched generation, parent care, crossover effects

The work-family literature traditionally has focused on the conflict between work and family. Recently, this focus has given way to a more positive approach emphasizing work-family balance (e.g., Brennan & Poertner, 1997; Hall, 1990; Joseph & Hallman, 1996). This shift recognizes that people do not simply passively experience conflict between their work and family roles, but that they are active in their search for work-family balance and will seek to make the necessary accommodations to achieve that balance. These accommodations can be described as behaviors that entail an elimination, reduction, or change in the participation of one role to aid in the participation of another role.

Another recent development in work-family research involves studying the effects that stress and strain experienced by one member of the couple may have on his/her spouse or partner, known as crossover effects (Hammer, Allen, & Grigsby, 1997; Westman & Vinokur, 1998). This research utilizes a systems perspective, which considers the interdependence of elements in a system (e.g., the family) (Bronfenbrenner, 1977) and recognizes that the actions of one member of the system (e.g., spouse) influence the behaviors and attitudes of the other member of the couple. This article joins these two lines of research by examining how individuals' job and family satisfaction are impacted not only by the accommodations they themselves make at home and at work, but also by the accommodations made by their spouses.

ACCOMMODATIONS MADE AT WORK AND AT HOME

For the purposes of this study, accommodations at work and at home are defined as a behavioral subset of coping mechanisms. These behaviors entail either an elimination, decrease, increase, or other change in the level of participation in one role to provide more flexibility and perhaps to engage in other aspects of that role or other life roles. People make accommodations in their work or family roles to try to achieve a balance between the two, or to balance various roles within the family or at work. Examples of accommodations made at work include cutting back on work hours, limiting business travel, and changing work hours to spend more time in other activities at home. Examples of accommodations made at home include hiring a house cleaning service, taking children to school early, and missing some of the children's activities due to other demands. Although the research on accommodations made at work and at home is sparse, a few studies have examined some antecedents and consequences of such accommodations, which are described as follows.

Research on accommodations made at home has focused primarily on the division of labor in the home. Researchers have consistently found that women spend more hours in housework and household management than do men (Baruch & Barnett, 1986; Gutek, Searle, & Klepa, 1991; Mederer, 1993). Dancer and Gilbert (1993) found that the employment status of wives had a significant effect on husbands' levels of family participation. Specifically, involvement of husbands and wives appeared to be more equal among dual-career and dual-earner couples than in traditional families, where the wife was not employed outside the home.

Two studies have examined accommodations at work, or what was termed "restructuring" at work. Brett and Yogev (1988) researched the types of accommodations made at work by dual-earner couples with children. At least one of the members of the couple was either a professional in advertising, law, or accounting. Overall, wives did significantly more work restructuring than did husbands, and those individuals who were more involved at work made fewer accommodations at work. It should be noted that this sample did not include part-time workers. Voluntary part-time work may be an accommodation that people make at work, in part, to spend more time in the family domain.

Karambayya and Reilly (1992) collected both qualitative and quantitative data in which both members of 39 dual-earner couples reported on specific work restructuring behaviors in which they engaged, such as changing work schedules, limiting business travel, and limiting weekend work. Couples were also asked if they had made special "one-time" arrangements at work to accommodate a child's or spouse's activity. As in Brett and Yogev's study (1988), wives did more accommodating at work, overall, than did husbands. Husbands, however, reported making more special "one-time" arrangements to meet family demands than did wives.

In summary, the limited research on accommodations made at home indicates that wives spend more hours doing house- and family-related tasks compared to husbands. In addition, research suggests that in general, wives make more accommodations at work to enable them to meet their family demands than do husbands (Brett & Yogev, 1988; Karambayya & Reilly, 1992). Little research, however, has been conducted examining the outcomes of making such accommodations, either at work or at home. The present study attempts to fill this void by examining the effects of making such accommodations on both job and family satisfaction.

Crossover Effects

A criticism of many work-family studies has been these studies' exclusive focus on the individual and their failure to consider the social context, such as the individual's spouse, children, or coworkers (Westman & Vinokur, 1998). A recent line of research has addressed this omission by examining how spouses' behaviors and attitudes influence one another; these have been termed "crossover effects" (Hammer et al., 1997; Westman & Etzion, 1995). This is a perspective adapted from systems theory, which emphasizes the important role that context plays in outcomes and recognizes the reciprocal influences and feedback loops within a system (e.g., Bronfenbrenner, 1977; Grzywacz & Marks, 2000).

Westman and Vinokur (1998) suggest that crossover effects occur via three potential mechanisms: (1) stressors that are common to both partners (e.g., life events), (2) direct transmission from one spouse to another, and (3) indirect transmission, in which the relationship is mediated by the interaction processes of the partner. For instance, because certain stressors are present, one spouse may develop a more conflictual style, which then increases the stress level of the partner.

Studies thus far have documented the influence that one spouse can have on the other in terms of stress and strain. Westman and Etzion (1995) determined that the level of burnout experienced by a sample of male Israeli military officers was positively related to their spouse's level of burnout, after controlling for the officer's own job stress and coping resources. This finding also applied in the opposite direction, from wives to husbands. Additionally, Hammer et al. (1997) found that, after controlling for an individual's own work- and family-related antecedents, the level of conflict between work and family reported by his or her spouse accounted for a significant amount of variance in the individual's own work-family conflict. Hammer, Bauer, and Grandey (1999) also reported a positive relationship between husbands' and wives' work-family conflict, specifically family interfering with work, and a measure of work withdrawal, including lateness and interruptions at work, thus demonstrating crossover effects on work-related outcomes.

The present study adds to this stream of inquiry by examining the effect of behaviors (i.e., work and family accommodations) by one spouse on the work- and family-related attitudes (i.e., job and family satisfaction) of the other spouse. Existing research has examined the effects of attitudes of one spouse on those of the other (e.g., Hammer et al., 1997; Westman & Etzion, 1995), or the effects of attitudes of one spouse on certain work-related behaviors of the other (Hammer et al., 1999), but not how behaviors of one spouse may cross over and influence attitudes of the other spouse.

HYPOTHESES

Because so little research has been conducted on work and family accommodations, particularly in terms of the outcomes resulting from the accommodations, research from other areas of the work and family literature informs these hypotheses. It is anticipated that accommodations made at work will be constrained by many organizational factors. Work is generally viewed as less flexible than family, due to work's structure, so it may not be possible for many individuals to make certain accommodations at work, such as working at home or changing one's schedule. For this reason, those individuals who are able to make these accommodations at work may have more positive feelings toward their organization. This is, in fact, what is argued by social exchange theory, which states that organizations and employees are engaged in an exchange of commitments (Sinclair, Hannigan, & Tetrick, 1995). When employees perceive that their organization is sympathetic toward their needs and allows them the flexibility which can ameliorate some of their stress, employees will respond in kind by increasing commitment and attachment to the organization, as manifest in increased levels of job satisfaction. Also, making these accommodations at work may increase one's sense of control at work, which has been shown to increase job satisfaction (Thomas & Ganster, 1995). Furthermore, it is expected that these positive feelings will spill over and affect family satisfaction as well, as models of the work-family interface have demonstrated (e.g., Frone, Russell, & Cooper, 1992). This is because the increased flexibility afforded by making accommodations at work enables workers to better meet their family demands, thereby increasing family satisfaction. Thus, we made the following predictions concerning the effects of *accommodations made at work:*

> *H1a.* The use of accommodations at work will be *positively* related to family satisfaction, such that those individuals making more frequent accommodations at work will experience higher levels of satisfaction at home.

> *H1b.* The use of accommodations at work will be *positively* related to job satisfaction, such that those individuals making more frequent accommodations at work will experience higher levels of satisfaction at work.

The relationships between accommodations made at home and job and family satisfaction are very different from those between accommodations made at work and both types of satisfaction. As stated previously, work tends to be much more structured than family life. As a result, it may not be possible to make accommodations at work. Individuals may then feel compelled to make certain accommodations at home, such as spending less time with family members or missing certain events (e.g., a child's baseball game or recital), in order to meet their work demands. In this way, people may feel a lack of control, because they perceive that they have no choice but to make accommodations at home. This, in turn, may lead to lower levels of satisfaction with the family. Also, the relative inflexibility of work may be seen as the source of the trouble, leading people to experience lower job satisfaction.

Therefore, we hypothesized the following concerning the effects of *accommodations made at home:*

H2a. The use of accommodations at home will be *negatively* related to family satisfaction, such that those individuals making more frequent accommodations at home will experience lower levels of satisfaction at home.

H2b. The use of accommodations at home will be *negatively* related to job satisfaction, such that those individuals making more frequent accommodations at home will experience lower levels of satisfaction at work.

We also expected that the extent to which a spouse made accommodations at work for home would be likely to cross over and have positive effects on an individual's family satisfaction, due to the greater input and help that the spouse would be providing in the family. At the same time, we expected that the use of accommodations at home for work by one's spouse would negatively impact an individual's level of family satisfaction, because that person may be left with more of the family responsibilities. For example, if a spouse makes accommodations at home because of work, such as spending less time doing yard work or taking care of the children, typically, those responsibilities will fall on his or her partner. Thus, we proposed the following hypotheses concerning the *crossover effects of accommodations on family satisfaction* of work and family accommodations made by one's spouse:

H3a. The use of accommodations at work by one's spouse will be *positively* related to one's own family satisfaction, such that those individuals whose spouse makes greater use of accommodations at work will experience higher levels of satisfaction at home.

H3b. The use of accommodations at home by one's spouse will be *negatively* related to one's own family satisfaction, such that those individuals whose spouse makes greater use of accommodations at home will experience lower levels of satisfaction at home.

Because of limited theoretical rationale, we could not make specific predictions concerning the effects of spouse's work and family accommodations on individuals' level of job satisfaction. Therefore, we posed the following research questions concerning the *crossover effects of accommodations on job satisfaction:*

> *Research Question 1a:* Is spouse's use of accommodations at work related to one's own level of job satisfaction?

> *Research Question 1b:* Is spouse's use of accommodations at home related to one's own level of job satisfaction?

METHOD

Participants

The participants in this study consisted of couples who were part of the first wave of a larger study involving dual-earner couples in the sandwiched generation. Specifically, these were working couples who had children at home and who also were caring for aging parents, and thus were "sandwiched" between their child care and parent care responsibilities. To be included in the study, both members of the couple had to participate. Also, participants had to (a) have been living together for at least one year, (b) have at least one child 18 or under living at home three or more days per week, (c) be providing care for one or more aging parents for a minimum of three hours per week, (d) be working (i.e., one member 35 or more hours per week and the other at least 20 hours per week), and (e) have a combined household income of $40,000 or greater. This final criterion was stipulated due to the specific interest of the project's primary funding source in middle- and upper-income families. It should be noted that, although not a criterion for eligibility in the study, all participants were heterosexual couples.

Sample description. The average age of couples for the sample was 44 for husbands and 42 for wives. The sample was fairly well educated, with husbands reporting an average of 14.7 years of education and wives with slightly more education at 15.3 years. The sample was also mostly White, with 95.3% of husbands and 93.2% of wives reporting their ethnicity as Caucasian. Couples reported a median annual household income of $62,500. Husbands worked an average of 49.0 hours per week, whereas wives worked 37.7 hours per week. Couples had an average of 1.6 children, and the average age of the youngest child was

10.6 years of age. Couples reported an average of 16.5 hours per week of providing care to an aging parent (median = 10.5 hours).

Sampling Procedure

Sampling was accomplished via telephone screening using a Computer Assisted Telephone Interviewing (CATI) system and a purchased list of telephone numbers of households across the United States targeted to contain an adult aged 30 to 60. If a couple met the eligibility criteria (excluding income), the respondent was asked if both members of the couple might be willing to complete a mailed survey. If so, a packet containing two cover letters, two copies of the survey instrument, and two separate self-addressed and stamped envelopes was mailed to the couple. After both members had returned their surveys, the couple was mailed a check for $40 as a token of appreciation.

Of the 8,268 apparently working, non-business numbers originally called, a total of 741 households (8.97%) contacted met the criteria for participation (except for income–96 respondents reported household incomes below $40,000, and 35 refused to say). Of these, 624 couples agreed to consider participating in the study and were mailed surveys. Both members of 360 couples returned surveys, but 22 couples (6.1%) no longer met the study criteria. Applying this ineligibility rate of 6.1% to the 741 couples initially identified as eligible yields a base of 696 households identified and eligible. Thus, the response rate was 48.6% (338 couples out of 696) of those identified and eligible, or 57.7% of those who were actually mailed surveys and would have been expected to remain eligible (338 couples out of 586) at Wave 1. Of the 338 couples who returned useable surveys, 309 ($N = 618$ individuals) met the income criterion and served as the sample for this study.

Measures

Work and family accommodations. The measures of work and family accommodations were developed specifically for this study. To do this, 17 focus groups ($N = 63$ participants) were held locally with members of couples who met the eligibility criteria. Focus group participants were asked: "What accommodations do you or your spouse make at home with regard to your home and social life? What things do you do differently, or more or less of, to help you manage both your work and your family responsibilities for your children and your parents?" They were also asked this question with regard to accommodations they made at work. The tapes from the groups were transcribed and coded to ascertain the full spectrum of work and family accommodations being made by working couples in the sandwiched generation, as well as general coping mechanisms, which are often internalized or more generalized plans of attack (see Amatea & Fong-Beyette, 1987). From the coded transcripts, items for the mailed survey then were developed. For the present study, items were chosen that reflected behavioral accommodations made either at work or at home. Several of the original items were ambiguous in nature as to where the accommodation was being made (e.g., "I plan how I'm going to use my time and energy."), so those items were omitted. The remaining items for each scale (i.e., accommodations at home and at work) were analyzed for their internal consistency. Several items had low inter-item correlations with the others and resulted in a severe decrement in the internal reliability, so those items were dropped. The resulting internal-consistency reliability coefficients for the family accommodations scale were $\alpha = .66$ for husbands, and $\alpha = .60$ for wives. Those for the work accommodations scale were $\alpha = .52$ for husbands and $\alpha = .42$ for wives. The low reliabilities are recognized as a potential limitation of the study and are addressed in the Discussion. (See Appendix A for specific items.)

In the survey, participants were asked to indicate the degree to which each statement described how they act in response to their work and family demands. Responses were on a three-point scale (1 = "never"; 2 = "sometimes"; 3 = "most or all of the time"). Separate mean scores were calculated for the three-item work accommodations scale and the six-item family accommodations scale.

Satisfaction measures. Job satisfaction was measured using the five-item General Job Satisfaction scale (husbands: $\alpha = .72$; wives: $\alpha = .69$), which is part of the Job Diagnostic Survey (Hackman & Oldham, 1975). Examples of items include, "Generally speaking, I am very satisfied with my job," and "I frequently think of quitting my job" (reverse scored). The family satisfaction scale (husbands: $\alpha = .72$; wives: $\alpha = .65$) is a modification of three items from the job satisfaction scale, substituting the word "family" for "job," and making a few other minor changes to make the context more logical. Kopelman, Greenhaus, and Connolly (1983) used this same method. The three items were: "I frequently think

I would like to change my family situation" (reverse scored), "Generally speaking, I am very satisfied with my family," and "I am generally satisfied with the role I play in my family." For both measures, high scores indicate high satisfaction.

Control variables. Several demographic variables were controlled for in the analyses, including years of education, perceived adequacy of household income, number of children aged 18 or under living at home, total number of hours of parent care provided per week by the respondent, and number of hours worked per week by the respondent.

Analyses

Descriptive statistics and bivariate correlations were computed for the primary variables in the analyses. In addition, t-tests were conducted to test for differences between wives and husbands in the accommodation scores and in the dependent variables. To test each of the hypotheses, separate hierarchical regressions were run for husbands and for wives in the sample. To test the within-individual effects (Hypotheses 1a, 1b, 2a, and 2b), the individual's control variables were included in the first step of the regression, followed in the second step by the individual's own scores on each of the two accommodation measures. To test the crossover effects (Hypotheses 3a, 3b, and the two research questions), the individual's control variables were included in the first step of the regression, and his or her spouse's scores on the two accommodation measures were included in the second step.

RESULTS

Descriptive Statistics and Gender Differences

Table 1 lists the mean scores on the descriptive variables for wives and husbands, and Table 2 contains the correlations between study variables. Examination of these two tables yielded several interesting findings. Overall, wives more frequently made accommodations at work ($t = -6.67, p < .001$) and at home ($t = -3.80, p < .001$) than did husbands. An interesting pattern emerges, however, when the differences between wives' and husbands' use of accommodations at home and at work are examined. While wives made similar use of accommodations

TABLE 1. Means and Standard Deviations for Levels of Accommodation and Satisfaction

Variable	Range	Wives (N = 308)		Husbands (N = 308)	
		Mean	SD	Mean	SD
Family Accommodations*	1-3	2.04	.33	1.95	.34
Work Accommodations*	1-3	2.01	.47	1.77	.45
Job Satisfaction	1-5	3.50	.66	3.46	.72
Family Satisfaction	1-5	3.98	.70	4.03	.73

*Indicates a significant difference between Wives and Husbands ($p < .001$)

at work and at home ($t = -.80$, $p = .43$), husbands made significantly greater use of accommodations at home than accommodations at work ($t = 5.79$, $p < .001$). Wives' and husbands' levels of family satisfaction and job satisfaction did not differ significantly.

Examination of the bivariate correlations also revealed some noteworthy findings (see Table 2). First, there was a statistically significant correlation for wives between the frequency of accommodations made at work and at home ($r = .12$, $p < .05$), suggesting that wives who are making accommodations at work are also making accommodations at home. This was not true for husbands, as there was no correlation between the frequency of making accommodations at work and the frequency of making accommodations at home. In addition, there was a significant, positive correlation between the extent to which wives and husbands were making accommodations at home ($r = .27$, $p < .001$), but this was not the case for accommodations at work, suggesting that couples may be categorized either as those who tend to make family accommodations or those who tend not to make family accommodations.

Tests of the Hypotheses

Within-individual effects (Hypotheses 1a and 1b and Hypotheses 2a and 2b). As summarized in Table 3, for wives in the study, the frequency of making accommodations at work was a significant, positive

TABLE 2. Correlations Between Wives' and Husbands' Accommodation Frequencies and Satisfaction

Variable	1	2	3	4	5	6	7	8
1. Family accommodations–wives	---							
2. Family accommodations–husbands	.27***	---						
3. Work accommodations–wives	.12*	−.08	---					
4. Work accommodations–husbands	.02	.04	.05	---				
5. Job satisfaction–wives	−.16**	−.09	.08	−.07	---			
6. Job satisfaction–husbands	−.08	−.10	.00	.08	.07	---		
7. Family satisfaction–wives	−.33***	−.15**	.09	−.06	.13*	.17**	---	
8. Family satisfaction–husbands	−.26***	−.32***	−.08	−.03	.04	.31***	.38***	---

*** $p < .001$, ** $p < .01$, * $p < .05$

predictor of family satisfaction ($\beta = .12$, $p = .04$), but was not a significant predictor of job satisfaction ($\beta = .10$, $p = .09$). For husbands, the frequency of making accommodations at work was not a significant predictor of either job satisfaction ($\beta = .06$, $p = .27$) or family satisfaction ($\beta = -.02$, $p = .70$). Thus, Hypothesis H1a was supported for wives but not for husbands, and Hypothesis H1b was not supported for either wives or husbands.

For wives, as predicted, making more frequent accommodations at home was a significant, negative predictor of both family satisfaction ($\beta = 2.31$, $p < .001$) and job satisfaction ($\beta = -.15$, $p = .01$). Similarly, for husbands, making more frequent accommodations at home was a negative predictor of family satisfaction ($\beta = -.31$, $p < .001$), but this was not the

TABLE 3. Results of Within-Individual Analyses: Own Work and Family Accommodations Predicting Own Job and Family Satisfaction

	Wives					
	Job Satisfaction			Family Satisfaction		
Variable	β	R^2	ΔR^2	β	R^2	ΔR^2
Step 1:		.02	.02		.06	.06**
Years of education	.07			.08		
Number of children	.02			.03		
Parent care hours	.03			−.08		
Hours worked	.01			−.07		
Income adequacy	.10			.13*		
Step 2:		.04	.03*		.15	.09***
Family accommodations	−.15*			−.31***		
Work accommodations	.10			.12*		

	Husbands					
	Job Satisfaction			Family Satisfaction		
Variable	β	R^2	ΔR^2	β	R^2	ΔR^2
Step 1:		.04	.04		.03	.03
Years of education	.11			.10		
Number of children	.04			.00		
Parent care hours	.00			.02		
Hours worked	.08			.01		
Income adequacy	.10			.08		
Step 2:		.05	.01		.12	.10***
Family accommodations	−.10			−.31***		
Work accommodations	.06			−.02		

***$p < .001$, ** $p < .01$, * $p < .05$

case for job satisfaction ($\beta = -.10, p = .11$). Therefore, Hypothesis H2a was supported for both wives and husbands, and Hypothesis H2b was supported for wives, but not for husbands.

Crossover effects (Hypotheses 3a and 3b and Research Question 1a and 1b). Hypothesis 3a predicted that greater use of work accommodations by one's spouse would be associated with higher levels of family satisfaction for the individual. As shown in Table 4, however, the extent to which a spouse made accommodations at *work* had no significant impact on family satisfaction for either wives or husbands. Thus, no support was found for Hypothesis 3a.

Hypothesis 3b predicted that greater use of family accommodations by one's spouse would negatively affect an individual's level of family satisfaction. The findings revealed that the extent to which their spouse made accommodations at *home* was indeed a significant, negative predictor of family satisfaction for both husbands ($\beta = -.26, p < .001$) and wives ($\beta = -.12, p < .05$). While the incremental R^2 in the final step of the regression did not reach a significant level for husbands, the regression coefficient did. Thus, Hypothesis 3b was supported for both husbands and wives.

Research questions 1a and 1b concerned the crossover effects of a spouse's use of work and family accommodations on an individual's level of job satisfaction. The exploratory analyses failed to show significant crossover effects of spouse's use of either type of accommodations on job satisfaction for either husbands or wives.

DISCUSSION

In this study, we examined the extent to which accommodations were made at home and at work by members of dual-earner couples in the sandwiched generation and the impact of making those accommodations on family and job satisfaction. We found that wives were making more frequent accommodations both at work and at home than were husbands. These findings are consistent with previous research on accommodations made at work (Brett & Yogev, 1988; Karambayya & Reilly, 1992). To our knowledge, however, no prior research has explicitly examined accommodations made at home. Theoretically, it makes sense that women would be making more frequent accommodations at work because of the stronger association women traditionally

TABLE 4. Results of Crossover Analyses: Spouse's Work and Family Accommodations Predicting Own Job and Family Satisfaction

	Wives					
	Job Satisfaction			Family Satisfaction		
Variable	β	R^2	ΔR^2	β	R^2	ΔR^2
Step 1:		.02	.02		.06	.06**
Years of education	.06			.04		
Number of children	.01			.00		
Parent care hours	.02			−.11		
Hours worked	.00			−.08		
Income adequacy	.11			.17**		
Step 2:		.03	.01		.08	.02
Husband's family accommodations	−.08			−.12*		
Husband's work accommodations	− .07			− .05		

	Husbands					
	Job Satisfaction			Family Satisfaction		
Variable	β	R^2	ΔR^2	β	R^2	ΔR^2
Step 1:		.03	.03		.03	.03
Years of education	.12*			.13*		
Number of children	.04			.02		
Parent care hours	.00			.03		
Hours worked	.07			− .01		
Income adequacy	.10			.09		
Step 2:		.04	.01		.10	.08***
Wife's family accommodations	−.08			−.26***		
Wife's work accommodations	.02			−.07		

*** $p < .001$, ** $p < .01$, * $p < .05$

have with the home (Major, 1993). Similarly, this finding is consistent with research demonstrating that men generally are still perceived as the principal breadwinners of the family, while women who work are viewed as providing "supplementary" income (Dancer & Gilbert, 1993). This would also explain why men were making a greater frequency of accommodations at home than at work, as well, since work is conventionally viewed as the male's primary role. This rationale, however, does not explain why wives were also making accommodations at home to a greater extent than were husbands. It may be that wives were actually making accommodations at home at a similar or even lower rate relative to husbands, but they over-reported such accommodations due to the greater psychological impact of making those accommodations for women than for men. That is, the salience of having to withdraw behaviorally from family activities may have been stronger for women than for men. This argument is consistent with that presented by Gutek et al. (1991), who hold that gender role expectations distort one's perceptions of time spent in work and family roles. Because women are socialized to believe that their main responsibility is for family obligations, they notice it more when they are not able to spend the amount of time they would like in family roles.

In our focus groups, a fairly consistent theme, particularly among women, was the deliberate effort to balance work and family as much as possible. As one woman in our focus groups explained, "I can decide not to take on work because a lot of family things are coming up . . . or I take on less during the summer." Another woman and her business partner consciously sought a work site that was close to both of their homes and their children's school. "It wouldn't be so hard to pick up someone from home and take them to school or take them to soccer or whatever," she stated.

We found support for Hypothesis 1a, which predicted that making more accommodations at work would positively influence family satisfaction, but for wives only. The extent to which wives were making accommodations at work was a significant, positive predictor of family satisfaction. Presumably, making accommodations at work makes it easier for wives to fulfill their family obligations, thus increasing their level of satisfaction in that area. Our hypothesis that making more accommodations at work would also be associated with greater job satisfaction (Hypothesis 1b), however, did not hold for wives. While the regression weight was in the expected direction (i.e., positive), it did not reach significance. It is possible that the work role is not as salient for women as the family role, and for this reason, the impact of making accommodations at work is stronger on family, rather than job, satisfaction.

For husbands, we found no significant relationship between the making of accommodations at work and either job or family satisfaction. We did find, however, that husbands were making accommodations at work significantly less often than were wives. It may be that the nature of the accommodations husbands make at work is distinct from that of the accommodations made by wives. As Karambayya and Reilly (1992) found, men reported that the accommodations they made at work were "one-time" or special arrangements, whereas the accommodations wives made at work were more ongoing or permanent. For this reason, perhaps the extent to which accommodations are made by husbands at work has less impact on outcomes such as job or family satisfaction.

Of all the hypotheses tested, we found the most support for Hypotheses 2a and 2b, which predicted that making accommodations at home would negatively affect individuals' family and job satisfaction. As expected, for both husbands and wives, level of family satisfaction was negatively impacted by the extent to which they made accommodations at home. This was reflected in comments made during the focus groups as well. One husband remarked, "It's difficult to find time in which the whole family is together because we're trading off the child care in order to run this errand or do that task and the like. So, there's little time for us as a whole, and we have to systematically plan that." Additionally, for wives, the frequency with which accommodations were made at home had a negative impact on their job satisfaction. Wives who made more frequent accommodations at home reported lower levels of both family and job satisfaction. Some women in our focus groups resented having to quit their jobs or cut back on hours. One working mother said, "I've considered at times not working. After giving birth I didn't and I realized I needed that outside stimulation . . . for my own self-concept." We found no support for this hypothesized negative relationship between making accommodations at home and job satisfaction, for husbands, however.

As predicted, our examination of crossover effects indicated that the extent to which one's spouse made accommodations at home did have a significant negative impact on one's own level of family satisfaction for both husbands and wives. These are the first such findings of the crossover effects of behaviors on attitudes, although it is important to note that these are self-reported, as opposed to objective, measures of behavior. Our findings demonstrate that people are very likely to feel the impact when their spouse spends less time in the family role. This is probably especially true for those individuals who have high family role demands, as with our sandwiched sample of couples caring not only for children but also for aging parents. A husband and father in our focus groups was concerned about how the demands of his and his wife's busy lives were impacting the marriage. "I've been working days, [my wife] basically works evenings. I run home, she goes off to work, so she's got the kids in the day, I have them in the evening. We don't see each other a lot. So, we haven't had to deal with the financial impact of child care, or for feeling that somebody else is bringing up our kids. At the same time . . . I think our relationship has been sacrificed."

Additionally, our findings are consistent with those in Arlie Hochschild's seminal study, *The Second Shift,* which found that women with families entering the work force were essentially working two jobs, one at work and another at home (Hochschild & Machung, 1989). Many women, both in our study and in the Hochschild study, expressed frustration with the inequities they perceived in their marriages. Since, for the most part, men are not participating in the household management on par with women, even when women are engaged in paid employment, these women feel compelled to do most of the rearranging of their schedules. This sentiment was echoed by one of the women who participated in our focus groups: "Do I need to be a wife first, a mother first, a daughter first? I tried to evaluate whose needs were the most crucial right now, and you feel like pieces are being taken out of you."

Limitations and Future Research

This study has provided important insights into how women and men attempt to find a balance between their work and family lives and the effect on their job and family satisfaction. At the same time, there are several shortcomings which must be noted. First, the scales for accommodations at work and accommodations at home developed for this study are preliminary and could benefit from additional work in terms of demonstrating their reliability and validity. In particular, the reliability coefficients were lower than the generally accepted standard of $\alpha = .70$ (e.g., Landy, 1989). Thus, the findings should be viewed with caution.

At the same time, it may be that internal consistency is not the most appropriate measure of reliability for these scales, since a person may choose one type of accommodation at the exclusion of others. For instance, reducing the number of hours one works may effectively solve one's work-family balance problem, making other accommodations unnecessary. A test-retest coefficient may be a more appropriate measure.

Another possible limitation associated with the accommodation measures is that participants were asked to respond to the items in light of their work and family duties, but they were not asked to indicate if the accommodation was made specifically in response to their family demands or to work demands. It could be that accommodations were being made to balance within-role demands. For instance, at work one might cut back on some supervisory duties in order to complete other projects. In the family domain, one might spend less time with one's spouse or partner because of child or elder care demands. In general, there are fewer roles to fulfill in the work domain than in the family domain, so it is likely to be safer to say that accommodations made at work are being made for the sake of the family. In the family domain, however, and particularly for sandwiched-generation couples, there are multiple family-related roles (e.g., spouse, parent, adult child, self), and the specific reason an individual is making an accommodation at home cannot be assumed. If a wife spends less time with her husband, is it because of work-related reasons, because of other family demands, or even a combination of work and other family demands? Do people react differently if they are making an accommodation at home for family-related reasons than if it is for work-related reasons? If accommodations are made for multiple reasons, disentangling the relationships between the accommodations made and the outcomes of interest will be even more challenging. Future research should investigate the motivations behind the accommodations being made, and how these motivations affect different outcomes.

A final possible limitation is that the findings presented here pertain to working couples in the sandwiched generation with household incomes of $40,000 or above. Additionally, the sample was predominantly White (about 94%), thus preventing comparisons across ethnic or racial groups. Future research will need to determine if the findings can be generalized to other racial groups and to other types of families, such as those with child or parent care responsibilities only, single-parent families, childless couples, or couples with very low incomes. In this study, however, there is a wide range in the ages of the participants' children, as well in the range of hours of elder care provided, and the gross household income criterion was set fairly low. This increases the probability that the results would generalize to other samples.

In addition to the research topics mentioned above, future studies should focus on other variables that could affect or be affected by accommodations made at work and at home. For instance, what are the antecedents of making certain accommodations at work and at home? What is the relationship between role involvement or role salience, work-family conflict, and the making of accommodations at work and at home? Also, the effects of making work and family accommodations on other outcome variables, such as role performance and mental health (i.e., depression), should be examined.

IMPLICATIONS AND CONCLUSIONS

There are several practical and theoretical implications of this study. First, these findings suggest that making more family accommodations is related to decreased levels of family satisfaction for both women and men and related to decreased job satisfaction for women. Greater availability of community and organizational supports for working couples who have high family demands might help to reduce the need to make family accommodations and thus improve both family and job satisfaction. Couples also need to gain a better understanding of who is making the bulk of the accommodations in the family and in which arena these accommodations are being made. Support from one's spouse has been shown to be a buffer against stress (e.g., Repetti, 1989), and a loss of, or a reduction in, that support could be detrimental to a marriage. These findings provide further support for the connection between work and family role responsibilities. They suggest that if employers help employees better manage their role demands, they will reap the direct benefits that result from higher levels of job satisfaction.

From the standpoint of work-family theory development, our findings demonstrate the importance of widening the focus of studies to include not just the individual, but the larger family context, and in particular, the spouse. Our findings provide the first demonstration of crossover effects where behaviors on the part of one spouse have an effect on attitudes of the other. Our finding that increased family accommodations by one's spouse is related to lower levels of family satisfaction for both husbands and wives appears to be a clear indication that the family system may suffer when one member makes adjustments that reduce his or her behavioral involvement in family roles. This finding also has important implications for systems theory in clinical practice, by recognizing that individual behavior is best understood in its context, which is in this case the family system.

In conclusion, this article has added to the body of knowledge in work-family research by examining the extent to which accommodations are made by wives and husbands at work and at home, and the effects of these accommodations on individuals' levels of job and family satisfaction. Furthermore, this research has augmented understanding of how behaviors of one spouse affect the other spouse. Future work remains to further refine the measures of work and family accommodations and elucidate the mechanisms by which making these accommodations affect not only individuals but also their spouses.

REFERENCES

Amatea, E. S., & Fong-Beyette, M. L. (1987). Through a different lens: Examining professional women's interrole coping by focus and mode. *Sex Roles, 17*, 237-252.

Baruch, G. K., & Barnett, R. C. (1986). Consequences of fathers' participation in family work: Parents' role strain and well-being. *Journal of Personality and Social Psychology, 51*, 983-992.

Brennan, E. M., & Poertner, J. (1997). Balancing the responsibilities of work and family life: Results of the family caregiver survey. *Journal of Emotional and Behavioral Disorders, 5*, 239-249.

Brett, J. M., & Yogev, S. (1988). Restructuring work for family: How dual-career couples with children manage. In E. B. Goldsmith (Ed.), *Work and family: Theory, research, and applications.* A special issue of *Journal of Social Behavior and Personality, 3*(4), 159-174.

Bronfenbrenner, U. (1977). Toward an experimental ecology of human development. *American Psychologist, 32*, 513-531.

Dancer, L. S., & Gilbert, L. A. (1993). Spouses' family work participation and its relation to wives' occupational level. *Sex Roles, 28*, 127-145.

Frone, M. R., Russell, M., & Cooper, M. L. (1992). Antecedents and outcomes of work-family conflict: Testing a model of the work-family interface. *Journal of Applied Psychology, 77*, 65-78.

Grzywacz, J. G., & Marks, N. F. (2000). Reconceptualizing the work-family interface: An ecological perspective on the correlates of positive and negative spillover between work and family. *Journal of Occupational Health Psychology, 5*, 111-126.

Gutek, B. A., Searle, S., & Klepa, L. (1991). Rational versus gender role explanations for work-family conflict. *Journal of Applied Psychology, 76,* 560-568.

Hackman, J. R., & Oldham, G. R. (1975). Development of the Job Diagnostic Survey. *Journal of Applied Psychology, 60,* 159-170.

Hall, D. T. (1990). Promoting work/family balance: An organization-change approach. *Organizational Dynamics, 18,* 5-18.

Hammer, L., Allen, E., & Grigsby, T. (1997). Work-family conflict in dual-earner couples: Within-individual and crossover effects of work and family. *Journal of Vocational Behavior, 50,* 185-203.

Hammer, L. B., Bauer, T. N., & Grandey, A. A. (1999). *The relationship between work-family conflict and withdrawal behaviors at work among dual-earner couples: Individual-level and crossover effects.* Poster presented at the Annual Meeting of the Society for Industrial/Organizational Psychology, Atlanta, GA.

Joseph, A. E., & Hallman, B. C. (1996). Caught in the triangle: The influence of home, work, and elder location on work-family. *Canadian Journal on Aging, 15,* 393-412.

Karambayya, R., & Reilly, A. H. (1992). Dual earner couples: Attitudes and actions in restructuring work for family. *Journal of Organizational Behavior, 13,* 585-601.

Kopelman, R. E., Greenhaus, J. H., & Connolly, T. F. (1983). A model of work, family, and interrole conflict: A construct validation study. *Organizational Behavior and Human Performance, 32,* 198-215.

Landy, F. J. (1989). *The psychology of work behavior (4th Ed.).* Pacific Grove, CA: Brooks/Cole.

Major, B. (1993). Gender, entitlement, and the distribution of family labor. *Journal of Social Science Issues, 49,* 141-159.

Mederer, H. J. (1993). Division of labor in two-earner homes: Task accomplishment versus household management as critical variables in perceptions about family work. *Journal of Marriage and the Family, 55,* 133-145.

Repetti, R. L. (1989). Effects of daily workload on subsequent behavior during marital interaction: The roles of social withdrawal and spouse support. *Journal of Personality and Social Psychology, 57,* 651-659.

Sinclair, R. R., Hannigan, M. A., & Tetrick, L. E. (1995). Benefit coverage and employee attitudes: A social exchange perspective. In L. E. Tetrick & J. Barling (Eds.), *Changing employment relations: Behavioral and social perspectives* (pp. 163-185). Washington, DC: American Psychological Association.

Thomas, L. T., & Ganster, D. C. (1995). Impact of family-supportive work variables on work-family conflict and strain: A control perspective. *Journal of Applied Psychology, 80,* 6-15.

Westman, M., & Etzion, D. (1995). Crossover of stress, strain and resources from one spouse to another. *Journal of Organizational Behavior, 16,* 169-181.

Westman, M., & Vinokur, A. D. (1998). Unraveling the relationship of distress levels within couples: Common stressors, empathic reactions, or crossover via social interaction? *Human Relations, 51,* 137-156.

APPENDIX A

ACCOMMODATIONS AT WORK

1. I plan my work hours around my child(ren)'s, parent'(s), or spouse's or partner's schedules.

2. I plan to work at home so that I can be close to my family.

3. When necessary, I take time off work to care for a child or a parent.

ACCOMMODATIONS AT HOME

1. I limit my social activities.

2. I limit my personal time for reading, exercise, or other leisure activities.

3. I spend less time with my spouse or partner.

4. I spend less time with other family members.

5. I limit the number of my child(ren)'s activities that I attend.

6. I attend activities separately from my spouse or partner because of conflicting schedules or responsibilities.

1 = Never; 2 = Sometimes; 3 = Most or all of the time.

Family Organizational Labor: Who's Calling the Plays?

Toni Schindler Zimmerman
Shelley A. Haddock
Scott Ziemba
Aimee Rust

SUMMARY. Many dual-earner couples are striving for equality in their marital or intimate partnerships as a way to balance family and work successfully. Despite substantial advances in achieving equality in many aspects of marital or intimate partnerships, such as housework and child care, many couples struggle to equitably divide responsibility for family organizational tasks, such as maintaining the family calendar, managing the household, and organizing the children's activities, schedules, and care. Data for this study were drawn from 47 middle-class, heterosexual, dual-earner couples who perceive themselves as successful in balancing family and work. The couples were interviewed to investigate their philosophies and strategies for successful work-family balance. The pur-

---

Toni Schindler Zimmerman, PhD, is Associate Professor in the Human Development and Family Studies (HDFS) Department at Colorado State University (CSU). Shelley A. Haddock, PhD, is Assistant Professor at Colorado State University and Director of the Center for Family and Couple Therapy. She is with the Human Development and Family Studies (HDFS) Department. Scott Ziemba, MS, and Aimee Rust, MS, are graduate students of the HDFS Department at CSU; both are research assistants on this project.

The first two authors are the principle investigators for the grant entitled, Successfully Balancing Family and Work, funded by the Alfred P. Sloan Foundation. They share first authorship on this publication and all subsequent grant-related publications.

[Haworth co-indexing entry note]: "Family Organizational Labor: Who's Calling the Plays?" Zimmerman et al. Co-published simultaneously in *Journal of Feminist Family Therapy* (The Haworth Press, Inc.) Vol. 13, No. 2/3, 2001, pp. 65-90; and: *Balancing Family and Work: Special Considerations in Feminist Therapy* (ed: Toni Schindler Zimmerman) The Haworth Press, Inc., 2001, pp. 65-90. Single or multiple copies of this article are available for a fee from The Haworth Document Delivery Service [1-800-HAWORTH, 9:00 a.m. - 5:00 p.m. (EST). E-mail address: getinfo@haworthpressinc.com].

pose of this article is to describe how these couples divided responsibility for family organization. Although the vast majority of these couples reported that striving for marital equality was foundational to their successful work-family balance, most reported that wives were primarily responsible for family organization. Organization is discussed as a factor of equality that warrants more research and as an important remaining barrier to the achievement of couples' equality. Clinical implications are provided. *[Article copies available for a fee from The Haworth Document Delivery Service: 1-800-HAWORTH. E-mail address: <getinfo@haworthpressinc. com> Website: <http://www.HaworthPress.com> © 2001 by The Haworth Press, Inc. All rights reserved.]*

KEYWORDS. Work, family, balance, equality, invisible labor, dual-earner couples

In the past four decades, as the number of dual-earner couples in the United States has steadily increased, researchers have become interested in studying the interface between family and work. Recently, researchers have focused on understanding dual-earner couples' adaptive strategies for balancing family and work (Edgell Becker & Moen, 1999). The current study extends this body of research by documenting the adaptive strategies of 47 middle-class, heterosexual, dual-earner couples with children who self-identify as successful in balancing family and work. The study was designed to discover the philosophies and strategies that these couples utilize at home and work in successfully balancing family and work.

As previously reported (Haddock, Zimmerman, Ziemba, & Current, in press), the majority of couples interviewed for this study emphasized that their philosophy of striving for marital equality was central to their successful work-family balance. However, through qualitative analyses of interview data, it became apparent that, even in these couples who enjoy relatively high levels of equality and successful work-family balance, organizational labor was primarily the responsibility of female partners. This article describes the strategies that these couples used for organizing family life, the disproportionate allocation of responsibility for organizational tasks to female partners, and the couples' explanations for this inequitable division of responsibility for the organization of family life.

LITERATURE REVIEW

In previous decades the number of dual-earner couples has increased dramatically; in fact, dual-earner couples now outnumber traditional male breadwinner/female homemaker families nearly three-to-one (Hayghe, 1990; U.S. Bureau of the Census, 1998). Despite this increased labor force participation, women continue to be primarily responsible for the majority of household labor and child care (Williams, 2000). This inequitable division of labor persists even in families where women work outside the home (Demo & Acock, 1993; Shelton & John, 1993).

Hochschild and Machung's (1989) research on dual-earners couples forever changed discourse regarding household labor and egalitarianism. They coined the term "second shift" to describe a previously unrecognized phenomenon that had been occurring in families for decades. They found that women in dual-earner couples were typically responsible for two work shifts–one shift outside of and another shift inside of the home. Hochschild and Machung (1989) contributed to making a previously invisible part of family life more easily identifiable and recognizable. Their research also illustrated the detrimental aspects of women's second shift, catalyzing change among dual-earner couples in the United States.

Although women still perform considerably more domestic labor than men, research from the past decade has revealed a trend toward increased sharing of housework and parenting among dual-earner couples (Barnett & Rivers, 1996; Schwartz, 1994). Unlike earlier periods in history, many couples now believe in the importance of maintaining an egalitarian relationship in which family and household labor are the equal responsibility of both spouses (DeStefano & Colasanto, 1990; Rosenbluth, Steil, & Whitcomb, 1998). There is a growing recognition that an equitable division of domestic labor is particularly important for couples in which both partners work outside the home (Barnett & Rivers, 1996).

Equality has been described as a partnership in which partners tend to share responsibility for duties such as household tasks, economic labor, child care, and decision making (Schwartz, 1994). It has been measured in previous research by assessment scales emphasizing division of task responsibilities, such as housework and child care (Demo & Acock, 1993; Shelton & John, 1993). As research on this topic has evolved, additional facets of family labor are beginning to emerge as vital to overall equality. Current research is beginning to focus on two dimensions of family labor that have received insufficient attention: emotional labor and organizational labor. These responsibilities have been referred to as invisible labor by some family scientists (DeVault, 1987; Seery & Crowley, 2000) and are becoming more readily recognized as obstacles to egalitarianism (Mederer, 1993). In fact, even among couples who are attentive to protecting fairness in division of domestic tasks, inequality often persists in these less conspicuous relationship dimensions.

To date, research on invisible forms of family labor has focused primarily on the area of emotional labor. Emotional labor has been defined as "behaviors performed to improve the emotional well-being in others and to create cooperative and positive social relationships" (Strazdins, 2000, p. 41). Traditionally, men and women have been socialized from an early age to place different value on social relationships. Men are often encouraged to value and maintain independence while avoiding deep emotional connections with others (Duncombe & Marsden, 1995), and thus lack opportunities to develop the sensitivity and observational skills vital to performing emotional labor. On the other hand, women are taught to enjoy the companionship of others and develop skills beneficial in maintaining relationships with friends and loved ones. As a result, women often accept primary responsibility for the emotional labor necessary to maintain family well-being (Higgins, Cook, Werner-Wilson, & Berger, 1997; Seery & Crowley, 2000). In addition, the subtleties of this form of labor often contribute to difficulties in its identification, delegation, and division. As such, this type of labor often remains unnoticed and underappreciated by men as well as by the women who typically perform it (Duncombe & Marsden, 1995; Erickson, 1993).

Responsibility for organizational management of the family is a second type of invisible labor that is becoming more readily recognized as a duty traditionally and primarily performed by women (Barnett & Baruch, 1987; Hawkins, Roberts, Christiansen, & Marshall, 1994; Leslie, Anderson, & Branson, 1991; Mederer, 1993; Rasmussen, Hawkins, & Schwab, 1996; Risman & Johnson-Sumerford, 1998). This form of labor involves identifying household tasks in need of completion and taking steps to insure that the work is accomplished properly and in a timely fashion (Rasmussen et al., 1996). Levine (2000) referred to this primarily female-performed labor as "The Dreaded Tape." "It's like a ticker tape: don't forget that the kids need to go to the doctor . . . you have a meeting tomorrow with seven executives . . . you have to pick up the cleaning . . . you have to get clay to make the volcano for the 5th grade science project" (Levine, 2000).

Women left responsible for organizational labor can be likened to family quarterbacks who are expected to call the appropriate play for a given situation, remain cognizant of each teammates' location on the field, set teammates up for the pass, and accurately throw the ball. In this role, women are expected to accept the tremendous responsibility of insuring that the team runs smoothly and ultimately experiences success. However, the additional responsibility the family quarterback carries has yet to be investigated in great detail.

The relative lack of attention in popular and academic writings has been primarily due to complications in identification and measurement of organizational labor. Previous measures of division of domestic labor have failed to examine household organizational management in a meaningful way. These instruments focus primarily on the division of household tasks that produce a tangible and identifiable result (e.g., changing diapers, washing dishes, cooking, vacuuming) and as a result are more easily quantifiable (Demo & Acock, 1993; Ferre, 1991). Organizational labor is primarily planning (e.g., coordinating schedules, planning family meals for a week, planning holiday traditions and festivities) and is difficult to measure through traditional quantitative techniques. Even naturalistic observations have created difficulties in the measurement of organizational labor. As DeVault (1987) noted, the invisible labor of planning and managing family meals is often not readily obvious. For example, insuring that a family meal runs smoothly often appears similar to simply enjoying the companionship of family, while menu planning often appears similar to sitting and resting. As a result of these difficulties in identification and measurement, inequality in organizational labor has persisted among couples with minimal effort to intervene on the part of many professionals.

In addition to the difficulties with measuring this form of labor in research studies, couples themselves also encounter difficulties recognizing the daily and weekly effort expended on organizational management and determining how to split these responsibilities (Duncombe & Marsden, 1995; Trebilcot, 1983). Furthermore, couples may not articulate imbalance in division of organizational management as a form of inequality. Hawkins et al. (1994) studied the effectiveness of an intervention program designed to assist dual-earner couples in sharing family labor and found that women generally accepted greater responsibility for family organizational labor, even in couples who had made concerted efforts to insure the equitable division of tasks.

A number of hypotheses have been developed to account for observed difficulties in equitably sharing responsibility for invisible labor. One explanation attributes inequality in invisible labor to fixed personality characteristics believed to endow a person with a set of skills or abilities well-suited to the completion of certain tasks. In families, these individual characteristics are thought to prepare women and men for different family and household responsibilities (Allen & Hawkins, 1999; DeVault, 1987). For instance, the personalities of many women are considered more skillful in managing details, multi-tasking, and organizing family schedules. Conversely, the personalities of men often are considered to be more relaxed, laid back, spontaneous, and flexible with regard to family life. Such an argument is frequently offered as justification for family arrangements in which a majority of the invisible labor is completed by women (DeVault, 1987). These personality characteristics are often discussed in the context of permanence and inflexibility, and this argument is based on an assumption that these traits are inseparable from an individual's identity. The fatalistic nature of this argument often provides ample justification for many couples to continue unequal division of household management.

Another explanation explores the influence of gender socialization on the roles and responsibilities adopted by women and men in families. Societal expectations have long portrayed forms of invisible labor as the responsibility of women. Simultaneously, men are often depicted in the role of household assistant, coming to the aid of their wives only when the responsibilities of the family become too much for one person to handle alone. Further, gender messages transmitted by the popular media often portray women in the roles of secretaries, nurses, and clerks who are primarily responsible for insuring that proper organization is maintained for their, typically male, superiors. These media images have helped to create and reinforce societal assumptions that women are more appropriate to fulfill these roles. This explanation argues that gender messages have a powerful influence upon what many men and women adopt as the standard of acceptable masculine and feminine behavior, thereby shaping roles adopted in the family. As such, patterns of gender socialization implicitly or explicitly predispose couples to accept a traditional division of invisible labor, despite the inequality often associated with such an arrangement (Seery & Crowley, 2000; Tingey, Kiger, & Riley, 1996).

In light of the invisibility of family organizational labor, it is not surprising that couples experience difficulty in its identification and division, even when striving for equality in domestic labor (Hawkins, 1994). As mentioned, this study on organizational labor in families is part of a larger research investigation of dual-earner couples who self-identify as successfully balancing the demands of family and work. The majority of these couples described their efforts to achieve equality as foundational to their success (see Haddock et al., in press; Haddock, Zimmerman, Current, & Ziemba, in progress). However, even in these highly equitable couples, organizational labor was still a problem.

METHOD

Participants

Participant couples were residents of three major urban population centers in Colorado. A variety of recruitment efforts were utilized to obtain participants of a diverse population (e.g., diversity in race, income, and career type). Recruitment efforts included: distribution of fliers to parents of children in early childhood learning facilities, preschools, daycare facilities, and public elementary and middle schools; articles appearing in two major daily newspapers; stories broadcast by two television news programs; posters displayed in a variety of retail shops, family activity centers, and large businesses and universities; e-mails distributed to employees of large businesses and universities; and distribution of postcards to alumni from a major university and members of the Women's Chamber of Commerce in this state. Despite efforts to recruit a diverse population, the couples that contacted us were relatively homogenous with regard to income levels.

Upon expressing interest in the study, potential participants were screened during a phone conversation to determine eligibility. Couples were considered eligible if: (a) they were married, (b) each spouse completed at least 35 hours per week of paid employment, (c) the couple had at least one child 12 years of age or younger who resided with them at least half of the time, and (d) both partners wanted to participate in the study. In addition, couples had to agree that all of the following statements were descriptive of them: (a) my spouse and I experience more positives than negatives from the opportunity to fill both work and family responsibilities; (b) my spouse and I believe that we are skilled in balancing the many responsibilities in our lives (e.g., spouse, parent, employee); (c) my spouse and I have found and continue to find creative ways for balancing work and family; (d) my spouse and I would be described as skilled in balancing work and family; (e) my spouse and I believe we have quality and quantity time with each other and our children, and are mostly satisfied with our performance at work and home.

One hundred and thirteen couples originally expressed interest in the study, of which 50 were found not to meet screening criteria primarily because of demographic considerations (e.g., not married, children older than 12), 11 withdrew prior to screening, and 5 couples withdrew from the study following successful screening. Forty-seven couples participated in the study. The average age was 38 years old for women and 40 years old for men. On average, the couples had 2 children, ranging in age from 6 months to 23 years of age. The average age of the youngest child was 5 years old and the average age of the oldest was 9 years old. For 38 women and 40 men, this was their first marriage, and the average length of marriage for the couples was 12.75 years.

Together, the couples earned an average aggregate income of $105,022.70 (excluding the income of two outlying couples), with a range in combined incomes from $34,000 to $220,000. On average, wives earned less than husbands did; women earned $45,530 compared to men's average income of $63,320, with a range of $10,000 to $105,000 for women, and $20,000 to $190,000 for men. Twelve individuals were self-employed, 39 worked at companies that had 50 or fewer employees, 11 worked at companies that employed 50 to 200 individuals, and 42 worked at companies with 200 or more employees. The wives in the study worked fewer hours, with an average of 40 hours a week compared to the husbands' 45 hours per week. The occupations of the participants were diverse, ranging from billing clerks and secretaries to executives and chief financial officers for large corporations.

Of the individual participants, 77 identified as Caucasian, 8 as Hispanic-American, 4 as African-American, 1 as Asian-American, 1 as Caucasian-Native American, and 1 as "Other." Participants attained relatively high levels of education, with the average participant completing some graduate study. In terms of highest level of education completed, 5 individual participants graduated high school, 13 attended some college, 27 graduated college, 7 attended some graduate study, and 40 attained graduate degrees.

Procedure

Participant couples were asked to complete a written questionnaire and a conjoint interview. The questionnaire included a battery of instruments, including basic demographic information and assessments of work, family, marital, and personal variables. The results presented in this article were drawn exclusively from the interview data. The interview followed a semi-structured format, including a broad spectrum of open-ended questions regarding philosophies and strategies that have contributed to the couple's overall success. For example, the following questions were asked: (a) What are the primary factors that contribute to your successful balance of family and work? (b) Do you have philosophies that are central to the way in which you manage family and work responsibilities, and if so, what are they? (c) What are some of the strategies that you use at home and at work to successfully balance family and work? Although specific questions about organizational labor were not directly asked, participants described their process for organizing family life as an important aspect of how they balance family and work. The majority of interviews–which lasted approximately 90 minutes–were conducted in participants' homes. Couples received $30 as compensation for their participation.

Data Analysis

A grounded theory approach was adopted for analysis of the qualitative interview data (Strauss & Corbin, 1990). Consistent with grounded theory method, an inductive, cross-case strategy was utilized. No one truth, theory, or set of conclusions was sought after; themes were generated largely from participants' experiences, rather than attempting to impose interpretations on the data or procure support for a particular worldview. The intent and goal was to let the data speak for themselves.

Consistent with grounded theory methodology, data collection and analysis occurred simultaneously using a qualitative data analysis program, Atlas/ti. Data categories were collapsed and clarified by constantly comparing new data with previously generated hypotheses

(Strauss & Corbin, 1990). Theoretical saturation was achieved with the creation of a common lexicon of terms, diminished category modification, and conceptual crystallization (Strauss & Corbin, 1990). Recruitment efforts were terminated upon reaching saturation in interview data.

Ensuring Validity

To insure the integrity of qualitative research, Creswell (1998) advised investigators to utilize at least two commonly accepted strategies. We used four primary strategies to enhance the trustworthiness of our findings, described as follows. Prior to interviewing couples, we clarified biases, perspectives, and orientations that we likely brought to our research. Commonly used by qualitative researchers, this process allows the researcher and consumer of research to be aware of the potential influence of their belief systems on the interpretation of findings. As family therapists, we have approached this study from a perspective shaped by feminist social philosophy and family systems theory.

To insure the validity of the emerging code structure, we adopted a team approach to data analysis. Each interview was conducted by one member of the research team, reviewed by another, and systematically analyzed by two others. This process allowed each member of the research team to achieve high levels of familiarity with the data. The team met regularly to discuss the emergent themes.

The use of Atlas/ti allowed us to create an online audit trail of our findings so that we could trace codes back to discrete units of text in the interview transcripts. This process allows us to reexamine units of coded data to insure that generated data categories have remained true to the voices of the participants. Finally, in reporting our results, we have made an effort to offer a rich, detailed description of the findings. Quotations from a cross section of interviews allow for a clearer understanding of the findings.

RESULTS

While varying in degree of marital equality, findings emerging from this study indicate that, as a group, participant couples enjoyed a relatively high level of equality compared to societal norms (Haddock et al., in progress). Yet, while successfully balancing family and work and dividing the task responsibilities required for daily household operations, most couples left the duties of family organization and household management to the wives. This section will accomplish two specific tasks: (a) describe this phenomenon utilizing direct quotations from participant interviews and (b) explore a common explanation among couples for why this dynamic occurred.

Inequality in Organizational Responsibility

Family calendar. The most prominent organizational aspect of family life for which most wives were responsible was the family calendar. Given the full lives led by many couples, the family calendar was vital in tracking social obligations, school functions, doctor's appointments, and family/child activities. Quite often, the calendar was a central strategy that allowed couples to successfully balance the various demands of their lives.

> (Wife): We keep a calendar. I keep the calendar, actually. I'm the administrator. And we track all the stuff that the kids are doing and what we're doing. If we lose it, we're dead because it has key phone numbers, and things we have to get done in a particular time frame. It's been very helpful to keep that. And by writing it down, sometimes it frees up our thinking [so] we can move on and stop thinking about it.

In addition, some wives also appeared responsible for reminding their husbands about family obligations, taking primary responsibility for insuring their husbands were abreast of the family's schedule.

> (Husband): Becky leaves me messages on weekends, and I don't even know that she's on the cell phone. "Who are you talking to?" "Oh, I'm leaving you a message." Then I'll write it on my calendar when I get to work.... As a matter of fact, if you ask me right now what we're doing this weekend, I would not have a clue until I ask Becky. She's pretty much organized, and I like that. That way I don't have to think about it. At work I have to do a lot of organizing and stuff and I'd probably get burned out on it. Becky's awesome at it . . .

(Wife): . . . we have a calendar. We have it up and change it every month and write down major events and things. And then I have my own planner and he has his own planner. But I tend to be the one that has to organize all the different activities and make sure things fit. So I'll pretty much just tell Karl, here's what we have to do this weekend and here's where we have to go. And he says, "OK."

In another example, one couple demonstrated that the wife was responsible not only for the family calendar, but also for organizing her husband's schedule as well.

(Husband): Julie writes everything down in her daytimer and I [have to] ask her. I'm not very good at that at all. So, I'll say, "OK, when is this house closing [for my real estate business]?" and she'll know. She knows everything well in advance, socially and [my] important work days. And anytime people ask me stuff, to come over for dinner or to go to a Bronco game or anything, I just say, "Check with Julie, because she knows." That's her total responsibility.

Household management. While couples in this sample have demonstrated roughly equal division of household labor (i.e., "task equality"), evidence suggests that most wives are more responsible for insuring these tasks are completed. In other words, it appears that many wives' duties include establishing an organizational system and providing a predictable structure in which household labor can be completed in a timely and efficient manner.

(Husband): Carmen is the consummate manager. It seems like we do a lot by the seat of the pants, but we don't. She's thinking two weeks ahead, and it frustrates her because I get used to her thinking, so I don't. But I think that's a big piece of it, the structure really helps the boys.

In the following example, a female participant describes the task lists she creates for the entire family, demonstrating the additional level of responsibility often involved in monitoring household management for the family.

(Wife): One thing that comes to mind for me immediately, and I'm probably the instigator of this, is lists. They're kind of checklists. I tend to be the one that knows who's doing what, when, and why, and who's got what homework, and I'm just the one that pays a little more attention to that. And John will be the enforcer sometimes, but he doesn't know when math is due, or whatever, but I do. So I tend to be kind of the one that keeps track of a lot of the details. So, therefore, I'll make lists, checklists, or whatever, and say, "OK, here's the things you gotta get done tonight," and I'll send him little notes in the morning, "Don't forget to run by the bank and call your mom," and whatever, because we have very complicated jobs that involve lots of information. It just helps us all relax a little because it's written down and you can just check them off and know that it's done. If I have it written down, I can forget about it, and if he's written it down, he doesn't have to worry about it because I wrote it down. So, that's a huge thing for us.

In one couple, the wife's organizational system allowed her organizational presence to be felt even when away on business trips.

(Wife): At night he'll usually place the call before I leave work to ask what's on the menu for dinner, if I haven't left something out, and then he just goes right with it. And I really try to set it up good when I travel. I will go as far, if it's a two-night trip, I will leave two outfits out [for each of our children], just to make it easy for him. I tend to be overboard, where he can completely handle it without me. And I think I'm getting better because I'm travelling more for some reason lately. Before it was like, I'd leave notes and do this and do that, and now he's like, "I've got it."

While an extremely rare occurrence among our sample, the wife in this couple expressed the negative emotional consequences she experiences as a result of fulfilling the "family organizer" role.

(Wife): I love it when company comes over because that's when Shawn cleans, because you have to do it fast, right? . . . I definitely do more on the end of the organizing and the strategy, but the thing is that he works on the car or he works late at work. He does stuff that I wouldn't even want to think about doing. So I kind of feel like, [to husband] don't listen too closely to this, but I kind of feel like it's OK, and sometimes I get resentful, but that's not answering your question.

Organizing for children. Among this sample of dual-earner couples, fathers were clearly involved in the lives of their children. Repeatedly, fathers demonstrated a clear willingness to participate in caring for their children. However, similar to the distinction between household tasks and household management, interviews also suggested that most women in these couples were primarily responsible for organizing and staying in touch with the lives surrounding their children.

> (Husband): I usually get home before Cheryl. . . . and I'm really bad on making the kids do their work and homework and stuff. I don't know where they're at. Cheryl knows where they're at in school and stuff.

> (Husband): . . . we agree on most things, but if we have something to talk about, she usually initiates it more . . . like about whatever plans we have for the kids or if we need to think about vacation planning and stuff. And she's real good about organizing, you know, a lot of different things . . .

The following quotation demonstrates this father's willingness to take an active role for his children. Yet, in this passage he also alludes to the fact that he typically accompanies his children to the doctor or dentist if his wife is unable to do so first. In this respect, he appears to consider his role in managing these responsibilities secondary to that of his wife.

> (Husband): I think we both take a big part in [taking care of the kids], and I think that helps out a bunch. If Krista can't be with the kids or take them somewhere, then I always make sure that I'm there. Dentist appointments, doctors appointments, that type of stuff. I think that's the major part of it.

Again, this example suggests that both spouses are involved in their children's school activities and lunch preparation, yet, it also appears that the wife is primarily responsible for coordinating schedules by making note on the family calendar.

(Wife): When the school newsletter comes out I immediately get out my day timer and I start marking everything down that night. In the pantry I keep the calendar from their school. And because they don't have a hot lunch program, they just kind of started one that you can select certain days for them to have something, it's not like an everyday thing. So I keep it in there. I write for the month what days they have hot lunch and cold lunch and that way, if either of us are doing lunches, we know.

Personality Differences as Explanations for Division of Organizational Responsibility

The female "organizer personality." Based on impressions from the interview data, most couples appeared cognizant of their difference in organizational responsibility, and many considered this a natural consequence of differences in their personalities. Couples reported that the wife assumed the role of primary organizer because her personal qualities were better suited to managing such responsibilities. In essence, such explanations portrayed wives as ideal to fulfill the role of "family organizer," since "it was in her nature," "that's the type of person she is," or "she's really good at it because that's the way she is."

(Husband): Diane is really well organized, so that really helps. One of her qualities is that she's able to say, "OK, here are the things that we really need to get done" or whatever, and that really helps. I'm not as much that way, but I'm a lot more flexible. So, if there's a change in what needs to happen, it doesn't bother me as much.

(Husband): . . . she's an extreme organizer. Most of the stuff that we do probably wouldn't get done except for the fact that she's extremely well-organized and she's a driven person. A lot of things are more of a competition, even to herself. A lot of things that I might let slide because it's just okay either way, you know, she's going to see that it gets done because she just wants to see something better. . . . she's not happy to be in one place. [laughter] With a lot of the . . . business-type things that we've really stepped into and are even talking about right now . . . I've actually come up with and said, "Well, this is something I really would like to do." But a lot of times I don't really know how to go about getting it accomplished, and she has that ability to be able to break things down and not just take it as this great big picture but be able to put it into little blocks so that each one gets accomplished, so that when you're done, "Oh, well that wasn't hard at all." She's good at breaking it down and helping you to see how to break it down.

The male "flexible personality." As alluded to in the above quotations, many couples found themselves fulfilling complementary roles with regards to family organization. Not only did most wives possess an "organizer personality," but many husbands were described as more flexible and relaxed in comparison.

(Wife): But I think our personalities, too, complement each other, because I'm very high strung and he is very laid back. So he keeps me grounded. He's like, "You know what? It's not that big of a deal." And sometimes, I'm like, "Yeah, you're right, it's not."

(Husband): I think the combination we have is really good because I'm really optimistic and a little more happy-go-lucky, but Teresa's very careful. You know, I'd go spend five thousand dollars on a boat tomorrow, but she's like, "Alright, hold on. How are we going to do this, this, and this to do that?" So, it's a good combination.

"Personality" interactions. Interview data seemed to indicate that the development of these two organizational styles produced a cycle of behavioral interactions between spouses. In other words, when a couple believes that one partner is more organized, they begin to assign more organizational tasks to this person and develop a belief that the other partner is less capable of organization.

(Husband): Basically Nicole's more organized; that's a quality. One of the bad qualities is she gets very high strung, and I can understand it at times, but sometimes it spills over to things that she shouldn't be high strung about, so that gets in the way. But conversely, sometimes I'm too relaxed, so she's gotta kick me in the rear end.

However, given the tendency of couples to attribute these differences to personality types, this cycle of interaction was seemingly overlooked and appeared to take on a self-sustaining quality in marriages. Given that couples were recruited for this study on the basis of their ability to successfully balance family and work, it is not surprising that these roles were often offered as support for couples' ability to work together as teammates and for a "goodness of fit" between spouses' personality types, rather than being considered problematic.

> (Husband): . . . I think a personality trait of mine that helps a lot is that I've always been a team player, and I've always been–I don't know what the right word is–a leader, without ever being elected. I think it comes down to sort of leading by example. And that plays very well with Judy's personality, and she brings the other traits of the organization and she's got the big picture at all times. Whereas I might be, you know, jumping into the little things. Judy keeps sort of the big part together. In that sense, it's not obvious all the time, but we're sort of using each other's strengths to sort of walk around.

> (Husband): . . . I hate the term, but it's right, it's anal retention. I mean she manages the whole corporation here [the family]. I mean this company wouldn't work as well if she weren't around. Because I just don't do some of the stuff that is required to make a family run well. And she will take the time and make it happen, and she knows how to coerce me to get it done, too. It was funny when she was filling out the forms before you got here, and [our son] Timothy said, "Why are you and Mommy so good as a couple?" I said, it's really easy, "Mommy's smart and I work hard." So, it's a good team.

DISCUSSION

In interpreting the results of this study, it is important to remember that, despite efforts to obtain a more diverse sample, the couples who participated in this study were predominantly highly educated, middle-class couples with at least one child under the age of 12. Despite the resultant limits to generalizability, the results of this study suggest that inequality in household organizational labor is a common occurrence among dual-earner couples–even among those who demonstrate a relatively high level of equality in other relationship dimensions. The couples in this sample made efforts to approach equality in housework, child care, the value placed on each spouse's paid employment, emotional labor, and communication (Haddock et al., in progress). However, despite these efforts, inequality in organizational labor was common.

While the interview protocol for this study assessed many dimensions of family and work balance (including philosophies and strategies of success), interview after interview revealed that household organization was a domain that had been implicitly deemed "women's work" by many couples. Interestingly, the women in these couples rarely reported or demonstrated dissatisfaction with the overall imbalance in division of organizational responsibilities. In fact, across the sample, interviews revealed that spouses were happily married, felt emotionally connected to one another, and considered themselves to be partners.

Several possible explanations may account for the fact that women in this sample did not often express dissatisfaction with the division of organizational management. These hypotheses are similar to those utilized to explain the occurrence of this phenomenon in the first place, and seem to suggest that the process of explaining inequality in organizational labor is intimately connected to the process of justifying its continued existence. As such, critiques of these arguments will also follow in order to illustrate the inconsistencies in these explanations and attempt to interrupt the process of justification for continued inequality in organizational labor. The overall goal remains advocating for change in this domain of marital labor.

The first explanation is the one most often and most explicitly articulated by couples in this sample; many couples interpreted inequality in division of organizational management as a function of personality differences between men and women, not merely as a facet of marital equality. As seen previously, couples were more likely to describe husbands as flexible and spontaneous and wives as organized, uptight, and detail-oriented. These traits often led participants to believe that the wives were more naturally suited to fulfill the role of family organizer. Rather than questioning the accuracy and validity of this argument, couples often portrayed these personality differences as complementary traits that allowed husbands and wives to compensate for one another and also created the formula for spouses to work together as teammates.

The fact that many of the couples in this sample explained division of organizational labor on the basis of personality differences is consistent with previous research on egalitarianism among dual-earner couples. Hochschild and Machung's (1989) findings indicated that many dual-earner couples believe that men and women are well-suited for different types of labor. She referred to such beliefs as "family myths"– "versions of reality that obscure a core truth in order to manage family tension" (p. 19)– and found that these explanations played a significant role in rationalizing, justifying, and maintaining inequitable division of second shift labor. Deutsch (1999) also discussed the power of personality and gender myths to excuse otherwise blatant inequalities among married couples. The results of the current study are congruent with both Hochschild and Machung's (1989) and Deutsch's (1999) work, as women in this sample rarely complained about inequality in organizational responsibility due to rationalizations that considered this arrangement the result of fixed personality characteristics.

Such ideologies about the personality differences between women and men have been referred to as myths because previous research offers little to no support for these beliefs. In fact, a majority of research on this topic has produced findings contrary to the "common wisdom" contained in many gender myths. For example, Strazdins (2000) demonstrated that the frequency with which women and men perform caretaking behaviors and attend to emotional labor tends to vary with the expectations of life roles (e.g., spouse, parent, professional). The findings from Strazdins' (2000) work indicate that the labor involved in caring for others is often performed in professional roles (e.g., health care, service-oriented industries), regardless of an individual's biological sex. While women have traditionally been responsible for these forms of labor within families, these results suggest that demonstrating care for others in these ways is a function of role requirements rather than a function of sex or individual personality characteristics. Based in this contrast between family and professional roles, it appears that inequality in responsibility for family caretaking is primarily due to the differing expectations placed on men and women within families. Presumably, should these expectations continue to change over time, the division of this labor should also become more equitable regardless of the perceived personality traits involved.

Interestingly, participants in the current study did not explicitly connect the above personality differences to generalized differences between the genders. None of the couples attributed different personality characteristics between husbands and wives to global differences between men and women. As such, it appears that couples in this sample did not explicitly assign responsibility for the labor of organizational management on the basis of gender. Participant couples did not overtly endorse a perspective that considered organizational responsibility primarily "women's work." This comes as no surprise, given that couples also did not report that other domains of family labor (e.g., child care, breadwinning, emotional labor) were divided solely on gender lines (Haddock et al., in progress). Instead, perceived personality differences repeatedly provided the impetus for rationalizing women's continued responsibility for organizational labor within families. Yet, across the aggregate data pool, no couples described the woman as flexible and spontaneous *and* the man as organized and structured with respect to family labor. While these personality differences were discussed by participants as individual differences, considering the sample of participant couples as a whole suggests that couples' attributions for these personality differences were correlated with gender. These findings appear to be a clear indication that the above personality characteristics have become part of the socially constructed definitions of femininity and masculinity. Therefore, it appears that organizational management was implicitly "women's work" in most participant couples, yet justified and rationalized under the guise of personality differences between individual husbands and wives.

While many couples resorted to explaining inequality in division of organizational responsibility through individual personality differences (i.e., "That is just how I am," "She is that type of person," "He is a more relaxed person"), this explanation has the potential to obscure closer examination of the relationship dynamics surrounding this arrangement. As such, couples may fail to consider interactional patterns that can lead these roles to become complementary and self-reinforcing over time (i.e., the more organized and structured she is, the more flexible and relaxed he can afford to be; the more flexible and relaxed he is, the more organized and structured she is required to be). For many, focusing on personality differences can draw attention away from an evaluation of the overall fairness of this arrangement and create barriers to acknowledging organizational labor as equivalent to the labor involved in completion of household tasks. Without this acknowledgement, organizational labor will likely persist as a form of invisible labor and will avoid detection by couples focused on achieving egalitarianism.

While discussion of personality differences was the principle explanation overtly present in participant interviews, other possible explanations exist for why women in this sample did not express dissatisfaction with organizational labor. While not receiving direct mention in the interviews, these explanations may have evaded couples' awareness and had a more subtle influence on participants in this sample. These explanations deserve mention here so that therapists may have the opportunity to investigate and intervene with these more subtle influences concealing inequality in organizational labor.

Women in this sample may not have expressed dissatisfaction with unequal division of organizational management because they are appreciative of the help currently provided by their husbands in other areas of family labor. As previously reported, couples in this sample possessed a relatively high level of equality in the domains of housework, child care, emotional labor, and the importance placed on each spouse's paid labor (Haddock et al., in progress). Relative to expectations perhaps shaped by their fathers, other men in their support network, or traditional male stereotypes, men in these couples emerged as significant contributors to completion of household tasks. As such, it was of little surprise that interviews and survey data revealed that women experienced high levels of relationship satisfaction and expressed sincere praise for their husbands' efforts in the home.

To return to the football metaphor, women often may not mind playing family quarterback when their husbands have proven that they come prepared to play, have familiarity with the team's playbook, are willing to run the plays called by the quarterback, and will catch the ball when thrown in their direction. These efforts certainly helped reduce the overall burden placed on many wives, and many women may feel fortunate to play alongside a teammate who stands out as a superstar when compared to other players at that position. Yet, unlike the star quarterback who just won the big game, family quarterbacks often do not receive an analogous level of recognition for a similar level of responsibility and stress. Rather, family quarterbacks could be considered as unsung heroes, taking responsibility for duties that are largely invisible but pivotal to the overall outcome of the game.

Female gender socialization also may play a significant role in determining whether or not women experience frustration and dissatisfaction with inequality in organizational labor. Given that gender socialization has led many women to consider the job of family planning and organization a primary means for demonstrating care, many may not feel a sense of injustice from accepting primary responsibility for these duties. In demonstrating care for their families in these ways, they may derive feelings of personal fulfillment, satisfaction, and power.

Another explanation for why women may be left with the burdensome responsibility of household organization was recently highlighted in the popular media. A story in *Working Mother* magazine (2000) speculated that many women may not completely trust their husbands to adequately complete such duties. The article indicated that many women do not feel comfortable sharing family organization with their husbands, who often do not appear ready to manage the many details of family life. In essence, this article postulated that many working mothers remain the family's primary organizer as the safest strategy for insuring that important family details were not overlooked in the process of family planning and organization.

Clinical Implications

When dual-earner couples seek couple or family therapy, it is critical that therapists guide spouses or partners through a thorough assessment of their overall level of relationship equality (Haddock, Zimmerman, & MacPhee, 2000). This assessment can include more traditional aspects of family labor, such as housework, child care, and decision making, and also those that are typically more invisible, such as emotional and organizational labor. A comprehensive assessment of division of organizational labor should include investigation of at least six critical variables.

First, an investigation of the overall division of household tasks (e.g., child care, meal preparation, laundry, house cleaning) will provide a baseline reading of the level of achieved equality between spouses. Given that task labor is often easier for couples to identify than organizational management, an assessment in this domain will help indicate a couple's commitment to egalitarianism and predict a couple's readiness to divide organizational duties. Second, identifying the strategies or techniques that a couple utilizes in household organization (e.g., family calendar, chore charts, phone calls or voice mails during the work day, notes written to individual family members, family menu) will indicate a family's methods for insuring organization, delegation, and completion of household tasks. This process of identifying strategies will pay dividends in later sessions, by helping organizational labor become more concrete and easily visible for spouses.

Third, determining which spouse originally devised these strategies and presently insures their continued usage will help indicate which partner is primarily responsible for organizational labor for the family. Fourth, helping trace the origins of this arrangement will establish the lifespan of inequality in organizational labor, enhance understanding of the time period over which this issue has remained unrecognized, and shape realistic expectations for the ease with which this arrangement might be changed. Fifth, investigating the attributions couples utilize to explain division of organizational duties (e.g., personality, teamwork, gender differences) will help illuminate areas on which to focus with interventions. Finally, determining the meaning that change in this area might carry for individual spouses will indicate whether feelings of guilt, embarrassment, or discomfort will create emotional obstacles to change. As therapists assist couples in striving toward egalitarianism, investigating these six variables in a sensitive yet thorough assessment may be critical to the overall success of treatment.

Therapists can recommend strategies for couples designed to facilitate increased equality in division of organizational labor. For example, couples might divide responsibility for the family calendar on six-month intervals, with one spouse accepting total responsibility for its maintenance for six months and then passing it to the other for the following six months. Additionally, parental responsibility for organizing homework or devising the family menu can be divided on an alternating-week schedule. Beginning small, such as with rotating homework or meal-planning schedules, can enhance division of organizational labor in at least one aspect of their lives and ultimately help other forms of organizational labor become more visible over time. Another possibility might be for spouses to divide organizational duties across activities in which their children are enrolled. For instance, if a couple's daughters participate in ballet and soccer, one parent would manage all aspects of organization for ballet while the other manages the same aspects for soccer. While both parents would likely have a desire to attend recitals and games in order to support their children, spouses (most likely the wife) could enjoy these activities without the pressure of managing all of the organizational aspects for both.

The number of strategies for splitting organizational labor is countless, yet the particular strategy adopted is far less important than assisting couples in recognizing this form of labor as one in need of equal division, much like washing dishes and cleaning clothes. While organizational duties often do not produce a tangible result when compared to task labor, such labor involves keeping track of the details that help families remain balanced and on task. This labor is often both time consuming and extracts a tremendous mental burden when not divided equitably. The possibilities of increased mental relaxation, decreased organizational responsibility, and increased sharing of family details would certainly be a welcome relief to many women in charge of organizational labor. Sharing of the family quarterback role might effectively break the cycle of the "uptight, organized" mom and "flexible, laidback" dad, and more women would be able to enjoy the thrill of going out for the pass rather than always having to call the plays.

FUTURE RESEARCH

The area of organizational equality is relatively new and underresearched; thus further research is needed. For example, the long-term implications for being the organizer of the family are not known. Women who have been in charge of the family's organizational labor may not feel unsatisfied with this role over time. Additionally, comparative studies challenging the "personality" explanation are needed. For example, future studies could look at the organizational management in single father households, in gay and lesbian partnerships, and in families where the males are more responsible for the organizational labor. Determining how these arrangements were negotiated may assist therapists in addressing resistance in couples for whom the arrangement is problematic.

REFERENCES

Allen, S.M., & Hawkins, A.J. (1999). Maternal gatekeeping: Mothers' beliefs and behaviors that inhibit greater father involvement in family work. *Journal of Marriage and the Family, 61*, 199-212.

Barnett, R.C., & Baruch, G.K. (1987). Determinants of fathers' participation in family work. *Journal of Marriage and the Family, 49*(1), 29-40.

Barnett, R.C., & Rivers, C. (1996). *She works, he works: How two-income families are happy, healthy, and thriving.* Cambridge, MA: Harvard University Press.

Creswell, J.W. (1998). *Qualitative inquiry and research design: Choosing among five traditions.* Thousand Oaks, CA: Sage Publications.

Demo, D.H, & Acock, A.C. (1993). Family diversity and the division of domestic labor: How much have things really changed? *Family Relations, 42*, 323-331.

DeStefano, L., & Colasanto, D. (1990). The gender gap in America: Unlike 1975, today most Americans think men have it better. *Gallup Poll News Service, 54*(37), 1-7.

Deutsch, F.M. (1999). *Halving it all: How equally shared parenting works.* Cambridge, MA: Harvard University Press.

DeVault, M.L. (1987). Doing housework: Feeding and family life. In N. Gerstel & H.E. Gross (Eds.), *Families and work.* Philadelphia: Temple University Press.

Duncombe, J., & Marsden, D. (1995). "Workaholics" and "whingeing women": Theorizing intimacy and emotion work–the last frontier of gender inequality? *The Sociological Review*, 150-169.

Erickson, R.J. (1993). Reconceptualizing family work: The effect of emotion work on perceptions of marital quality. *Journal of Marriage and the Family, 55*, 888-900.

Haddock, S.A., Zimmerman, T.S., & MacPhee, D. (2000). The Power Equity Guide: Attending to gender in family therapy. *Journal of Marriage and Family Therapy, 26*(2), 153-171.

Haddock, S.A., Zimmerman, T.S., Current, L.R., & Ziemba, S.J. (in progress). Intimate partnership: The foundation to the successful balance of family and work.

Haddock, S.A., Zimmerman, T.S., Ziemba, S.J., & Current, L.R. (in press). Ten philosophies for work and family balance: Advice from successful families. *Journal of Marriage and Family Therapy.*

Hawkins, A.J., Roberts, T., Christiansen, S.L., & Marshall, C.M. (1994). An evaluation of a program to help dual-earner couples share the second shift. *Family Relations, 43*, 213-220.

Hayghe, H.V. (1990). Family members in the work force. *Monthly Labor Review.*

Higgins, M.R., Cook, A.S., Werner-Wilson, R., & Berger, P. (1997). The effects of emotion management performance on the work and marital satisfaction of marriage and family therapists. Presented at the 59th Annual Conference of the National Council on Family Relations, Arlington, Nov. 7-10, 1997.

Hochschild, A.R., & Machung (1989). *The second shift.* New York: Viking.

Leslie, L.A., Anderson, E.A., & Branson, M.P. (1991). Responsibility for children: The role of gender and employment. *Journal of Family Issues, 12*(2), 197-210.

Levine, S.B. (2000). *Father courage: What happens when men put family first.* New York: Harcourt.

Mederer, H.J. (1993). Division of labor in two-earner homes: Task accomplishment versus household management as critical variables in perceptions about family work. *Journal of Marriage and the Family, 55*, 133-145.

Rasmussen, K.S., Hawkins, A.J., & Schwab, K.P. (1996). Increasing husbands' involvement in domestic labor: Issues for therapists. *Contemporary Family Therapy, 18*(2), 209-223.

Risman, B.J., & Johnson-Sumerford, D. (1998). Doing it fairly: A study of postgender marriages. *Journal of Marriage and the Family, 60*(1), 23-40.

Rosenbluth, S.C., Steil, J.M., & Whitcomb, J.H. (1998). Marital equality: What does it mean? *Journal of Family Issues, 19*(3), 227-244.

Schwartz, P. (1994). *Love between equals: How peer marriage really works.* New York: Free Press.

Seery, B.L., & Crowley, M.S. (2000). Women's emotion work in the family: Relationship management and the process of building father-child relationships. *Journal of Family Issues, 21*, 100-127.

Shelton, B.A., & John, D. (1993). Does marital status make a difference: Housework among married and cohabiting men and women. *Journal of Family Issues, 14*, 401-420.

Strauss, A., & Corbin, J. (1990). *Basics of qualitative research: Grounded theory procedures and techniques.* Newbury Park, CA: Sage Publications.

Strazdins, L.M. (2000). Integrating emotions: Multiple role measurement of emotional work. *Australian Journal of Psychology, 52*(1), 41-50.

Tingey, H., Kiger, G., & Riley, P. (1996). Juggling multiple roles: Perceptions of working mothers. *The Social Science Journal, 33*(2), 183-191.

Trebilcot, J. (1983). *Mothering: Essays in feminist theory.* Totowa, NJ: Rowman & Allanheld.

Williams, J. (2000). *Unbending gender: Why family and work conflict and what to do about it.* New York: Oxford University Press.

Therapists' Approaches to the Normative Challenges of Dual-Earner Couples: Negotiating Outdated Societal Ideologies

Shelley A. Haddock
Stephanie Weiland Bowling

SUMMARY. The majority of American couples with minor children are dual-earners, and research indicates that, in general, the members of these families are thriving. Yet, outdated societal ideologies and practices place stressors on these families. Dual-earner couples, particularly working mothers, may experience guilt and/or concern about their family arrangement. Additionally, these couples may experience tensions in renegotiating gender expectations. A national, random sample of clinical members of AAMFT was surveyed to find out how family therapists are responding to the normative challenges of dual-earner couples in therapy. Results suggest that many therapists are unaware of the related empirical literature regarding the benefits and challenges of dual-earner

Shelley A. Haddock, PhD, is Assistant Professor, Human Development and Family Studies Department, Colorado State University and Director, Center for Family and Couple Therapy. Stephanie Weiland Bowling, MS, is a doctoral student in the Marriage and Family Therapy Program at St. Mary's University.

Partial funding for this project was generously provided by the Coalition of Labor Union Women.

Address correspondence to: Shelley A. Haddock, Department of Human Development and Family Studies, Colorado State University, Fort Collins, CO 80523.

[Haworth co-indexing entry note]: "Therapists' Approaches to the Normative Challenges of Dual-Earner Couples: Negotiating Outdated Societal Ideologies." Haddock, Shelley A., and Stephanie Weiland Bowling. Co-published simultaneously in *Journal of Feminist Family Therapy* (The Haworth Press, Inc.) Vol. 13, No. 2/3, 2001, pp. 91-120; and: *Balancing Family and Work: Special Considerations in Feminist Therapy* (ed: Toni Schindler Zimmerman) The Haworth Press, Inc., 2001, pp. 91-120. Single or multiple copies of this article are available for a fee from The Haworth Document Delivery Service [1-800-HAWORTH, 9:00 a.m. - 5:00 p.m. (EST). E-mail address: getinfo@haworthpressinc.com].

families. Further, many therapists remain unaware of how the societal context often promotes guilt and inequity among today's couples. Implications for family therapists are discussed, including the need for therapists to become more familiar with recent research about dual-earner families, equality in intimate partnerships, and child care. *[Article copies available for a fee from The Haworth Document Delivery Service: 1-800-HAWORTH. E-mail address: <getinfo@haworthpressinc.com> Website: <http://www.HaworthPress.com>* © *2001 by The Haworth Press, Inc. All rights reserved.]*

KEYWORDS. Dual-earner couples, family therapy practice, work-family balance

Modern American families are being challenged to respond to one of the most significant cultural transformations in the past four decades (Coontz, 2000). The rise in dual-earner couples–or, more precisely, the increased participation of women in the paid labor force–has led to significant changes in middle-class Americans' experiences of work and family. Although women–particularly those with lower incomes–have routinely participated in the paid labor force, the influx of middle-class women into the external work force in recent decades strikes at the heart of cultural assumptions about the American economy, marriage, notions of "good" parenting, and the personal identities of women and men (Williams, 2000).

Often, in ways that are unrecognized, these societal changes shape the daily experiences and inform the major decisions of parents as they strive to create healthy and meaningful lives for themselves and their children. Although cultural changes have created more opportunities for persons of both genders, many social and structural dynamics operate to constrain people's choices and personal and relationship well-being (Barnett & Rivers, 1996; Williams, 2000). Despite the fact that 68% of couples with children under the age of 18 are dual-earners (Barnett & Rivers, 1996), the structure and supporting ideologies of American social institutions continue to be based on an assumption that the "traditional" breadwinner father/homemaker mother family arrangement is the norm.

The purposes of this study were threefold: (a) to examine family therapists' treatment approaches for dual-earner couples experiencing normative challenges, (b) to learn the amount of graduate training therapists receive on this topic and the other sources of relevant information they utilize, and (c) to determine if certain educational and personal factors are related to the quality of their treatment approaches.

LITERATURE REVIEW

To fully appreciate the opportunities and constraints of today's dual-earner couples, one must examine them within a historical, sociocultural, and economic context. The institution of family underwent dramatic changes as a result of the industrial revolution in the 19th century (Skolnick, 1991). As the economy moved from a subsistence to a monetary base, paid work became distinct from non-paid work at home. This revolution gave rise to the ideology of domesticity–a gender system that justifies and sustains a separation in the "public" and "private" spheres of life. It is important to recognize that the ideology of domesticity is class linked; poor women have routinely worked outside the home for pay (Coontz, 2000). As an ideology, domesticity often does not reflect many people's lives, but it has a powerful influence in shaping cultural expectations and practices that affect the lives of all Americans.

As described by Williams (2000), domesticity is an "entrenched, almost unquestioned, American norm and practice" (p. 1) with several defining characteristics. First, it presupposes an ideal-worker norm–an expectation that workers do not have care-giving responsibilities (because they are handled by a spouse), and, therefore, can work overtime, relocate, and avoid taking time off for childbearing or rearing. Second, it holds that men are "naturally" suited for employment and women for relationship maintenance, child care, and homemaking. In this way, men's and women's identities are informed by domesticity as each gender is assigned characteristics that would make them successful in their respective realms. Third, domesticity produced shifts in child rearing norms, whereby expectations developed that children ideally need almost constant supervision and stimulation by their mother.

The ideology of domesticity was at its strongest in the 1950s; women were encouraged to "return home" after increased numbers had participated in the paid labor force as part of the war effort (Skolnick, 1991). It is this family–as depicted on TV as Ozzie and Harriet Nelson and Ward and June Cleaver–that came to be viewed as the ideal family arrangement and informs current nostalgic notions of "family" (Coontz, 1992). Yet, when viewed from a historical perspective, most family historians agree that the breadwinner family was really an aberration that emerged only in a brief stage of history.

In the past several decades, as economic and social conditions neces-sitated and allowed couples to deviate from the breadwinner-home-maker model, women's labor force participation increased by record numbers. In fact, the number of dual-earner married couples overtook "traditional" (i.e., breadwinner father/homemaker mother) families in number as early as the mid-70s (Hayghe, 1990). In 1998, dual-earner couples outnumbered "traditional" families nearly three-to-one (U.S. Bureau of the Census, 1998). This increase is a result of many factors, including economic; many scholars (e.g., Galinsky, 1999) argue that most families require two incomes to be economically viable.

Despite these changes, the norms of domesticity continue to be ac-cepted unquestionably by many. These norms reinforce cultural as-sumptions that the traditional family is the preferred family. In contrast, because it exists "in violation" of each norm of domesticity, the dual-earner family often is rendered lacking in some way or inferior in comparison. As the dual-earner families challenged deeply rooted be-liefs about gender, marriage, and workplace norms, it was expectable that cultural dissention and anxiety would result from their increased number. These changes have spawned heated and often polarized pub-lic and private debates. Some segments of society have welcomed the challenges to domesticity (Faludi, 1991). However, many have as-sumed that maternal employment would result in negative outcomes for families (Holcomb, 1998).

Holcomb (1998) argued that, despite ample empirical evidence to the contrary, the media has perpetuated negative and often false informa-tion about dual-earner couples, particularly working mothers. Dual-earner couples are often depicted as time-crazed, lacking time for one another, their children, and their employer; their children are frequently portrayed as desperate for parental love and attention while being "raised" by child care providers. These couples are portrayed as selfish, ambitious, and materialistic. The media also is replete with alarming and inaccurate information about the outcomes for children of em-ployed mothers (Holcomb, 1998; Galinsky, 1999).

Not only have cultural ideologies–as represented and reinforced by the media–been slow to respond to dual-earner couples, so, too, have the structure and norms of the American economy (Barnett & Rivers, 1996). In many workplaces, work norms continue to be structured around an assumption that paid employees have a full-time adult (i.e., wife) at home who takes care of all non-paid labor (Coontz, 2000). For instance, average work hours continue to increase; in fact, Americans work an average 47-hour work week, 3 1/2 hours longer than 20 years ago and more than persons in any other country in the world (Coontz, 2000).

Given these outmoded and inhospitable structural and ideological dynamics, how are dual-earner families generally faring? According to the latest research, in dual-earner families "the men and women are doing well, emotionally and physically, and the children are thriving" (Barnett & Rivers, 1996, p. 1). Aside from the obvious financial benefits associated with dual earning, research has found many benefits of dual earning for women, men, and children. Most dual earners report that the benefits of their family arrangement outweigh the costs (Barnett & Rivers, 1996; Galinsky, 1999; Holcomb, 1998; Williams, 2000). For instance, many women find paid employment to be a source of independent identity, increased self-esteem, enhanced social contacts, and inherent interest (Barnett & Baruch, 1985; Coleman, Antonucci, Adelmann, & Crohan, 1987). The outcomes for male dual earners have received less attention; however, benefits for many men include decreased breadwinning pressure and increased opportunities for family involvement (Barnett & Rivers, 1996; Schwartz, 1994). Additionally, women's increased labor force participation has contributed to the development of a new cultural ideal of marriage–one that is more egalitarian and companionate (Ferree, 1990; Rabin, 1996). Schwartz (1994) argued that because dual-earner couples have smaller economic differentials, they have a greater possibility for achieving an egalitarian relationship, which has been associated with positive relationship outcomes. For instance, in his 20-year longitudinal study, Gottman (1999) found that sharing power is essential for a successful marriage.

A significant body of research conducted over several decades has concluded that maternal employment in and of itself has very little impact on children (Galinsky, 1999)–and, that when there is an impact, it is generally positive. Research has consistently reported that maternal employment does not affect the mother-child bond (NICHD Early Child Care Research Network, 1997), does not diminish the influence of parents on children (Fuligni et al., 1995; NICHD, 1997), and does not influence children's assessment of the quality of their mothers' parenting (Galinsky, 1999). The effect of maternal employment depends on a number of factors, such as parental attitudes about maternal employment; the income that working brings to the family; the mother's warmth and sensitivity to her children; the quality of parents' jobs; and the quality of child care (Fuligni et al., 1995; Galinsky, 1999). This literature has revealed that, contrary to popular beliefs, employed parents spend more time now with their children than they did 20 years ago (Galinsky, 1999). And, finally, the use of child care cannot be judged either "good" or "bad" for children; its effects depend on other factors, such as the quality of the care (NICHD, 1997).

Despite evidence that dual-earner families as a whole are successful and faring well, Holcomb (1998) argues that "no serious researcher [would] deny that real conflicts exist between work and family duties today" (p. 120). However, these conflicts are not exclusive to dual-earner families; all families experience such conflict, but perhaps in different ways. Secondly, work-family conflicts are not inevitable for dual earners, nor are they a result of qualities intrinsic to the dual-earner family; instead, they reflect a lag in changes to social ideologies and structural dynamics (Williams, 2000).

For the purpose of this study, two struggles that are experienced by many dual-earner couples as a result of lagging social and structural dynamics will be discussed. First, many dual-earner couples–particularly working mothers–experience concern and guilt about their family arrangements. This guilt is not a personal problem, indicating some kind of personal pathology, but rather a natural response to having one's choices, motivation, and quality of parenting consistently called into question (Holcomb, 1998). The second challenge that appears to be shared by many dual-earner families is that of renegotiating gender expectations for their relationship. Although a move towards less traditional gender norms can benefit dual-earner men and women in many significant ways, it can prove challenging (Barnett & Rivers, 1996; Schwartz, 1994). As Coontz (1992) wrote, "few Americans want to return to the days of segregated gender roles and legal inequality, but they are not sure how to build male-female intimacy in the midst of continuing inequities" (p. 3). It appears that one of the areas with which dual-earner couples typically struggle is dividing household labor and child care equitably. Several researchers have found that although men as a group contribute more than they did in the past, their contributions still fall short of those of their wives (e.g., Barnett & Rivers, 1996; Hochschild, 1989).

Family therapists can be a powerful source of accurate information about the two-income family arrangement and child care, assisting families in developing strategies that will allow them to glean the benefits and minimize the challenges of this family arrangement. It is unclear, however, how therapists are treating the normative challenges of dual-earner families and to what degree therapists are prepared to effectively assist these families. This study is guided by three primary research questions: (a) What are the therapeutic practices of therapists in working with dual-earner couples who are experiencing normative challenges? (b) What are their perceptions of the amount of related training they received in graduate training programs, and what sources do they currently use to gain information about dual-earner families? (c) Are key training and personal experiences related to the quality of therapeutic practices? Because the first two questions are descriptive, hypotheses were generated for the third question only. The hypotheses were: (a) therapists' perceptions of the amount of relevant training provided in their graduate program will be positively related to the quality of their reports of therapeutic approaches, (b) therapists' use of the scholarly literature to gain information about related topics will be positively related to the quality of their reports of therapeutic approaches; (c) therapists' use of the popular media to gain information about related topics will be negatively related to the quality of their reports of therapeutic approaches; and (d) therapists' membership in a dual-earner family as an adult will be positively related to the quality of their reports of therapeutic approaches.

METHOD

Sample

Surveys were mailed to two hundred clinical members of the American Association for Marriage and Family Therapy (AAMFT) randomly selected from the 1999 AAMFT membership directory. Surveys that were returned because of incorrect address (N = 6) or inability to complete (N = 8) were replaced. Reminder postcards were mailed three weeks after the original mailing. Eighty-two completed surveys were returned, resulting in a 38% response rate.

Sixty percent of the participants were women. The respondents' mean age was 49.08 ($SD = 9.52$). The sample was ethnically homogeneous, with 92.7% identifying as Caucasian, 3.7% identifying as Native American, and 3.7% identifying as "other." Regarding educational background, 40.2% earned an MS or MA degree, 22% earned an MSW degree, 20.7% possessed PhDs, 4.9% earned an EdD, and 12.2% earned some other degree allowing them to clinically practice. Respondents earned these degrees between 1968 and 1999, with the average participant graduating in 1985 ($SD = 7.71$). Most participants (59.5%) were licensed in marriage and family therapy. Other licenses were as professional counselors (23.2%), social workers (20.7%), psychology (8.5%), and other licenses relevant to clinical practice (13.4%).

Clinical practice settings included private individual practice (41.5%), group practice (18.3%), private, non-profit agencies (22%), government agencies (3.7%), and some other kind of clinical practice setting (14.6%). Finally, respondents reported that, on average, their clinical population was comprised of adult individuals (42.8%), adolescent individuals (11.3%), and child clients (7.3%). On average, respondents reported that the 29.54% ($SD = 8.37$) of their couple cases during the past year involved difficulties associated with work-family balance.

Although 84.1% of respondents had children, fewer were members of a dual-earner couple when their oldest (43.9%) and youngest (31.7%) children were each under age six. In addition, only 18.3% of therapists had dual-earner parents when they were under the age of six.

Procedure

Participants received a self-administered questionnaire that contained questions about demographics, professional training and experiences, personal background, and a brief clinical vignette. A cover letter explained that the research study was designed "to explore different approaches used by family therapists for working with families who are struggling with work-related decisions." One dollar was enclosed with each survey.

Amount of relevant training in graduate program. To test the first hypothesis, respondents were asked to rate four items on a Likert scale, ranging from 1 (*none*) to 4 (*a lot*). Items were the amount of training they received related to (a) families and their work-related decisions, (b) the benefits and drawbacks of child care, and (c) the common experiences of dual-income couples. They also rated, from 1 (*not at all*) to 4 (*definitely*), to what extent they believed this training adequately prepared them to assist families of today in making work-related decisions and in managing family and work responsibilities. Given the high alpha reliability for the combined items (alpha = .85), they were combined as a single variable for analysis.

Use of the scholarly literature. To test the second hypothesis, on a scale of 1 (*never*) to 4 (*regularly*), respondents indicated how often they read professional journal articles and how often they read scholarly books on the topic. Given the high alpha reliability for the combined items (alpha = .77), they were combined as a single variable for analysis.

Use of the popular media. To test the third hypothesis, respondents identified sources from which they obtain information about these topics, including popular press books, news, popular media (TV, movies), magazines, other professionals, friends and family, clients, and personal experience. A count was performed on only those items related to popular media, indicating the number of popular press mediums used; scores ranged from 0 to 4.

Membership in a dual-earner family as an adult. To test the fourth hypothesis, respondents were asked if they have child(ren), and if so, if both they and their spouse worked at least 30 hours per week when their oldest child was under the age of 6 and when their youngest child was under the age of 6. Participants were coded as an adult member in a dual-earner family if both partners worked when either their oldest or youngest was under the age of 6.

Reports of therapeutic approaches. Coding participants' written responses to a vignette was used to discover therapists' treatment approaches. Based on the literature, the vignette (see Appendix A) described a heterosexual, dual earner couple who was struggling with normative challenges: division of household and parenting labor, and guilt and concern about maternal employment. Respondents were asked to describe their approach in working with this couple, focusing specifically on issues related to work-family decisions and child care. They were asked to describe: (a) the problems that were confronting the family; (b) their treatment approach; (c) the resources they would recommend; (d) the clinical or personal experiences they would share; and

(e) their response if the couple asked them what the typical benefits and drawbacks were for all members of dual-income families compared to "traditional" families.

Coding procedure. A coding scheme was developed to analyze responses to the clinical vignette. The coding scheme was organized into five areas: problem hypotheses, treatment plans, benefits and drawbacks, resources recommended, and personal experiences. Codes related to respondents' hypotheses about the problem were: the placement of responsibility for the problem (e.g., on Janie, Paul, or couple dynamics), whether problem definitions were pathologizing of Janie or Paul, the types of problems hypothesized, whether societal context was included in problem definition, and whether the complaints related to division of labor and Janie's guilt and concerns about working were addressed. In terms of treatment plan, codes included the target(s) of the intervention (e.g., Janie, Paul, couple), the type of intervention, whether the problems of division of labor and Janie's concerns about working were addressed, and whether the societal context was addressed. To code benefits and drawbacks mentioned and resources provided, lists of all responses were generated. Finally, for the personal experiences section, codes included whether information was shared and the nature of this information.

Quality of practice. Five variables were used to operationally define the *quality* of therapists' reports of practice for quantitative analysis. For "placement of responsibility," it was considered higher quality practice to place responsibility on both partners as opposed to disproportionately on Janie; because few therapists placed responsibility disproportionately on Paul, this value was not included in analysis. For "pathologizing of Janie," it was considered higher quality practice to actively resist pathologizing Janie than to remain neutral; actively pathologizing her was assigned the lowest value for this variable. For "recognition of societal context," it was considered higher quality practice to critically analyze the influence of the societal context in problem assessment than it was to fail to mention this context; reinforcing the negative influences of this context was assigned the lowest value for this variable. It was also considered higher quality practice to develop interventions intended to address the presenting problems; in other words, it was considered higher quality practice to address Janie's feelings of guilt than to ignore them, and to address division of labor than to ignore it.

Interrater reliability. The second author coded all vignette responses. To determine interrater reliability, a second coder independently coded 20 vignette responses (24%). Using Cohen's Kappa, interrater ranged from .76 ($p < .001$) to 1.0 ($p < .001$) with a median of .88.

RESULTS:
RESPONSES TO THE CLINICAL VIGNETTE

Therapists' Assessments of the Case

To whom was responsibility for the problem attributed? Approximately 37% of participants attributed responsibility for the problem to a combination of Janie and couple dynamics, and 6.1% of therapists saw the problem as residing solely with Janie. For example, one respondent wrote:

> [The problems are] ambivalence of the mother due to conflict between her desire for work and its resulting benefits and the sense of loss or abandonment of child . . . . There is not a problem with couple balance [because] the husband is willing to cooperate. Hers is the primary conflict; she needs to decide what she thinks is most important.

A relatively large percentage of therapists (28%) attributed responsibility to couple dynamics or to *both* partners individually and couple dynamics (25.6%). A small minority of respondents (2.4%) located the problem as a combination of couple dynamics and Paul.

Did problem conceptualizations pathologize clients? Participants were much more likely to pathologize Janie (40.2%) than Paul (2.4%) or the couple (8.5%). A response was coded as "pathologizing" when it attributed the problem solely to pathology or deficits as opposed to recognizing a systemic context. An example of a pathologizing hypothesis is:

> [The problems are] Janie's need for recognition, or productivity, or money, or all three; Janie's need to please everyone else in her life, excluding her own needs; Janie's lack of self-confidence in her own ability to find an acceptable solution; Janie's lack of education around her need to set boundaries for herself and others.

Another respondent indicated that Janie many need to be "redirected" toward her husband.

> Many times, women need [to be] redirected toward the husband [after the birth of a baby] . . . Emotionally, a man often feels abandoned with the primary relationship in the family switching from being him and his wife to him and wife and their new child. Men often feel it goes from friendship and good sex to having a role to play as child care provider and home maintenance person. If he wanted a job at a day care, he would apply for one. If he wanted a maintenance job on top of his regular job, he would apply for one.

Were the primary presenting problems addressed in therapists' problem formulations? The vignette centered on two primary presenting problems: guilt and worry about working and using child care, and inequities in division of household and parenting labor.

Attention to concerns about child care. The vast majority of respondents (87.8%) did not include Janie's concern that child care would have a "negative impact" on her family in their conceptualizations of the problem. Approximately 9% of therapists mentioned and reinforced these concerns. A very small percentage of respondents (3.7%) mentioned child care in a realistic or research-based manner. For example, one participant, who appeared familiar with the research on child care, indicated concern that the couple was "unaware of the literature indicating that the mother's attitude about working outside the home greatly determines the child's adjustment."

Attention to Janie's feelings of guilt that were exacerbated by others' comments. Most of the respondents (57.3%) did not address Janie's feelings of guilt in their problem formulations. Of the remaining therapists who did address these comments, 22% appeared to find fault in Janie and/or the couple for allowing these comments to influence them, for instance, by describing the problem as "Janie's concern about what others think." Almost 21% of respondents tended to normalize and empathize about the influence of these comments on Janie and/or the couple. For example, one participant wrote: "This is a very typical situation of a couple [being] caught between their true values and societal pressures. . . . Philosophically, this couple has to decide between what's *best* for their family and what's *expected* by others."

Attention to inequitable division of labor. About half (51.2%) of the participants included inequitable division of household labor and child care in their problem formulation.

What other problems were hypothesized as part of problem conceptualization? Given that many respondents did not refer to the two most salient presenting problems in the vignette, how did they view the problems in this family? Table 1 lists the problems hypothesized with the percentage of therapists who mentioned each.

Did therapists conceptualize the couple's problems within a societal context? The majority of therapists (68%) did not mention the societal context in their assessments. Twenty-two percent of therapists appeared to recognize and analyze critically the constraining ideologies embedded in society. For instance, one therapist wrote: "This is a typical dilemma for women–a psychosocial stressor. With the freedom to have a career, women have to balance strong cultural ideas about motherhood, their child's individual needs, and their own career plans." Approximately 9% of therapists mentioned the influence of the societal context, but appeared to accept societal myths about dual earners. For instance, one therapist wrote: "I believe that this 'problem' is a societal one: we are brainwashed by popular culture to believe we need a higher standard of living than we can comfortably support."

Therapists' Treatment Approaches

Who was the target of therapists' interventions? Despite the large number of participants who attributed responsibility to Janie and the couple, the majority of therapists (74.4%) targeted their interventions to the couple's relationship or to each partner and the relationship (9.8%). Only 2.4% of therapists targeted their intervention to Janie, and 9.8% to Janie and couple dynamics. Two percent of therapists targeted their intervention to Paul and couple dynamics.

Was the presenting problem of guilt addressed? What interventions were recommended? Only 14.6% of therapists addressed Janie's feelings of guilt and concern about working and child care, and these therapists used various methods for assisting the couple in managing these feelings. Approximately 9% of participants stated that they would provide research-based information on child care or suggest that the couple explore the relevant literature. One therapist stated that she would provide research-based information on dual-earner couples. Surprisingly,

TABLE 1. Therapists' Assessment of the Case

Type of Problem	% Who Mentioned
Problems Attributed to Couple Dynamics	
Different and/or unclear values about work and family	57.3
Unequal division of labor	36.6
Communication or conflict resolution difficulties	35.4
Family-of-origin patterns and/or expectations about gender	28.0
Financial issues	20.7
Life cycle changes and transitions	17.1
Stepfamily issues	14.6
Not enough intimacy and/or couple time	7.3
Ineffective time management skills and/or time constraints	7.3
Power struggle between couple	4.9
Influenced too much by consumerist values	3.7
Problems Attributed to Janie	
Guilt about working and/or child care	42.7
Ambivalence between roles of professional and mother	31.7
Low self-esteem	14.6
Difficulty setting boundaries; overly influenced by others	14.6
Lack of confidence as a parent and/or in parenting outcomes	8.5
Overfunctioning as a parent and/or spouse	8.5
Grief and loss about not being able to be a stay-at-home parent	6.1
Difficulty balancing family and work	3.7
Exhaustion	3.7
Need for personal fulfillment	2.4
Depression	2.4
Problems Attributed to Paul	
Not functioning as a partner in parenting or household labor	12.2
Inability to understand his wife's feelings	7.3
Traditional gender ideology	4.9
Unwillingness to compromise	2.4
Unwillingness to stand up to his parents in support of Janie working	2.4

Note: Only problems that were mentioned by more than one therapist are included.

only one therapist indicated that they would address the prevalence of guilt-inducing messages in our society (e.g., media, news reports) as part of their treatment plan.

Thirteen percent of therapists referred specifically to the guilt-inducing comments from family and friends in their plans for intervention. Strategies for intervention reflected varying degrees of recognition of the prevalence of these negative messages in our society and empathy for their effects. One respondent would have suggested or brainstormed with the couple concrete ways to respond to these kinds of comments. Another strategy was to focus on clarifying the couple's beliefs to lessen the effect of the comments, for example, "Family and peer pressure aside, I would want to help this couple focus on their own goals and needs." Some therapists appeared to believe that Janie's guilty feelings were indicative of some kind of deficit within her or the family rather than a normal response to cultural messages. For instance, one therapist wrote: "I would address the family's guilt first by trying to understand why a social worker who presumably studied child development would feel *that* guilty." Others hypothesized that these comments were not freely offered and, therefore, believed that a solution resided in "refrain[ing] from getting advice from anyone else including family, friends, etc."

Was the complaint about inequitable division of household and parenting labor addressed in treatment plans? While 51.2% of therapists included division of labor in their conceptualization of the problem, only 26.9% of participants included it as part of their intervention plan. Some therapists (17.1%) attended to this problem within a couple context, such as in the following example: "The initial problem appears to be one of setting appropriate boundaries within the family around what issues or assignments of the workload can be given to Paul . . . A division of the workload (a list) each week might work to manage everyone's anxiety." Approximately 10% of therapists targeted this aspect of their intervention to Paul; for instance, one therapist stated that she would "gently confront Paul on his willingness to be home less (work two jobs) rather than actively participate more at home, [and then] identify chores and parenting that he can and will do to increase his involvement with Jesse."

What other kinds of interventions were included in treatment plans? As shown in Table 2, interventions were organized into those targeted at the couple and each partner. The most common intervention was to as-

TABLE 2. Therapists' Proposed Interventions

Intervention	% Who Mentioned
Interventions Targeted to Couple	
Assist couple in clarifying their values	46.3
Improve couple's communication and conflict resolution skills	25.6
Consider changes to work-family arrangement (i.e., Janie works part-time or from home)	18.2
Assist couple in dividing household labor and parenting more equitably	17.1
Explore family-of-origin patterns regarding work-family arrangements and gender expectations	17.1
Assist couple in setting boundaries with family and friends	11.0
Improve the couple's intimacy	9.8
Interventions Targeted to Janie	
Address guilt/concerns about working and using child care	14.6
Assist Janie in clarifying her values regarding work and family	6.1
Assist Janie in clarifying her beliefs about women's roles	4.9
Increase her self-esteem	3.7
Normalize her ambivalence about working	3.7
Validate her desire to work	3.7
Interventions Targeted to Paul	
Encourage Paul to equitably share household and parenting responsibilities	9.8
Assist him in developing his sensitivity to Janie's response to societal messages	2.4

Note: Only problems that were mentioned by more than one therapist are included.

sist the couple in identifying and clarifying their work-family values. For instance, one therapist stated: "[I'd] help them clarify *their* values around the full-time mothering vs. working issue. It might be difficult to stay objective as a counselor. I would recommend lots of communication between the couple, monitoring the effect on the child of full-time day care."

It is noteworthy that another common intervention, suggested by 18.2% of therapists, was to suggest changes to–or exploration of changes to–the couple's present work-family arrangement. Interestingly, almost all of these therapists suggested consideration of changes to Janie's schedule, such as working part-time or working from home.

Therapists' Perceptions of the Typical Benefits and Drawbacks of Dual-Earner Families

Therapists were asked to describe their response if Paul and Janie were to ask them: "What are the *typical* benefits and drawbacks for women, men, and children in dual-income families compared to traditional families (where the father is employed and the mother stays at home)?" The results to this question are summarized in Table 3.

The most common response (approximately 29% of therapists) was to take a neutral approach by stating that benefits and drawbacks depend on the particular family; most then indicated that they would assist the couple in exploring their own beliefs on this topic. One respondent stated: "Benefits and drawbacks are relative to the couple's value system; this couple has a lot of work to do to define the values that will drive their lifestyle."

Benefits of dual-earner family arrangements. By far the most frequently cited benefit for any family member was that of increased personal fulfillment and self-esteem for women. All other benefits for any family member were mentioned by fewer than 25% of therapists. An illustrative quote related to the benefits for children is: "more social contacts at daycare, more intellectual stimulation; if mother enjoys her work, she may be more loving and less depressed."

Drawbacks of dual-earner arrangements. Therapists indicated that these benefits were not free of costs. For instance, one therapist stated: "I would emphasize the difference between 'the ideal' and 'the reality' of dual-income families–generally, somewhere something has to give or is sacrificed (i.e., quality time with children, someone's career, etc)." For instance, approximately 25% of therapists indicated that dual earning typically results in women experiencing fatigue and stress from a busy lifestyle.

A surprising number of therapists (13.6%) indicated that they would reinforce the beliefs that fuel Janie's guilt and worry about working and using child care. For instance, one therapist indicated that she would say

TABLE 3. Therapists' Perceptions of the Typical Benefits and Drawbacks of Dual-Earning

Benefits and Drawbacks Mentioned	% of Participants Who Mentioned
Benefits for Women	
Increased personal fulfillment/self-esteem	46.3
Increased support system/decreased isolation	23.2
Increased autonomy (financially and/or emotionally)	17.1
Greater marital equality and involvement in decision making	15.9
Increased family relationship quality/appreciate family time more	12.1
Drawbacks for Women	
Less time for children and family life/parenting suffers	35.4
Fatigue and/or stress from busy lifestyle	29.3
Doing the second shift at home	24.4
Guilt/conflict/ambivalence about being a working mother and/or about child care	24.4
Less time for self-care and social support	7.3
Decreased marital satisfaction/decreased couple time	7.3
Benefits for Men	
More family involvement and opportunity to be in a nurturing role	23.2
Decreased financial pressure to be the sole breadwinner	20.7
Happier, more fulfilled wife	12.2
Increased marital equality/marital satisfaction	11.0
Less pressure to be sole emotional support of spouse	7.3
Drawbacks for Men	
Increased household/parenting responsibilities	28.0
Gender role conflict/difficulty seeing wife as equal partner	11.0
More chaotic, stressed, hurried lifestyle	11.0
Not enough attention from wife/feel neglected	7.3
Benefits for Children	
Increased peer interaction/better social skills	19.5
Learn flexible gender expectations and behaviors from parents	17.1
Day care is positive for children	13.5
Greater access to fathers	11.0
Increased responsibility/independence/adaptability/flexibility	11.0
Happier parents/happier mother	9.8
Drawbacks for Children	
Children experience less or a lack of parental attention and time	24.4
Day care is negative for children	13.4
Children are too rushed and hurried	12.2
Decreased closeness and/or attachment between child and parents (typically mother)	11.0
Children feel unvalued, unloved, and/or neglected	9.7
Children are unsupervised more often–raised by others and television	9.7

the "benefits for women include self-development in a career, increased independence, and increased opportunities for income over a lifetime. Drawbacks include stress on women and on the whole family, less family time, negative impacts on children and the marriage." Almost 25% of therapists indicated that they would explain to the couple that children in dual-earner families have less or even a *lack* of parental attention and time. For instance, one therapist wrote, "Parents are stressed out at the end of the day and have little left to give." An additional 9.7% of therapists saw the situation for children as dire, stating that they would tell the couple that children typically felt unvalued, unloved, and neglected. For instance, one therapist stated that children "feel abandoned or neglected, miss parents." Another noted the "deprivation, neglect, [and] rushed/stressed lifestyle" that are typical of the lives of dual-earner children. Another respondent wrote that children in dual-earner families are "raised in daycare, which is never as high quality as own parents; [have] less time w/parents; [are] home alone many times without supervision; lack control; can feel unloved." One therapist focused on the long-term effects; she would explain to the couple that "children suffer from parental absence. These kids are more prone to turn to drugs, sex, and alcohol at an earlier age." Interestingly, some therapists appeared to view the resulting benefits for children as those borne from enduring hardship. For instance, one therapist indicated that they would explain to the couple: "Children learn to adjust in working families. They learn how to overcome shyness and make new friends. They learn assertiveness and leadership skills simply as a result of being forced to take initiative in order to survive." The presumption here is that child care is something one is *forced* to *survive*.

Dual-earner husbands also were frequently viewed as disadvantaged. The most frequently cited drawback for men was having additional family responsibilities (28%). In fact, more therapists mentioned this drawback than mentioned the benefits of increased family involvement and decreased breadwinning pressure. Several respondents (7.3%) indicated that men typically feel less valued and even ignored or neglected when their wives work.

Finally, one of the most obvious benefits for all members of a dual-earner family is increased income. However, 67.1% of participants did not mention this benefit. Only 25% of respondents mentioned that two incomes are often necessary for family necessities and well-being. Approximately 9% of participants who addressed financial benefit described it in terms of increased money for luxuries, vacations, or conveniences.

Resources Recommended

Sixty-one percent of therapists did not list any resource that they would recommend to the couple. Only 7.1% of therapists listed a resource relevant to work-family balance, child care, equitable marriages, working mothers, or dual-earner families; and the majority of these therapists (3.7%) listed the *Second Shift* (Hochschild & Machung, 1989). Most of the resources recommended were not directly related to the couple's primarily presenting problems; 10% of therapists listed books on marriage, 5% on parenting, and 3% on general family well-being.

Sharing of Clinical or Personal Experiences

Most respondents (58.5%) wrote clinical or personal experiences that they would share with the couple during the course of therapy. Approximately 18% of therapists shared experiences that were encouraging of dual-earner families, and 18% shared experiences that were discouraging. The remainder shared information that appeared neutral.

Respondents' Perceptions of Graduate Training and Other Sources of Information

Nearly half of participants stated that their training either prepared them "not at all" (8.5%) or "minimally" (35.3%) for assisting families with work-family issues. The remainder believed they were "mostly" (39%) or "definitely" (17.1%) prepared to offer this kind of assistance to families. Over half of participants reported that they received "no" or a "little" training on work-related decisions in families (56.1%), the benefits and drawbacks of child care (62.2%), and the common experiences of dual-earner couples (51.2%). Most respondents (80.5%) reported learning how to assist families with these issues from personal experience and from therapeutic experiences with clients. A lesser number of therapists reported learning about work-family balance issues from professionals (72%), friends and family (67.1%), the news media (51.2%), magazines (39.0%), the popular media (34.1%), and popular press books (20.7%). Thirty-four percent of therapists indicated that they read journal articles sometimes or regularly; 40.2% reported reading professional books sometimes or regularly.

Association Between Therapists' Training and Personal Factors and Vignette Responses

To test all hypotheses, Spearman correlations were performed to determine the association between four training and personal experience variables and five variables that operationally define the quality of therapists' reports of therapeutic practice. The training and experience variables were: (a) therapists' perceptions of the amount of relevant graduate training they received, (b) therapists' use of the empirical literature to gain related information, (c) therapists' use of the popular media to gain related information, and (d) therapists' membership in a dual-earner family as an adult. The five quality of practice variables were: (a) placement of responsibility, (b) pathologizing of Janie, (c) inclusion of societal context in problem formulation, (d) intervention related to the presenting problem of guilt, and (e) intervention related to the presenting problem in inequities in division of labor. No significant associations were found at an adjusted *p*-value of .01.

DISCUSSION

The central premise of this article is that to successfully assist dual-earner families with normative challenges, therapists must be attentive to societal context. As such, therapists must be knowledgeable of the empirical literature so that they can understand and evaluate the messages that often inform "popular wisdom" about dual-earner families. This premise is consistent with a growing recognition in the field of the importance of attending to the societal context in working with all clients. However, many scholars (e.g., Bograd, 1999) have argued that, in practice, family therapists tend to focus on the family as a relatively closed system.

Unfortunately, one of the most striking and troubling findings of this study is the failure of most therapists to conceptualize the case within its social context. In fact, almost 80% of therapists either did not mention societal context factors or reinforced the negative societal myths about dual-earner families. Equally disturbing are the many indicators in the data that the majority of therapists were largely unfamiliar with the empirical literature. This is consistent with more than half of the sample's perceptions that they received minimal training relevant to this topic. As could be expected, most therapists reinforced the inaccurate beliefs about dual-earner families that, in part, prompted this couple to pursue therapy in the first place—by either not addressing the beliefs, remaining neutral about them, or actively reinforcing them. Perhaps the nonsignificant differences based on therapists' perceptions about aspects of training and adult membership in a dual-earner family can be explained by the prevalent nature of these societal messages; in other words, unless people are engaged actively in critical analysis, they accept them as "what we all know" about these families.

Implications of Inattention to Context and the Empirical Literature for Case Assessment

When therapists underestimate the influence of the social context, they tend to pathologize clients for normative responses to oppressive experiences (Bograd, 1999). This tendency was evidenced in the finding that a majority of therapists either ignored Janie's experience of guilt or hypothesized that these feelings resulted from a personal deficit (i.e., "low self-esteem," "an atypical dependence on others' opinions," "a lack of self-confidence," or "depression") instead of as a normative response to negative societal messages.

Another potential result of minimizing context in the practice of therapy is the resultant tendency to accept societal gender norms that hold women primarily responsible for family well-being, thus assigning a disproportionate amount of responsibility to them for problem formation and resolution (Avis, 1988). Although many therapists placed responsibility for change on both partners, the majority emphasized Janie's culpability for the couple's problems. It is important to recognize that the tendency of therapists to pathologize and/or hold Janie primarily responsible for the couple's difficulties is likely to exacerbate the couple's problems by *increasing* Janie's feelings of guilt and *reinforcing* the power differential between the couple whereby she is more responsible for emotion, household, and parenting work.

Implications of Inattention to Context and the Empirical Literature for Treatment Plans

Although not inherently problematic, the three most frequently cited interventions (values clarification, communication skill building, and work schedule changes) could reflect many therapists' inattention to the social context and empirical literature. For instance, communication enhancement may be a helpful aspect of intervention, but probably insufficient in a social environment that promotes guilt among working mothers and inequities between partners.

Values clarification. By far the most frequently mentioned intervention was to assist the couple and/or Janie with values clarification. Although this is likely to be a helpful therapeutic activity, the effectiveness of this intervention seems contingent on, first, assisting the couple in evaluating critically the "source" of their values (e.g., society), and second, providing them with accurate information upon which to make informed decisions about these values. Most parents place their children's well-being above all else; about this value, they are typically not ambivalent (Rosenfeld, 2000). What is less clear to many parents is how to live consistently with this value. However, no therapist suggested (or indicated knowledge of) a recent, research-based book related to the effects of maternal employment and child care, and only 10% recommended that the couple explore research on this topic.

It is important to recognize that viewing the couple's decision for Janie to work as primarily a reflection of their values ignores potential economic realities. This inattention is consistent with the fact that two-thirds of the therapists did not mention the financial benefits of dual earning, and another 9% indicated a belief that women work for "luxuries."

A predominant focus on values also minimizes the gender oppression made evident in the fact that, unlike mothers, fathers often are not called upon to justify or clarify their values when seeking employment, or to choose between a career and (guilt-free) parenthood. Although not evident in many therapists' responses, discussions about values within the context of working mothers often are characterized by simplistic and unnecessary polarizations, such as "the value of money versus children's well-being," and "the value of women's self-fulfillment versus her family's health and happiness." In actuality, women's employment benefits their children just as does men's employment (Galinsky, 1999; see the effects of poverty), and it is typically not necessary or healthy for the well-being of one family member (i.e., mother) to be sacrificed on behalf of others.

Exploration of possible changes to the couple's work arrangements. The third most commonly cited intervention–and perhaps the most troubling–was a suggestion that the couple consider a change to their work-family arrangement, which typically involved a recommendation for Janie to explore working part-time or from home. Again, although such a decision would not be inherently negative, several aspects of this intervention are problematic. First, it was made without first providing the couple with factual information from which they could make an informed decision about what was best for their family. Second, in neglecting the economic realities of this family, possible negative effects of the decision were not addressed. For instance, it is likely that a change to Janie's employment would result in additional work responsibilities for Paul, which is troubling for two reasons. Research has documented that men's well-being is just as intimately tied to family connection, particularly the quality of the parent-child relationship, as is women's (Barnett & Rivers, 1996), and it is with *fathers*–not working mothers–that children report that they want more time (Galinsky, 1999). Third, the intervention is based on an insufficient understanding of the literature related to part-time employment. Contrary to popular belief, reducing one's commitment to work–through part-time employment or minimizing investment–has been associated with increased psychological distress for women (Barnett & Rivers, 1996). And finally, the intervention ignores Janie's expressed enjoyment of her career. From a social justice perspective, women should not be expected to choose between parenthood and a career; sadly, only 4% of the sample validated Janie's desire to work.

Achieve an equitable division of household and parenting responsibility. Two-thirds of therapists did not indicate plans to directly address the inequities in the couple's division of household and parenting responsibility. We propose several possible explanations for this finding. First, as feminists have argued (e.g., Avis, 1988), an inattention to social context leads many therapists to ignore (or actively reinforce) power differentials and accept (or actively reinforce) cultural gender norms about personal identity and division of labor. Second, because more therapists perceived increased family responsibilities as a typical drawback for dual-earning men than did those who mentioned any benefit, perhaps many therapists were attempting to "protect" Paul. Such "protection," however, may be a reflection of socially sanctioned male privilege, which is "often so subtle and unremarkable in practice that it is easily missed" (Orton, 1993, p. 35); it also may come at the expense of Janie and the family's well-being.

Again, this finding may reflect therapists' lack of familiarity with the empirical literature, which has found that equity is essential for relationship satisfaction, sustained intimacy, and deep friendship in marriage (Rabin, 1996; Schwartz, 1994). More specifically, researchers have found that when couples achieve an equitable division of labor, wives *and* husbands experience less work-family conflict (Blair, 1993; O'Neil & Greenberger, 1994) and higher marital satisfaction (Gottman, 1999; Yogev & Brett, 1985). Additionally, women report higher levels of personal well-being and less depression (Schwartzberg & Dytell, 1996), and men report greater feelings of involvement and competence as fathers (Barnett & Rivers, 1996).

Assist Janie in managing her feelings of guilt and concern. Therapists' inattention to societal context and the professional literature also may have influenced their responses to Janie's expressed concerns about working. Although the vignette closed with Janie's statement that she enjoyed her employment "if only it didn't have a negative impact on her family," an astonishing 88% of therapists did not include the likelihood of her being misinformed about the effects of maternal employment and child care as part of their assessment. Only one-fifth of therapists normalized and empathized with Janie's feelings in their assessment of the case, and fewer indicated that they would assist the couple in addressing Janie's concerns.

It is likely that many therapists did not intervene to help Janie manage or realistically evaluate her concerns because they themselves are uninformed or misled about the typical experiences of dual-earner families. Such an explanation seems plausible when examining the number of therapists who–probably unwittingly–would actively reinforce Janie's feelings of guilt and worry through various interventions (such as suggesting she change to part-time work prior to considering other alternatives) or by directly relaying negative and unsubstantiated information about the typical drawbacks of dual-earner families for children and husbands. As shown in Table 3, many therapists appear to have accepted the myths that have been perpetuated by the media. For instance, several therapists indicated that children of dual-earner families experience limited time with parents, and are less emotionally close or influenced by parents. These beliefs have been disputed by research (see Galinsky, 1999).

Worse, a startling number of these professionals (10%) claimed that children of dual-earner families *typically* feel "unloved," "unvalued," and/or "neglected." The empirical literature does not support these claims. It is important to recognize that these are words that are typically used to describe the behaviors of abusive parents–those who do not feed, bathe, dress, or attend to the emotional needs of their children–not the behaviors of parents who work, in part to ensure their children's short- and long-term well-being. Furthermore, given empirical evidence that beliefs such as these are a significant source of stress for dual-earner parents and children (Barnett & Rivers, 1996), they are likely to cause harm–which is the last thing that most therapists intend to or should do.

Neutrality. A significant theme in the responses of therapists was their intention to take a neutral stance in working with this couple. For instance, one therapist said that they would not answer the couple's question about the typical benefits and drawbacks of dual-earner families, explaining, "It's not a therapy question. Anyone can provide an answer based on [one's] own perspective." While it is important for therapists to manage their power and influence, feminist scholars (e.g., Avis, 1988) have argued that therapy is inherently political, and neutrality impossible and undesirable. They argue that when a therapist remains silent in instances of oppressive ideological positions or practice, they in effect condone or reinforce them. Instead, feminist scholars argue that it is therapists' professional responsibility to educate clients, helping them critically analyze oppressive social ideologies. We are not arguing that therapists should state their personal opinions or condone one family type over another; however, we do believe that clients should be offered relevant research-based information that may be helpful to them.

IMPLICATIONS AND CONCLUSION

We are concerned that so many therapists' assessment and treatment plans were characterized by misinformation about dual-earner families, particularly given that the vignette portrayed normative challenges of the majority family type in our society. Professional standards require therapists to be familiar with the professional literature and pursue opportunities for continued learning. Therapists have an obligation to be aware of important issues affecting families and prepared to use this knowledge in the service of their therapeutic role. The results of this study indicate that therapists could benefit from more exposure to professional training and literature related to work-family interface, dual-earner families, child care, and equitable intimate partnerships. Although it is outside the scope of this article to provide an exhaustive review of the relevant literature, a list of research-based books has been provided in Appendix B. These books are appropriate for therapists and clients.

With greater knowledge, therapists can be helpful to dual-earner couples that are challenged by the lag in social ideologies. A more sophisticated understanding of these ideologies allows therapists and clients to "take this conversation to a new level," avoiding some of the simplistic, unhelpful, and unnecessarily polarized thinking that often surrounds this topic. Rather than arguing if one family form is superior to another, or if child care is "good" or "bad" for children, or if an unemployed woman is a better mother than an employed one, therapists and clients can grapple with more complex, realistic, and helpful questions. As Galinsky (1999) argued, the more realistic and empirically validated answer to these questions is, "It depends"–it depends on other important variables. For instance, when people stop debating whether child care is good or bad, they can begin researching the factors that characterize high-quality child care to evaluate their child care situation. And, when people learn that parental attitudes about working are a key factor in determining child care outcomes, they can develop strategies for communicating a positive attitude to their children.

Limitations

Although the 38% response rate is adequate, a higher response rate would allow more confidence in the generalizability of the findings. Additionally, as noted by Kazdin (1986), analogue research does not always yield results similar to real-life situations. Therefore, the validity of the response tendencies must be tempered by the fact that, in working with an actual family, therapists may respond in different ways. However, this study provided information about therapists' assumptions and beliefs about dual-earner couples in general; it is likely that these assumptions and beliefs influence their work.

REFERENCES

Avis, J. M. (1988). Deepening awareness: A private study guide to feminism and family therapy. *Journal of Psychotherapy and the Family, 3,* 15-46.

Barnett, R. C., & Baruch, G. K. (1985). Women's involvement in multiple roles and psychological distress. *Journal of Personality and Social Psychology, 49,* 135-145.

Barnett, R. C. & Rivers, C. (1996). *She works, he works: How two-income families are happy, healthy, and thriving.* Cambridge, MA: Harvard University Press.

Blair, S. L. (1993). Employment, family, and perceptions of marital quality among husbands and wives. *Journal of Family Issues, 14,* 189-212.

Bograd, M. (1999). Strengthening domestic violence theories: Intersections of race, class, sexual orientation, and gender. *Journal of Marital and Family Therapy, 25,* 275-289.

Coleman, L. M., Antonucci, T. C., Adelmann, P. K., & Crohan, S. E. (1987). Social roles in the lives of middle-aged and older Black women. *Journal of Marriage and the Family, 49,* 761-771.

Coontz, S. (1992). *The way we never were: American families and the nostalgia trap.* New York: Basic Books.

Coontz, S. (2000, June). *Inventing today's families.* Paper presented at the annual conference of the American Family Therapy Association, San Diego, CA.

Faludi, S. (1991). *Backlash: The undeclared war against American women.* New York: Doubleday.

Fuligni, A. S., Galinsky, E., & Poris, M. (1995). The impact of parental employment on children. New York: Families and Work Institute.

Galinsky, E. (1999). *Ask the children: What America's children really think about working parents.* New York, NY: William Morrow & Co.

Gottman, J. M. (1999). *The marriage clinic: A scientifically-based marital therapy.* New York: W. W. Norton & Co., Inc.

Guarnaccia, P. J., Angel, R., & Worobey, J. L. (1991). The impact of marital status and employment status on depressive affect for Hispanic Americans. *Journal of Community Psychology, 19,* 136-149.

Hayghe, H. V. (1990). Family members in the work force. *Monthly Labor Review, 113*(3), 14-19.

Hochschild, A., & Machung (1989). *Second shift: Working parents and the revolution at home.* New York: Penguin USA.

Holcomb, B. (1998). *Not guilty: The good news about working mothers.* New York: Scribner.

Kazdin, A. E. (1986). The evaluation of psychotherapy: Research design and methodology. In S. L. Garfield & A. E. Bergin (Eds.), *Handbook of psychotherapy and behavior change (3rd edition)* (pp. 23-68). New York: John Wiley.

NICHD Early Child Care Research Network (1997). The effects of child care on infant-mother attachment security: Results of the NICHD study of early child care. *Child Development, 68*(5), 860-879.

O'Neil, R., & Greenberger, E. (1994). Patterns of commitment to work and parenting: Implications for role strain. *Journal of Marriage and the Family, 56,* 101-118.

Rabin, C. (1996). *Equal partners, good friends: Empowering couples through therapy.* London: Routledge.

Rosenfeld, A., & Wise, N. (2000). *Hyper-Parenting: Are you hurting your child by trying too hard?* New York: St. Martin's Press.

Schwartz, P. (1994). *Love between equals: How peer marriage really works.* New York: Free Press.

Schwartzberg, N. S., & Dytell, R. S. (1996). Dual-earner families: The importance of work stress and family stress for psychological well-being. *Journal of Occupational Health Psychology, 1*, 211-223.

Skolnick, A. (1991). *Embattled paradise: The American family in an age of uncertainty.* New York: Basic Books.

Williams, J. (2000). *Unbending gender: Why family and work conflict and what to do about it.* New York: Oxford University Press.

Yogev, S., & Brett, J. (1985). Perceptions of the division of housework and child care and marital satisfaction. *Journal of Marriage and the Family*, 609-618.

APPENDIX A: CLINICAL VIGNETTE

Janie and Paul are a middle-class couple in their late 30s. They have a one-year-old daughter, Jesse. Janie also has a child (Robert, age 12) from a previous marriage who lives with Janie and Paul. Paul works full-time in the construction business. Janie was a social worker, but quit her job of eight years when Jesse was born. She recently obtained a full-time counseling position with the school district.

The couple has come to therapy because of marital difficulties, and Janie's concerns about working. They also indicate that they have been arguing a lot about housework and parenting because Janie feels that she is carrying a disproportionate amount of housework and parenting responsibility. The couple also reports that Janie has been emotionally distressed about her decision to work, feeling guilty and worrying about the possible effects on Jesse. Although Janie's family is very supportive of her decision to work, Paul's parents and Janie's stay-at-home friends have made comments that have increased her feelings of guilt and worry.

Paul doesn't share Janie's worries about child care, saying that he thinks child care is beneficial and enjoyable for Jesse. He states, however, that he is willing to obtain an additional part-time job if Janie decides she would rather not work. Janie admits that she likes working in the community—"if only it didn't have a negative impact on her family."

APPENDIX B. Some Good Resources for Therapists and Dual-Earner Couples

For Therapists and Clients

Barnett, R. C., & Rivers, C. (1996). *She works, he works: How two-income families are happy, healthy, and thriving.* Cambridge, MA: Harvard University Press.

Chira, S. (1999). *A mother's place: Choosing work and family without guilt or blame.* New York: Harper Collins.

Deutsch, F. M. (2000). *Halving it all: How couples share parenting.* Cambridge, MA: Harvard University Press.

Galinsky, E. (1999). *Ask the children: What America's children really think about working parents.* New York, NY: William Morrow & Co.

Gottman, J., & Silver, N. (1999). *The seven principles for making marriage work.* New York: Crown.

Holcomb, B. (1998). *Not guilty: The good news about working mothers.* New York: Scribner.

Levine, J. A., & Pittinsky, T. L. (1997). *Working fathers: New strategies for balancing work and family.* New York, NY: Addison-Wesley.

Peters, J. K. (1999). *When mothers work: Loving our children without sacrificing ourselves.* New York, NY: Harper Collins.

Rosenfeld, A., & Wise, N. (2000). *Hyper-Parenting: Are you hurting your child by trying too hard?* New York: St. Martin's Press.

Schwartz, P. (1994). *Love between equals: How peer marriage really works.* New York: Free Press.

For Therapists

Gottman, J. M. (1999). *The marriage clinic: A scientifically-based marital therapy.* New York: W. W. Norton.

Haddock, S., Zimmerman, T. S., & MacPhee, D. (2000). *The Power Equity Guide.* Attending to gender in family therapy. *Journal of Marital and Family Therapy, 26* (2), p 153-170.

Rabin, C. (1996). *Equal partners, good friends: Empowering couples through therapy.* London: Routledge.

Relocation as Potential Stressor or Stimulating Challenge

Martha E. Edwards
Peter Steinglass

SUMMARY. Guided by Rutter and Garmezy's model of risk, vulnerability, buffers, and resilience, the impact of relocations on children was examined, first in a literature review and then in an empirical study. The study assessed the impact of mobility on United States State Department families who had returned to the U.S. from life abroad. A history of mobility appears to put these children somewhat at risk. Factors that increase children's vulnerability to the risks of relocation include age, race, and a propensity to perceive social interactions as negative. A positive emotional climate in the family and a high functioning mother appear to buffer the negative effects of relocations. The skills children have learned in order to adjust to previous relocations may serve as resiliencies in adjusting to the current relocation. *[Article copies available for a fee from The Haworth Document Delivery Service: 1-800-HAWORTH. E-mail address: <getinfo@haworthpressinc.com> Website: <http://www.HaworthPress.com> © 2001 by The Haworth Press, Inc. All rights reserved.]*

KEYWORDS. Relocation, children, risk factors, resilience, balancing family and work

---

Martha E. Edwards, PhD, and Peter Steinglass, MD, are affiliated with the Ackerman Institute for the Family, 149 East 78th Street, New York, NY 10021.

[Haworth co-indexing entry note]: "Relocation as Potential Stressor or Stimulating Challenge." Edwards, Martha E., and Peter Steinglass. Co-published simultaneously in *Journal of Feminist Family Therapy* (The Haworth Press, Inc.) Vol. 13, No. 2/3, 2001, pp. 121-152; and: *Balancing Family and Work: Special Considerations in Feminist Therapy* (ed: Toni Schindler Zimmerman) The Haworth Press, Inc., 2001, pp. 121-152. Single or multiple copies of this article are available for a fee from The Haworth Document Delivery Service [1-800-HAWORTH, 9:00 a.m. - 5:00 p.m. (EST). E-mail address: getinfo@haworthpressinc.com].

121

OVERVIEW AND LITERATURE REVIEW

In the United States, one out of six families moves in any one year (U.S. Census Bureau, 2000). There are many reasons for these moves, but a significant number of relocations are job-related. Both adults and children report that moving is stressful, but adults typically underestimate the effects on children. Adults rate relocations 28th out of 43 potentially stressful life events on the Social Readjustment Rating Scale (Holmes and Rahe, 1967). Parents and teachers rated how stressful they thought moving was for children as 19th out of 43 (Chandler, 1981). But the children themselves rated it 7th out of 37 stressful life events (Hutton, Roberts, Walker, and Zuniga, 1987), following physical abuse and change in acceptance by peers and preceding marital separation of parents. Thus, while moving as a general event is moderately stressful for adults, it appears to be much more so for children, and its impact is typically underestimated by adults.

Does the stress of moving pose a risk for children's social or psychological functioning? When children move, they lose their sense of belonging as well as valued relationships and activities. They are faced with a general situation of uncertainty–which is more difficult for some than others to manage. There is uncertainty about how to adjust to the new surroundings, and whether they will regain a feeling of belonging and develop new friendships and engage in meaningful activities. Family routines are altered–perhaps permanently. Unlike other types of stressful situations, they no longer have direct support from friends. And, because parents may be distracted and under stress themselves, they may have less support from them to deal with the challenges of a new school and new peer group. As a result, children's functioning in significant areas of their lives may suffer–in their social adjustment, self-concept or self-esteem, school achievement, or emotional health and well-being–all areas on which researchers have examined the impact of relocations.

Drawing on the work of Rutter (1987), Masten and Garmezy (1985), Sameroff and Seifer (1990), and Richters and Weintraub (1990), Cowan, Cowan, and Schulz (1996) explicated a framework in which child outcomes are predicted as a function not only of risk factors, but also of vulnerabilities, buffers, and resiliencies. They define risks as processes that predispose individuals and populations to specific negative or undesirable outcomes. In this article, we address the degree to which relocations represent risks to children's social or psychological functioning, as well as vulnerabilities that heighten the risks, buffers that protect against the risks, and resiliencies that children develop as a result of their exposure to the risks of relocations. Each of the four domains of functioning (social adjustment, self-concept and self-esteem, school achievement, and emotional health and well-being) is examined separately as each has a different profile of risk, vulnerability, buffering, and resiliency.

Impact on Social Adjustment

Single relocations appear to have little negative impact on children's social adjustment (Young and Cooper, 1944; Smith and Demming, 1958; Bricker, 1973; Kantor, 1968; Barrett and Noble, 1974; Jones, 1973). Most children tend to make new friends rather quickly and adjust well to the new situation. What does pose a risk to social adjustment appears to be multiple relocations (Williams, 1965; Benson and Weigel, 1981; Benson, Haycraft, Steyaert, and Weigel, 1981; Douvan and Adelson, 1966; Khleif, 1973; Schaller, 1974; Moore, 1966). In these studies, highly mobile children had less sophisticated notions of friendships, were rated lower on social adjustment scales, and reported less participation in social activities than did their less mobile counterparts.

In examining the risks for specific negative outcomes, it is also important to identify particular vulnerabilities, defined as conditions that increase the probability of negative or undesirable outcomes in the presence of risks (Cowan, Cowan, and Schulz, 1996). Patterns of friendships in children tend to vary depending on age and gender and, thus, these constitute important areas in which to look for vulnerabilities.

With regard to age, adolescents tend to report more difficulty in making new friends and adjusting socially to moves than do younger children (Brett, 1983; Barrett and Noble, 1973). With regard to gender, the picture is a bit more mixed. In some studies, boys reported more difficulty in adjusting, particularly in leaving friends, making friends, adjusting to a new school, and experiencing rejection by peers (Lehr and Hendrickson, 1968; Brett and Werbel, 1980; Donohue and Gullotta, 1983; Vernberg, 1990). But Orthner et al. (1987) observed that girls were the ones who had more difficulty making new friends. By controlling for age and gender together (Raviv et al., 1990), it became apparent that younger (pre-adolescent) girls were most vulnerable, presumably because they tended to have one or two best friends and play in small groups of peers as contrasted to boys who tended to play in larger, more heterogeneous groups. A move for girls would constitute greater loss than for boys and it would be harder to meet and become intimate friends with other girls in the new location than it would for boys to find playmates. Thus, from the available data, it appears that both age and gender may constitute vulnerabilities that put mobile children at risk for difficulties with social adjustment. While the results are not entirely consistent, there is enough to suggest that these characteristics should be examined carefully to determine if they have an impact on who will and will not have difficulty adjusting to relocations.

Impact on Self-Concept and Self-Esteem

A second area of children's functioning for which relocations may pose a risk is their self-concept and/or self-esteem. Concern over the effect of relocations on children's self-concept stems from the view that its development depends on the child's relationship with the social and physical environment. Children develop a sense of who they are by: (1) feedback from others (Swann, 1983), (2) comparing oneself to others (Tesser and Campbell, 1983), and (3) playing various roles (Argyle, 1967), especially those in which one demonstrates mastery of the environment (Hendershott, 1989). Dramatic changes in one's milieu may temporarily result in a decrease in one's ability and confidence to master the environment. When this is accompanied by changes in feedback from significant others and the referents to which one compares oneself, the temporary decrements may become fixed in a more permanent negative self-concept.

The evidence is somewhat mixed as to the effect of relocations on self-concept or self-esteem. Children who move frequently sometimes score lower on self-esteem or self-esteem measures than non-mobile children (Bricker, 1973; Wooster and Harris, 1972; Shaw, 1979) and, in other studies, did not (Kroger, 1980; Hendershott, 1989). In a study of 26,000 sophomores, however, Sanders (1984) found that mobility interacted with socioeconomic status, race, and parental marital status in predicting self-concept. Since these studies did not control for these factors that could constitute vulnerabilities, nor the number of moves, age, or gender, whether moving is a risk for a child's self-concept is not entirely clear.

Impact on School Achievement

The third area of children's functioning examined by relocation researchers is school achievement, in which the data on the impact of moving on children's school achievement is even more mixed. Six studies show a negative impact (Gordon and Gordon, 1958; Greene and Daugherty, 1961; Benson, Haycraft, Steyaert, and Weigel, 1979; Benson and Weigel, 1981; Ingersoll, Scamman and Eckerling, 1989; and Temple and Reynolds, 1999); five studies show no relationship (Moore, 1966; Morris et al., 1967; Camer and Dorsey, 1970; Benson and Weigel, 1981; and Marchant and Medway, 1987); and four studies show a positive impact (Gilliland, 1958; Perrodin and Snipes, 1966; Kenny, 1967; and Inbar and Adler, 1976).

Examining the details of these and other studies suggests particular vulnerabilities that may make relocations more of a risk for some children. First, children who are already doing poorly in school do worse after moving than children who were doing well in school. Thus, prior academic difficulties are a vulnerability that adds to the risk of negative school outcomes in mobile children. Second, children who move while in elementary school tend to have more difficulty in school than either younger or adolescent children (Ingersoll, Scamman, and Eckerling, 1989; Inbar and Adler, 1976). Thus, moving when children are learning the basic academic skills of reading, writing, arithmetic makes them more vulnerable to the risks associated with relocations. Third, lower SES families tend to move more than higher SES families. The stresses and strains of poverty may make mobile children more vulnerable to the risks of relocations or there may simply be a spurious relationship between moving and school achievement that is accounted for by the relationship between SES and moving.

Thus, already having difficulties in school, moving during elementary school, and lower SES all appear to constitute vulnerabilities that make relocations even more risky for these children. The combination of these vulnerabilities was born out in a more recent, longitudinal study of low-income, elementary school children (Temple and Reynolds, 2000). In this study, students' prior achievement level as well as family SES and parent education level were controlled and there was still a negative impact of relocations on school achievement. They did not, however, control for the reasons for the moves. Did these highly mobile children move because of family breakup, death, loss of job? The vulnerability to relocations may have come about because of the effects of these transitions and stresses.

Tucker and his colleagues (1998) investigated this possibility by comparing the school achievement of mobile children living in a two-parent family structure with that of mobile children who, because of death or divorce, lived in a one-parent family structure. They found the latter group to be adversely affected by relocations but not the former group. Thus, having already gone through the stresses associated with divorce or death constitutes another vulnerability that puts a child at greater risk for negative effects of relocations.

Impact on Emotional Health and Well-Being

The fourth area of functioning that researchers have examined as sensitive to the potential risks involved in relocation is children's emotional health and well-being, where, again, there are mixed results. In two studies, there were no differences between mobile and non-mobile children in their emotional health (Pedersen and Sullivan, 1964; Hormuth, 1989). In one study, the vulnerability that pre-adolescent girls seem to have because of their patterns of friendships, discussed earlier, appeared to be responsible for their reported greater depression than mobile boys and non-mobile children (Brown and Orthner, 1990).

Contrary to many of the negative outcomes, the results from some studies suggest that mobility may actually be beneficial to some children, enabling them to develop resiliencies that they otherwise would not have developed–higher scores, for example, on the California Psychological Inventory (O'Connell, 1981) and greater tolerance for new and uncertain situations, and exhibition of less anxiety when in stressful situations (Mann, 1972).

This does not mean that relocations are not difficult, as children who have recently moved (within the last year) tend to be more depressed than children who have not moved (Hendershott, 1989). However, these same children who report being depressed also described their friendships as very close and supportive (Hendershott, 1989). Thus, if children have the capacity to become closely attached to friends, losing them repeatedly can be very difficult for them. This propensity to develop close relationships, however, can also be healing, as the same subjects also reported that if they moved recently and had supportive friends, they were less depressed than those who did not have supportive friends. Therefore, while the ability to make friends may be a sign of resilience in mobile children, it may actually make moving initially more difficult. It does not, however, appear to pose a long-term risk for these children.

Social support is an important mediator of risk in many types of situations and serves as what is often called a "buffer," defined as a protection that decreases the probability of a negative or undesirable outcome in the presence of a risk (Cowan, Cowan, and Schulz, 1996). The social support children receive from their families appears to be an important buffer in reducing the negative outcomes of relocations (Pittman and Bowen, 1994). The buffering influence may be more generalized as in a positive family emotional climate due to agreement about moving (Hormuth, 1989) and positive attitudes toward moving (Pedersen and Sullivan, 1964; Lehr and Hendrickson, 1968). The buffering may also be the result of mothers who exhibit good coping skills and are satisfied with their lives (Hormuth, 1989).

While positive family experiences appear to serve as buffers to the risks associated with relocations, it is important to note that the measures of family functioning in the reviewed studies came from self-reports of the family members. It is conceivable that since measures of the family and children's adjustment were often reported by the same respondent, that some of the results were due to commonalities of measurement. Since social support provided by the family is important both conceptually as well as practically as a buffer to the risk of relocations, it would be important to examine whether family functioning measured more objectively seemed to provide the same buffering influence.

In addition to the impact of family dynamics in buffering the risks of relocations, families can also play a specific role in helping their children with the move itself. Children reported that having input into the decision to move as well as planning their new rooms was a source of support in the relocation process (Raviv et al., 1990).

Social support from friends also factors into the relocation process. Both children and adults report that the most stressful thing about moving was the loss of social ties (Lehr and Hendrickson, 1968; Raviv et al., 1990; and Munton, 1990). Furthermore, when people move, they are less likely to become involved in social organizations (Butler et al., 1973). Thus, the loss of social connections and support is one aspect of what makes relocations risky. On the other hand, the ability to make friends–which may be a necessary skill developed as a result of frequent relocations–may be a resiliency that reduces the negative outcomes of relocations. Adolescents who made friends easily were more likely to report that a move had been easy (Brett and Werbel, 1978). The number of friends adolescents made after a move was related to the time it took for them to adapt to the move (Hormuth, 1989) and level of adjustment to the move (Lehr and Hendrickson, 1968). Young adolescents who move frequently and described their friendships as very close and supportive, however, tended to be more depressed (Hendershott, 1989). Thus, if children have the capacity to become closely attached to friends, losing them repeatedly can be very difficult for them. This propensity to develop close relationships, however, can also be healing as the same subjects also reported that if they moved recently and had supportive friends, they were less depressed than those who did not have supportive friends.

Summary of the Literature

Previous studies of family relocations have suggested the conditions under which relocations pose particular risks for families as well as vulnerabilities that might make these risks greater, buffers that might serve to reduce the risks, and resiliencies that individuals may develop as a result of exposure to these risks. While single relocations may be difficult for family members, they do not appear to pose risks to children's social or psychological adjustment. What seems to have an effect is the accumulation of stresses due to multiple relocations.

Particular characteristics of children make them more vulnerable to negative outcomes of relocations. With regard to social adjustment and self-concept, moves seem to be more difficult for adolescents than for elementary-school age children. Males and females may react differently and should be examined separately, although a consistent pattern was not seen. If children are already doing poorly in school, relocations tend to exacerbate their difficulties. Stresses associated with poverty, racial minority status, and experiencing death of a parent or divorce also appear to make children vulnerable to the stresses of relocations. This latter factor, however, was confounded by living with a single parent, and it is not clear whether the vulnerability emerges from previous traumatic experience (divorce or death) or from the current stresses of living in a single parent family.

In the short run, relocations may put children at risk for depression, but there does not appear to be long-term effect on their emotional health and well-being. In fact, moving may help some children develop resiliencies in the areas of dealing with stress and anxiety. The support that families provide to their children may also serve to buffer the risks associated with moving.

These results also suggest three areas of follow-up necessary in a new empirical study of relocations. First, factors that confound the impact of moving–reasons for moving and SES in particular–must be controlled for in an empirical study of relocations. Second, little attention has been paid to the impact of the process for any particular relocation, i.e., the decision to move, preparation, the move itself, and immediate aftermath. What happens in these phases of the relocation process may provide ideas for strategies to reduce the risks involved in moving. Third, support from the family appears to be a critical buffer of the risks of relocating. But none of the studies identified particular family dynamics assessed by observational methods to elucidate the mechanisms by which this buffering occurs.

In our empirical study, we build on the previous work by examining the impact of relocations in United States State Department families. This is an ideal population on which to study relocations, as the reasons for their moving as well as SES are both controlled. Families in the State Department move approximately every three years. Everyone knows that this will occur, and employees can put in a list of preferred locations for their next post. Families in this sample were all middle to upper-middle class. Furthermore, we examine the impact of the components of the relocation process (i.e., making the decision, preparation, the move itself, aftermath of the move) on children's adjustment. Finally, we assess family dynamics using both self-report and observational measures.

METHODS

The goal of the study was to carry out a within-group examination of potential risks to children of multiple relocations and the vulnerabilities, buffers, and resiliencies that might affect children's psychological and social adjustment to these relocations. Subjects were recruited via memo, displays in various State Department locations, and nominations from both State Department employees and other prospective subjects for the study. They consisted of families who had been living abroad and who had returned in the last two years to live in the United States. All data were collected in a three-hour block of time in which the family came to the Department of State office in Washington, DC.

Subjects

The sample consisted of 35 families comprised of 64 adults (29 men and 35 women) and 73 children (39 males and 34 females). Relevant demographic characteristics are summarized in Table 1.

To minimize the amount of time it took to collect data from the entire family, we limited the full participation to two children. All children over the age of six and living at home participated in the family interview and family task. However, only the youngest and oldest participating children were interviewed. In addition, the parents filled out the instrument measuring social adjustment on just these two children. The other children completed the rest of the questionnaires and their data were included in the analyses.

Instruments

The dependent variables, children's psychological and social adjustment, were measured by two questionnaire instruments. Children's psychological adjustment was assessed by the Piers-Harris Children's Self-Concept Scale (Piers and Harris, 1969). This scale is an 80-item self-report inventory designed to provide a standardized measure of children's self-esteem, confidence, and general satisfaction. Norms are available for children in school grades 3-12 and, thus, the children's scores on this instrument could also be compared to the children in the general population. It is one of the most widely used and validated measures of children's self-esteem available.

Children's social adjustment was measured by the Achenbach Child Behavior Checklist (CBCL) (Achenbach, 1978, 1979). The CBCL is a questionnaire listing 118 behavior problem items and 20 social competence items and is completed by the child's parents. It provides an excellent assessment of evidence of behavior disorders, developing psychopathological conditions, and social competencies of children aged 4-18. Each parent completed a checklist on each of the two target

TABLE 1. Demographic Characteristics of Subject Sample

	Adult	Child
Gender		
Male	29	39
Female	35	34
Age	Mean = 45.2	Mean = 11.7
	SD = 3.5	SD = 2.8
Ethnicity		
White	53	58
Asian/Pacific Island	6	8
Black	1	3
Hispanic	1	2
Arab American	1	2
Native American	1	
Education Level of Parents		
High school	1	
Some college	7	
College graduate	8	
Some graduate school	9	
Master's degree	24	
MD/PhD/JD	13	
Place of Birth of Parents		
United States	50	
Europe	8	
Asia	5	
Marital Status of Parents		
Married	62	
Separated	1	
Divorced	1	
Years Married	Mean = 18.4	
	SD = 3.7	
Number of Posts	N = 7.3	N = 5.7
	Range: 3-14	Range: 2-11
	SD = 2.2	SD = 2.11

Number of Children	In family	Living at home
One	2	4
Two	20	22
Three	10	9
Four	2	0
Five	1	0

children selected as full participants in the study. The responses from the two parents were averaged to result in a composite score representing both parents' views of each target child. Norms are available for this instrument and, thus, the children's scores could be compared to the general population to yield a measure of the degree to which foreign service families' children are different from or similar to other children.

The family interview was conducted with the entire family. They reported on the number and location of previous posts, what life was like at the previous post, and this most recent relocation process (including decision, preparation, nature of the move itself, and aftermath). This set the stage for the individual interviews in which both parents and target children reported on their satisfaction at previous posts, strategies they used to prepare for the move, their reactions to leaving the most recent post, and their views of family, school/work, and friendships at the most recent post and where they were currently living.

Three self-report measures provided a view of the family from an insider's point of view. Each family member completed a version of the Kvebaek Family Sculpture. In this procedure, the subject is given a blank piece of paper and a set of colored stickers with the names of each family member written on them. They are asked to "place the stickers on the paper in a way you feel describes your family now." Then they are asked whether they would like to see changes in the family from the way they represented them. If the answer is "yes" they are given a second set of stickers in a different color and asked to "place the stickers where you would like the family members to be." These arrangements were then analyzed by computer to determine the average distance among family members as a measure of family cohesion.

Each family member completed the Family Assessment Measure (FAM) self-rating scale. This is a 42-item, standardized questionnaire measuring seven dimensions of family life. Respondents endorsed items such as, "My family knows what I mean when I say something" (measuring communication); or "My family and I have the same views about what is right and wrong" (measuring values and norms); or "I keep on trying when things don't work out in the family" (measuring task accomplishment); or "I get angry when others in the family don't do what I want" (measuring control); or "When I'm with my family, I get too upset too easily" (measuring affective expression); or "I don't need to be reminded what I have to do in the family" (measuring role performance); or "I am available when others want to talk with me" (measuring affective involvement). The items can be combined into clusters or into an overall measure of perceived functioning in the family.

The parents completed the Dyadic Adjustment Scale (DAS), an instrument to assess the level of marital adjustment (Spanier, 1976). This is a 32-item, standardized questionnaire tapping each partner's view of the marriage via four scales: overall marital satisfaction, marital consensus, marital cohesion, and affectional expression. There have been, however, significant gender differences on these individual subscales and on the instrument itself (Kazak et al., 1988). Therefore, we used only the composite score for the entire instrument and reported each husband's and wife's score separately, i.e., did not combine them into a score for the couple.

An interactional task in which family process was observed and rated directly was used to obtain a more objective view of family functioning. In the Family Task, the members were first asked to write down where they would like the family to go on a family vacation, using only $500. Then they were to discuss the same question for a maximum of 12 minutes and come up with a family decision. A member of the family then wrote the family decision down. Each family member then rated, on a seven-point scale, their satisfaction with the family's discussion and the family's final decision. While they were working, the three observers watched their interactions and afterwards completed the Georgia Family Q-Sort (Wampler, Halverson, Moore, and Walters, 1989), sorting 43 descriptors of interaction that tap three dimensions of family functioning: (1) cohesion, e.g., "Enjoy being together" and "Expression of negative affect"; (2) problem solving/adaptability, e.g., "Disorganized" and "Use give and take in accomplishing task"; and (3) communication, e.g., "Listen to each other" and "Family does not talk much." The observers sort the descriptors into nine piles whose designations range from least characteristic to most characteristic of the family's interactions. The observers were trained for 1 and a 1/2 days to do these ratings. Their ratings on each of the 43 items were averaged to obtain a score that reflected their combined judgments.

Social support from each participant's extended family network and friendship network was assessed by the Social Network Inventory (Oliveri and Reiss, 1982). Here, each member was asked to list the family members they were not currently living with who were important to them and then list the friends or acquaintances who were important to them. For this analysis, the size of each network, calculated by the number of persons listed, was used.

Characteristics of the individual family members were measured by two instruments. The Shannan Sentence Completion Technique (Shannan, 1967, 1973) assessed the psychological coping styles of the family members. This instrument uses a semi-projective sentence-completion technique to measure personality-related dimensions thought relevant to overall coping style. The four dimensions that it measures are: (1) extent of differentiation in the person's aims and goals, (2) perception of sources of fear and frustration, (3) extent to which the person is ready to cope actively with novel or complex situations, and (4) the person's self-image.

The second instrument to measure individual characteristics was the Early Memories Inventory (Edwards, 1992). It assesses core aspects of the way subjects see themselves, their world, and the way they respond to it, based on the clinical technique of Alfred Adler (Adler, 1931). The procedure consisted of asking the subjects to write down, in as much detail as possible, two of their earliest memories. Then, for each memory, they were asked to complete the following sentence stems: I am . . . , Others are . . . , The world is . . . , Therefore I will. . . . Each memory was coded to quantify five aspects: (1) Activity, (2) Positive interactions, (3) Negative interactions, (4) Outlook, and (5) Attitude toward difficulty.

RESULTS

Three sets of analyses were conducted. In the first, measures of the psychological and social adjustment of State Department children were compared to children in the general population. In the second, a series of bivariate analyses were conducted to assess the relationship between the children's relocation history and experiences, individual demographic variables, family dynamics, social support, and individual characteristics and their psychological and social adjustment. This enabled us to determine factors that might serve to increase risk and vulnerability as well as serve as buffers and promote resiliency. In the third, multiple regression is used to determine which of these factors appear to be the most powerful predictors of children's psychological and social adjustment.

Comparison of State Department Children to General Population

Both measures of adjustment–the Piers-Harris Self-Esteem Inventory and the Achenbach Child Behavior Checklist (CBCL)–can be presented as standardized T-scores. This means that if the study sample followed a normal distribution in its scores, 67% of the children would fall in the "moderately adjusted" range, while 16.5% would fall in both the "high adjusted" and "low adjusted" categories. On the Piers-Harris instrument, twice as many State Department children as would be expected (34.5%) rated themselves as having a higher self-concept and none of the children rated themselves as having a low self-concept (see Table 2). The reports of the parents on the CBCL were more mixed. On the CBCL Competence scale, the distribution was as expected (13.8% rated as high adjusted; 72.3% rated as moderate adjusted; 13.8% rated as low adjusted). On the CBCL Problem scale, however, parents reported their children to be more symptomatic than would be expected (35.3%).

TABLE 2. Comparison of Standardized Adjustment Scores to Sample Adjustment Scores

	% High Adjusted	% Moderate Adjusted	% Low Adjusted
Norms	16.5	67	16.5
Sample Data			
Piers-Harris	34.5	65.5	0
CBCL-Competence Subscale	13.8	72.3	13.8
CBCL-Problem Subscale	12.3	52.3	35.3

Effect of Age, Race, Gender, Mobility History, and Time Back in the United States

In the literature review, a long history of mobility seemed to be what made relocations risky, as opposed to having experienced one or two moves. Gender, race, and age were identified as individual characteristics that could make children more vulnerable to the stresses of relocation. Furthermore, results from some who were studied varied depending on whether the children's short-term versus long-term adjustment was measured. Therefore, a number of correlations and t-tests were computed to test the relationship between these variables and children's psychological and social adjustment (see Table 3).

Two measures of relocation experience–the number of posts at which the children had lived and how long they had been back in the United States–were not related to either children's psychological or social adjustment. With the number of posts ranging from two to 11, and the mean at 5.7 (see Table 1), it is clear that the children in this sample had a long history of mobility and, thus, the level of risk does not appear to vary with the number of relocations children have experienced.

Two individual characteristics–age and race–do appear to be linked to adjustment. Parents of younger children describe them as exhibiting more problems than do parents of older children ($r = .2580$, $p < .05$). Non-Caucasian children (a grouping of Asian, Pacific Island, African American, Hispanic, and Arab racial groups) reported lower self-esteem ($x = 54.0$) than Caucasian children ($x = 59.6$; $p < .05$). The parents of non-Caucasian children also described them as less competent ($x = 43.8$) than did parents of Caucasian children ($x = 50.7$; $p < .001$). Contrary to the results from the literature review, boys and girls were not affected differentially by the move–there were no differences in their levels of adjustment.

Relocation Experiences, Individual Characteristics, Family Functioning, and Social Networks: Protective and/or Risk Factors

The literature review also suggested a number of factors that might either protect children or put them at greater risk for experiencing poor psychosocial adjustment following their move back to the U.S. Four categories of factors were examined and correlated with the children's

TABLE 3. Relationship Between Level of Adjustment and Age, Race, Gender, Number of Posts, and Years Back in U.S.

| | Correlations | | |
	Piers-Harris	CBCL Competence	CBCL Problem
Number of posts	.1100	.0275	.1529
Years back in U.S.	.1453	.0294	−.0260
Age	.1624	.0453	.2580**

* p < .05; ** p < .01 *** p < .001

| | T-Tests | | |
	Piers-Harris	CBCL Competence	CBCL Problem
Means for:			
Caucasian	59.6*	50.7***	45.7
Non-Caucasian	54.0	43.8	47.7
Means for:			
Males	57.5	47.4	48.4
Females	59.4	51.2	43.7

* p < .05; ** p < .01; *** p < .001

psychological and social adjustment: (1) relocation experiences, (2) individual characteristics, (3) social network characteristics, and (4) family characteristics.

Relocation experiences. In this category of factors are children's feelings about their previous experiences at postings as well as their experiences with this particular move (see Table 4). Children who reported having positive experiences at the last six posts had the higher adjustment scores on the Piers-Harris ($r = .2857$, $p < .02$) and CBCL ($r = .2256$, $p < .05$ on the Competence scale; $r = -.2279$, $p < .05$ on the Problem scale). Children who reported positive experiences at

TABLE 4. Relationship Between Relocation Experiences and Levels of Adjustment (Correlation)

	Piers-Harris	CBCL Competence	CBCL Problem
Mean ratings of experiences at last six posts	.2857**	.2256*	−.2279*
Rating of overall experience at most recent post	.2707**	.2153*	−.2082*
Ratings of feelings when first heard about assignment	−.1810	−.2281*	.2262*
Ratings of feelings about leaving when move occurred	−.3109*	−.1802	−.1879
Ratings of amount of input into decision to move	−.0088	−.0649	−.0145
Ratings of preparation for living in U.S.	.0015	−.0824	.0235
Ratings of difficulty of move	.0807	−.0039	.0776

* $p < .05$; ** $p < .02$; *** $p < .01$

the most recent post also had the higher adjustment scores on the Piers-Harris (r = .2707, p < .02) and CBCL (r = .2153, p < .05 on Competence scale; r = −.2082, p < .05 on the Problem scale).

There were also significant relationships between psychosocial adjustment and children's reactions to moving (see Table 4). The children with higher CBCL Competence and Problem scores had more negative reactions than did children with lower scores when they first heard that their families were moving (r = −.2281, p < .05) and (r = .2262, p < .05). Children with higher self-esteem had more negative feelings about moving at the time of the move than did children with lower self-esteem (r = −.3109, p < .05).

Finally, there were no relationships between characteristics of this particular move (i.e., input into the decision, preparation, and difficulty of the move) and the children's psychological or social adjustment (see Table 4).

Individual Characteristics. Only three of the 30 tested relationships between individual characteristics and adjustment were significant (see Table 5). Children who have higher self-esteem exhibit more active coping styles as measured by the Shannan Sentence Completion instrument (r = .2378, p < .05). Children with higher CBCL Problem scores had lower outlook scores (r = .2394, p < .05) and higher negative interaction scores (r = .3458, p < .01) on the Early Memories Inventory.

Social Network Characteristics. There were no relationships between the size of the current social network or ratings of current friendships and any of the adjustment measures (see Table 6). There was, however, a positive relationship between ratings of friendships at the post and self-esteem (see Table 6). Children with higher self-esteem tended to give their friendships at the last post higher ratings than did children with lower self-esteem (r = .2184, p < .05).

Family Characteristics. Four instruments were used to measure characteristics of the families as they related to adjustment of children in these families: (a) the Dyadic Adjustment Scale (DAS), which taps perceptions of the parents' marriage; (b) the Kvebaek Family Sculpture, a projective measure of family cohesion; (c) the Family Adjustment Measure (FAM), a broad-based questionnaire assessing how each member perceives his or her functioning within the family; and (d) a family planning task that observers used as the basis for ratings of family interactional style and about which family members rated their satisfaction

TABLE 5. Relationship Between Individual Characteristics and Levels of Adjustment (Correlation)

	Piers-Harris	CBCL Competence	CBCL Problem
Shannan Sentence Completion			
Aims and Goals	.0027	.0777	−.1743
Sources of Difficulty	−.1726	−.0611	.0727
Active vs. Passive Coping	.2378*	.0454	.1852
Self-image	.1974	.0250	−.0068
Total:	.1734	.0764	.0547
Early Memories Inventory			
Activity	.1806	−.0566	.1723
Positive Interaction	.0809	.1779	−.1092
Negative Interaction	−.0843	−.1477	.3468***
Outlook	.1363	.1235	−.2394*
Attitude Toward Difficulty	.1858	.0404	−.1206

* $p < .05$; ** $p < .02$; *** $p < .01$

with the discussion and family plan. The results of these analyses appear in Table 7.

Parents' marital satisfaction was not related to their children's level of adjustment. The Kvebaek measure of cohesion was related to children's adjustment on the CBCL in that children who reported more closeness in their family exhibited less problems ($r = −.2630$, $p < .05$, Problem scale).

TABLE 6. Relationship Between Ratings of Social Network and Level of Adjustment (Correlation)

	Piers-Harris	CBCL Competence	CBCL Problem
Size of current friendship network	.1563	.1661	−.0021
Ratings of current friendships	.1732	.0267	−.0335
Rating of friendships at last post	.2184*	.1627	.0872

* p < .05; ** p < .02; *** p < .01

The Family Assessment Measure tapped family members' perceptions of how they perceived their own functioning in the family. While a child's answers to these questions overlap too much with his or her measures of self-esteem, competence, or problems, the reports of the mother and father provide a measure of the family dynamics and their potential impact on the children's adjustment. Mothers' rating of their functioning in the family were highly correlated with all three measures of their children's adjustment ($r = -.3831$, $p < .01$ on Piers-Harris; $r = -.4710$, $p < .01$ on CBCL Competence scale; and $r = .3073$, $p < .01$ on CBCL Problem scale), and fathers' ratings were correlated with the CBCL Competence scale ($r = -.3675$, $p < .01$) and Problem scale ($r = .2447$, $p < .02$).[1]

The data from the observations of family interaction mirrors the self-report data. Two types of analyses of this observational data were performed. First, each family's q-sort was compared to an ideal family q-sort compiled by a group of family experts (Wampler, Halverson, Moore, & Walters, 1989). The degree to which a family met this ideal was related to children's self-esteem ($r = .2188$, $p < .05$) but not to their Competence or Problem scores on the CBCL (see Table 7).

Second, by performing factor analyses across two years of data, the authors of the instrument were able to group the 43 items into eight clusters with a minimum of internal consistency of .50. The scores on these eight clusters were then correlated with each of the children's three adjustment scores (see Table 7). Scores on three clusters were related to all three measures of the children's adjustment: Lively, Negative Affect, Chaotic. Scores on the Relaxed cluster were related to the chil-

TABLE 7. Relationships Between Family Functioning Variables and Children's Psychological and Social Functioning (Correlation)

	Piers-Harris	CBCL Competence	CBCL Problem
Self Report Measures			
Mother's DAS+	.0233	.0769	.0425
Father's DAS+	.1099	.2103	−.0210
Kvebaek Fam. Sculpture (Measure of cohesion)	−.0181	.0163	−.2630*
Mother's FAM+	−.3831***	−.4710***	.3073***
Father's FAM+	−.0294	−.3675***	.2447**
Interactional Task Measures			
Georgia Family Q-Sort+			
Correlation with ideal sort	.2188*	.0706	.0752
Positive affect cluster	.2723**	.1497	−.1120
Lively cluster	.3028***	.2780**	−.3114***
Relaxed cluster	.2148*	.2390*	−.1805
Negative affect cluster	.2019*	.2823***	−.3015***
Organized cluster	.1535	.2860***	−.1711
Chaotic cluster	.1987*	.2935***	−.2860***
Negotiation cluster	.0849	.0630	−.0222
Verbal cluster	−.1057	.1679	−.1931
Satisfaction with Discussion	.2505**	.3004***	.1038
Satisfaction with Plan	.1866	.0385	−.0954

* $p < .05$; ** $p < .02$; *** $p < .01$
+ Data at the family unique of analysis: n = 35.

dren's self-concept and their CBCL Competence scale. Scores on the Positive Affect cluster were related to self-concept, and scores on the Organized cluster were related to the CBCL Competence scale. More particularly, children whose families exhibited positive affect (r = .2723, p < 01), a lively interactional style (r = .3028, p < .01), a sense of being relaxed with one another (r = .2148, p < .05), low negative affect (r = .2019, p < .05), and a low level of chaos (r = .1987, p < .05) tended to have higher self-esteem. Children whose families exhibited a lively interactional style (r = .2780, p < .01), a sense of being relaxed with one another (r = .2390, p < .05), low negative affect (r = .2823, p < .01), high levels of organization (r = .2860, p < .01), and low levels of chaos (r = .2935, p < .05) tended to be more competent. Children whose families exhibited a lively interactional style (r = −.3114, p < .01), low negative affect (r = −.3015, p < .01), and low chaos (r = −.2860, p < .01) tended to display fewer behavioral problems.

Finally, children's ratings of their satisfaction with the family's discussion were related to both their self-esteem (r = .2505, p < .02) and to their Competence scores on the CBCL (r = .3004, p < .01). There were no relationships between children's ratings of the actual plan the family produced and their psychosocial adjustment.

Multiple Regression Analyses

Up to this point, all of the analyses have looked at bivariate relationships between hypothesized predictor variables (determinants of differential response to the relocation event) and adequacy of psychosocial adjustment. As has been seen, a large number of these relationships proved to be statistically significant, suggesting that multiple parameters of individual and family level characteristics play a role in determining adjustment of family members to the relocation. But are there weightings to these many factors, such that we can say that some variables are more important than others as determinants of ultimate levels of adjustment to the relocation event?

To explore this very important question, we performed a series of multiple regression analyses in which all the predictor variables found to be highly correlated with adjustment outcomes were now examined *together*. Three separate regression analyses were conducted, one for each of the three adjustment measures.

A combination of family level and individual variables predicted a relatively large amount of the variance in both psychological and social adjustment. The predictors of children's self-esteem are the positive affect displayed by the family in their interactions, accounting for 21% of the variance in self-esteem (see Table 8). Adding the child's feelings about leaving at the time of the move and the mother's scores on the

TABLE 8. Multiple Regression Analysis of Children's Psychological Adjustment (Piers-Harris)

Variables in the Equation	Beta	Adusted R²
Georgia Q-Sort–Positive Affect Cluster	.4808	.2092
Feelings about leaving at time of move	−.4071	.3606
Race	−.3454	.4673

Family Assessment Measure results in the ability to predict 47% of the variance in the child's self-esteem. That is, children who had negative feelings about moving at the time of the move and whose mothers rated themselves as functioning well in the family had higher self-esteem.

Regarding the children's Competence scores on the CBCL, a family-level variable, once again, proved to be the strongest correlate (see Table 9). The mother's score on the Family Assessment Measure accounts for 20% of the variance in her children's competence.[2] Adding the score on the Georgia Q-sort Lively Cluster increases the predictive power of these two variables slightly, accounting for 26% of the total variance in children's Competence scores.

The degree to which children exhibit problems is predicted by three variables. The strongest correlate is the Negative Interaction Scale on the Early Memories Inventory, accounting for 20% of the variance (see Table 10). Adding the children's feelings about the last post and the Georgia Q-sort Lively Cluster score increases the total variance accounted for to 34%. Children who felt positively about the last post and whose family members are involved with one another and display liveliness and use of humor in their interactions tend to exhibit less behavior problems.

DISCUSSION

Taken together, the results from this study make it possible to estimate the risks involved in multiple relocations for children in State Department families, and identify potential vulnerabilities that exacerbate the risks, as well as buffers and resiliencies that might attenuate negative outcomes. Compared to the general population, highly mobile State Department families are faring reasonably well, especially in their self-

TABLE 9. Multiple Regression Analysis of Children's Social Adjustment (CBCL-Competence Scale)

Variables in the Equation	Beta	Adusted R^2
Mother's Family Assessment Measure	−.4755	.2093
Georgia Q-Sort–Relaxed Cluster	.2666	.2601

TABLE 10. Multiple Regression Analysis of Children's Social Adjustment (CBCL-Problem Scale)

Variables in the Equation	Beta	Adusted R^2
Negative Interaction Scale (Early Memories Inventory)	.4681	.2001
Feelings about last post	−.3043	.2773
Georgia Q-sort–Lively Cluster	−.2747	.3360

esteem and general competencies, a finding somewhat different from others in the literature. One possible explanation for this finding is that the factors that typically confound the influence of moving–i.e., the reasons for moving–were controlled in this study. There were no instances of moving because of death, divorce, or remarriage. In fact, family members knew that moving was an integral part of their lives in the State Department. Whereas, in other studies, relocations themselves may not have been the primary risk factor, the relocations may have, instead, been merely a marker for a set of stresses associated with traumas and family transitions. Some children, however, do appear to be suffering from emotional and behavioral symptoms that may be the result of cumulative moves or the most current relocation back to the United States after living abroad. Thus, while the stresses of relocations do not appear to put children in as much risk as one might have predicted from the results of previous studies, it does appear that there may be some risk of negative outcomes to which these mobile children were exposed.

Three individual factors appear to make these mobile children even more vulnerable to negative outcomes. One of these factors is race–children who are not Caucasian exhibit more difficulties than Caucasian children. It is highly likely that both institutional racism and individual instances of racism to which non-Caucasian children are subjected are at the core of this vulnerability. The second factor that increases children's vulnerability is age–younger children have more difficulty adjusting to relocations than older children, displaying more emotional and behavior problems. A third vulnerability is a predisposition to viewing social interactions as negative. As a result of many interactions with family members and other significant figures in a child's life, he begins to make meaning of these interactions and internalize this meaning into a set of expectations for future interactions. Since adjusting to moves requires adjusting to a new social milieu, having negative expectations for the interactions in this new milieu would be a significant handicap to adjustment. Contrary to results, from previous studies, gender did not have an effect on the results, as boys and girls did not differ in their levels of functioning.

A mobile child's family appears to buffer his or her risk of negative outcomes. Based on observations of family process, children do better when their families' interactions are positive and lively and when members appear to be relaxed with one another. If the child's mother reports that she is functioning well in the family (and, possibly if the father reports functioning well in the family as well), their children do better–both from their perspective on the CBCL as well as the children's own reports on the Piers-Harris. On balance, then, the family appears to be a very important influence on the children's level of adjustment. Seen in the context of the other findings, this is a very important pattern. Almost none of the variables assessing individual characteristics, social networks, or characteristics of the most recent move (e.g., decision, preparation, difficulty of move) were related to adjustment. Although the parent data were not reported in this article, it is important to note that many measures of individual characteristics, social network, and characteristics of the most recent move were predictive of the *parents'* psychological and social functioning (Steinglass and Edwards, 1993). The contrast between the child and adult results is an important indication of just how much children rely on their families during times of stress. It appears, then, that these children have not yet developed adequate individual coping strategies to help them make the adjustment to a new location. Due both to their age and mobility, their social networks are not stable enough to provide the kind of support that might help them adjust. Thus, the family is the single most important current influence and appears to be a significant factor in protecting children from the stresses of relocation.

While in the bivariate analyses both the parents' self-reported levels of functioning in the family were related to their children's functioning, it was the mothers' levels of functioning that emerged as significant in the multiple regression analyses. This could have been due, in part, to a statistical anomaly (as the parents' FAM scores were moderately intercorrelated). But it is also possible that the mothers in this sample may have had a greater influence on their children than the fathers. In the majority of these families (30 out of 35), the father was the sole State Department employee. While some of these mothers have worked outside the home, living overseas for only three years at any one post makes it quite difficult for these women to sustain a stable career. As a result, it is likely that they spent more time with their children and may, thus, have had more of an influence on their social and psychological functioning. But even when both parents work outside the home, it is not uncommon for women to do substantially more than 50% of the work at home, including child care responsibilities. It is, therefore, possible that these families are not so different from non-State Department families living in the United States, where the influence of mothers on their children is greater than the influence of fathers.

The last two factors included in the regression equations point to resiliencies that the children may have developed to cope with their relocation experiences. Children who were functioning well tended to report positive feelings about living at the last post and negative feelings about leaving it. One could presume that these children had adjusted reasonably well to life at that post, which suggests some level of skill in adapting to new environments that may have been developed as a result of their numerous experiences with relocations. Consequently, it is equally plausible to assume that they then applied these skills to adjust to the current living situation, thus accounting for their higher scores on the measure of psychological and social adjustment.

Limitations

The purpose of this study was to examine the impact of work-related relocations on children and identify potential protective and risk factors that are connected with their psychological and social adjustment. Although a number of strong findings emerged from the study, there are three caveats that need to be considered when making final conclusions. First, because the group of families studied was comprised of volunteers, and hence not necessarily representative of the full cohort of State Department families, it is difficult to say if the findings are generalizable to the general population of such families. It is not unlikely that the families volunteering for the study were among the better adjusted families having recently returned to the U. S., and hence the prevalence rates of distress in the full cohort of families might be somewhat higher. Second, since this was a cross-sectional study with no control group, the associations between components of the relocation episode and children's adjustment are not causal relationships, and may be a function of something other than the relocation experiences. These associations may have causal implications, but the design of the study did not make it possible to determine this conclusively.

Third, the sample consisted of mostly Caucasian families where the husband was the sole State Department employee. While some of the wives worked outside the home, these families clearly understood that relocations occurred because of the husbands' employment situations. One woman in a focus group conducted before the study was done commented, "I reinvent myself every time we move." It is not entirely clear, therefore, how these results might generalize to a sample of two-earner families in which husbands and wives share more equally in the employee responsibilities and privileges. This presumably has more of an impact on the adults in the family, and it is unlikely that it would change the fact that the family as a whole, as well as either or both parents individually, has a significant impact on the social and psychological functioning of mobile children.

NOTES

1. The data from the Dyadic Adjustment Scale, Family Assessment Measure and Georgia Family Q-Sort are at the family unit of analysis, with an n of 35. The analyses relating these measures with children's adjustment may be slightly inflated as the two children's scores in each family are being correlated to the same family unit scores.

2. It is important to note, however, that in the bivariate correlations, both the mother's and father's self-reports on the FAM were correlated with their children's CBCL scores. The parents' FAM scores were positively correlated with one another $(r = .34, p < .03)$. Thus, while only the mother's FAM scores emerged in the regression analysis as a predictor of the children's CBCL scores, it is possible that the colinearity of the parents' scores masked the statistical influence of the fathers on their children's functioning.

REFERENCES

Achenbach, T.N. (1978). The Child Behavior Profile: I. Boys aged 6-11. *Journal of Consulting and Clinical Psychology*, 46:478-488.

Achenbach, T.N. and Edelbrock, C.S. (1979). The Child Behavior Profile: II. Boys aged 12-16 and girls aged 6-11, 12-16. *Journal of Consulting and Clinical Psychology*, 47:223-233.

Adler, A.A. (1931). *What life should mean to you*. New York: G.P. Putnam's Sons.

Argyle, M. (1967). *The psychology of interpersonal behavior*. Harmondsworth: Penguin Books.

Barrett, C.L. and Noble, H. (1973). Mother's anxieties versus the effects of long distance move in children. *Journal of Marriage and the Family*, 35:181-188.

Benson, G.P., Haycraft, J.L., Steyaert, J.P., and Weigel, D.J. (1979). Mobility in sixth graders as related to achievement, adjustment, and socioeconomic status. *Psychology in the Schools*, 16:444-447.

Benson, G.P. and Weigel, D.J. (1981). Ninth grade adjustment and achievement as related to mobility. *Educational Research Quarterly*, 5:15-19.

Brett, J.M. (1980). The effect of job transfer on employees and their families. In C.L. Cooper and R. Payne (eds.), *Current Concerns in Occupational Stress*, 99-135.

Brett, J.M. and Werbel, J.D. (1978). *The effect of job transfer on employees and their families: Baseline survey report*. Washington, DC: Employee Relocation Council.

Bricker, R.H. (1973). Effects of mobility on the social adjustment and self-esteem of middle and upper-middle class suburban children aged 8 through 11. Unpublished doctoral dissertation, Northern Illinois University.

Bronfenbrenner, U. and Ceci, S.J. (1994). Nature-nurture reconceptualized in developmental perspective: A bioecological model. *Psychological Review*, 101, 568-586.

Brown, A.C. and Orthner, D.K. (1990). Relocation and personal well-being among early adolescents. *Journal of Early Adolescence*, 10:366-381.

Butler, E.W., McAllister, R.J., and Kaiser, E.J. (1973). The effects of voluntary and involuntary residential mobility on females and males. *Journal of Marriage and the Family*, 35:219-227.

Carter, B.D. Family stress and social adjustment following geographic relocation: A study of the function of organizational policy and social network. Unpublished doctoral dissertation, University of Virginia.

Chandler, L.A. (1981). The Source of Stress Inventory. *Psychology in the Schools*, 18:164-168.

Connelly, S.L. (1978). *A study of executive mobility strategies for offsetting counter productive effects of relocation*. Arlington, VA: Resource Development Systems.

Cowan, P.A., Cowan, C.P., and Schulz, M.S. (1996). Thinking about risk and resilience in families. In E.M. Hetherington, and E.A. Blechman (eds.), *Stress, coping, and resiliency in children and families. Family research consortium: Advances in family research*. Mahwah, NJ: Lawrence Erlbaum Associates, Inc., 1-38.

Douvan, E. and Adelson, J. (1966). *The adolescent experience*. New York: John Wiley & Sons.

Edwards, M.E. (1992). The Early Memories Inventory Codebook. Unpublished codebook, Ackerman Institute for Family Therapy.

Garmezy, N. and Masten, A.S. (1986). Stress, competence, and resilience: Common frontiers for therapist and psychopathologist. *Behavior Therapy*, 17:500-521.

Gilliland, C.H. (1958). The relation of pupil mobility to achievement in elementary school. Unpublished doctoral dissertation, Colorado State College.

Gordon, R.E. and Gordon, K.K. (1958). Emotional disorders of children in a rapidly growing suburb. *International Journal of Social Psychiatry*, 14:85-97.

Greene, J.E. and Daugherty, S.L. (1961). Factors associated with school mobility. *Journal of Educational Sociology*, 35:36-40.

Gullotta, T.P. and Donohue, K.C. (1983). Families, relocation, and the corporation. In S.L. White (ed.), *Advances in occupational mental health*. San Francisco: Jossey-Bass, Inc.

Hendershott, A.B. (1989). Residential mobility, social support, and adolescent self-concept. *Adolescence*, 24:217-232.

Hinkle, L.E. (1973). The concept of "stress" in the biological and social sciences. *Science, Medicine, and Man*, 1:31-48.

Holmes, T.H. and Masuda, M. (1973). Life change and illness susceptibility. In B.S. Dohrenwend and B.P. Dohrenwend (eds.), *Stressful life events: Their nature and effects*. New York: John Wiley, 45-72.

Holmes, T.H. and Rahe, R.H. (1967). The Social Readjustment Scale. *Journal of Psychosomatic Research*, 11:213-218.

Hormuth, S.E. (1989). Psychological effects of geographical mobility on adolescents. Paper presented to United States Department of State.

Hutton, J.B., Roberts, T.G., Walker, J., and Zuniga, J. (1987). Ratings of severity of life events by ninth-grade students. *Psychology in the Schools*, 24:63-68.

Inbar, M. (1976). *The vulnerable age phenomenon*. New York: Russell Sage Foundation.

Inbar, M. and Adler, C. (1976). The vulnerable age: A serendipitous finding. *Sociology of Education*, 49:193-200.

Ingersoll, G.M., Scamman, J.P., and Eckerling, W.D. (1989). Geographic mobility and student achievement in an urban setting. *Educational Evaluation and Policy Analysis*, 11:143-149.

Jones, S.B. (1973). Geographic mobility as seen by the wife and mother. *Journal of Marriage and the Family*, 35:210-218.

Kantor, M. (1965). *Mobility and mental health*. Springfield, IL: Charles C. Thomas.

Kazak, A.E., Jarmas, A., and Snitzer, L. (1988). The assessment of marital satisfaction: An evaluation of the Dyadic Adjustment Scale. *Journal of Family Psychology*, 2:82-91.

Kenny, J. (1967). The child in the military community. *Journal of the American Academy of Child Psychiatry*, 6:51-63.

Khleif, B.B. (1970). *The schooling of military dependents*. Durham: New Hampshire University.

Kroger, J.E. (1980). Residential mobility and self concepts in adolescence. *Adolescence*, 15:967-977.

Lehr, C.J. and Hendrickson, N. (1968). Children's attitudes toward a family move. *Mental Hygiene*, 52:381-385.

McAllister, R.J., Butler, E.W., and Kaiser, E.J. (1973). The adaptation of women to residential mobility. *Journal of Marriage and the Family*, 35:197-204.

McKain, J.L. (1973). Relocation in the military: Alienation and family problems. *Journal of Marriage and the Family*, 35:205-209.

Mann, P. (1972). Residential mobility as an adaptive experience. *Journal of Consulting and Clinical Psychology*, 39:37-42.

Marchant, K.H. and Medway, F.J. (1987). Adjustment and achievement associated with mobility in military families. *Psychology in the Schools*, 24:289-294.

Moore, H.R. (1966). Geographic mobility and performance in high school: Part II. *Journal of Secondary Education*, 41:350-352.

Morris, J.L., Pestaner, M., and Nelson, A. (1967). *The Journal of Experimental Education*, 35:74-80.

Munton, A.G. (1990). Job relocation, stress and the family. *Journal of Organizational Behavior*, 11:401-406.

Newcomb, M.D., Huba, G.J., and Bentler, P.M. (1981). A multidimensional assessment of stressful life events among adolescents: Derivation and correlates. *Journal of Health and Social Behavior*, 22:400-415.

O'Connell, P.V. (1981). The effect of mobility on selected personality characteristics of ninth and twelfth grade military dependents. Unpublished doctoral dissertation, University of Wisconsin-Milwaukee.

Oliveri, M. and Reiss, D. (1981). The structure of families' ties to their kin: The shaping role of social constructions. *Journal of Marriage and the Family*, 43:391-407.

Orthner, D.K., Brody, G., and Covi, R. (1985). *Inside families of blue: A study of air force youth*. Washington, DC: U.S. Air Force.

Orthner, D.K., Giddings, M., and Quinn, W. (1987). *Youth in transition: A study of adolescents from air force and civilian families*. Washington, DC: U.S. Air Force.

Pedersen, F. and Sullivan, E. (1964). Relationships among geographical mobility, parental attitudes, and emotional disturbances in children. *American Journal of Orthopsychiatry*, 34:575-580.

Perrodin, A.F. and Snipes, W.T. (1966). The relationship of mobility to achievement in reading, arithmetic, and language in selected Georgia elementary schools. *The Journal of Educational Research*, 59:315-319.

Piers, E.V. and Harris, D.B. (1969). *Manual for the Piers-Harris Children Self-Concept Scale*. Nashville: Counselor Recordings and Tests.

Pinder, C.C. (1977). Multiple predictors of post-transfer satisfaction: The role of urban factors. *Personnel Psychology*, 30:543-556.

Pittman, J.F. and Bowen, G.L. (1994). Adolescents on the move: Adjustment to family relocation. *Youth & Society*, 26:69-91.

Raviv, A., Keinan, G., Abazon, Y., and Raviv, A. (1990). Moving as a stressful event for adolescents. *Journal of Community Psychology*, 18:130-140.

Renshaw, J.R. (1976). An exploration of the dynamics of the overlapping worlds of work and family. *Family Process*, 15:143-165.

Richards, S., Donohue, K.C., and Gullotta, T.P. (1985). Corporate families and mobility: A review of the literature. *Family Therapy*, 12:62-73.

Richters, J.E. and Weintraub, S. (1990). Beyond diathesis: Toward an understanding of high-risk environments. In J.E. Rolf and A.S. Masten (eds.), *Risk and protective factors in the development of psychopathology*. New York: Cambridge University Press, 67-96.

Rutter, M. (1987). Psychological resilience and protective mechanisms. *American Journal of Orthopsychiatry*, 57:316-33.

Sameroff, A. and Seifer, R. (1990). Early contributors to developmental risk. In J.E. Rolf and A.S. Masten (eds.), *Risk and protective factors in the development of psychopathology*. New York: Cambridge University Press, 52-66.

Sanders, D.W. (1984). Geographical mobility: A study of its relationship to self-concept and locus of control. Unpublished doctoral dissertation, University of Akron.

Schaller, J. (1974). Geographic mobility and children's perception of their school situation. *Goteborg Psychological Reports*, 21:20.

Schaller, J. (1976). Geographic mobility as a variable in *ex post facto* research. *British Journal of Educational Psychology*, 46:341-343.

Shannan, J. (1967). Active coping. *Behavior*, 16:188-196.

Shannan, J. (1973). Coping behavior in the assessment of complex tasks. *Proceedings of the 17th International Congress of Applied Psychology*, 1:313-321.

Shaw, J.A. (1979). Adolescents in the mobile military community. In S.O. Feinstein and P.O. Giovacchini (eds.), *Adolescent psychiatry: Developmental and clinical studies*. Chicago: University of Chicago Press, 191-198.

Shaw, J.A. and Pangman, J. (1975). Geographic mobility and the military child. *Military Medicine*, 140:413-416.

Smith, W.D. and Demming, J.S. (1958). Pupil mobility and adjustment. Unpublished manuscript, Florida State University.

Spanier, G.D. (1976). Measuring dyadic adjustment: New scales for assessing the quality of marriage and similar dyads. *Journal of Marriage and the Family*, 37:15-28.

Stokols & Shumaker (1982). The psychological context of residential mobility and well-being. *Journal of Social Issues*, 38:149-171.

Stubblefield, R.L. (1955). Children's emotional problems aggravated by family moves. *American Journal of Orthopsychiatry*, 25:120-126.

Swann, W.B. (1983). Self-verification: Bringing social reality into harmony with the self. In J. Suls and A.G. Greenwald (eds.), *Psychological perspectives on the self* (Vol. 2). Hillsdale, NJ: Erlbaum.

Tesser, A. and Campbell, J. (1983). Self-definition and self-evaluation maintenance. In J. Suls and A.G. Greenwald (eds.), *Psychological perspectives on the self* (Vol. 2). Hillsdale, NJ: Erlbaum.

U. S. Census Bureau. (2000). United States Government Printing Office.

Vernberg, E.M. (1990). Experiences with peers following relocation during early adolescence. *American Journal of Orthopsychiatry*, 60:466-472.

Wampler, K.S., Halverson, C.F., Moore, J.H., and Walters, L.H. (1989). The Georgia Family Q-Sort: An observation measure of family functioning. *Family Process*, 28:223-238.

Whalen, T.E. and Fried, M.A. (1973). Geographic mobility and its effect on student achievement. *The Journal of Educational Research*, 67:163-165.

Williams, R.C. (1965). The effects of school changes on service children. *Torch* (Journal of the RAEC).

Wooster, A.D. and Harris, G. (1972). Concepts of self and others in highly mobile service boys. *Educational Research*, 14:195-199.

Young, L.L. and Cooper, D.H. (1944). Some factors associated with popularity. *Journal of Educational Psychology*, 35:513-535.

Balance as Fairness for Whom?

Lynn Parker
Rhea Almeida

SUMMARY. Balance has been typically studied in the family therapy field as an issue for white, dual career, heterosexual couples dealing with responsibilities of work and family life. In this article, we argue for definitions that expand the discussion to include those who are often marginalized and, therefore, missing in such discussions. We suggest three broadly defined steps that feminist family therapists can take to redress issues of equity in family life and more broadly in society. *[Article copies available for a fee from The Haworth Document Delivery Service: 1-800-HAWORTH. E-mail address: <getinfo@haworthpressinc.com> Website: <http://www.HaworthPress.com> © 2001 by The Haworth Press, Inc. All rights reserved.]*

KEYWORDS. Feminist, equity, justice

Balance: To bring into or maintain a state of equilibrium; . . . harmony; . . . to be equal or equivalent (*American Heritage Dictionary*, 1982, pp. 152-153).

Lynn Parker, PhD, is Assistant Professor at the Graduate School of Social Work, University of Denver; faculty with the Family Training Center of CO; and in part time private practice. Address correspondence to: 748 S. Ogden, Denver, CO 80209. Rhea Almeida, MSW, is Founder/Director, Institute for Family Services, Somerset, NJ; and faculty, Multicultural Family Institute, Highland Park, NJ. Address correspondence to: IFS, 3 Clyde Road, Suite 101, Somerset, NJ 08873.

[Haworth co-indexing entry note]: "Balance as Fairness for Whom?" Parker, Lynn, and Rhea Almeida. Co-published simultaneously in *Journal of Feminist Family Therapy* (The Haworth Press, Inc.) Vol. 13, No. 2/3, 2001, pp. 153-168; and: *Balancing Family and Work: Special Considerations in Feminist Therapy* (ed: Toni Schindler Zimmerman) The Haworth Press, Inc., 2001, pp. 153-168. Single or multiple copies of this article are available for a fee from The Haworth Document Delivery Service [1-800-HAWORTH, 9:00 a.m. - 5:00 p.m. (EST). E-mail address: getinfo@haworthpressinc.com].

153

Equity: The state or quality of being just, impartial, and fair (p. 462).

Justice: Moral rightness, equity (p. 694).

As the authors reflected on the title for this special volume, *Balancing Family and Work*, we realized we needed to define what we mean by "balance," and balance for whom? We maintain that it is important to cast this discussion in a sufficiently broad field so that our definitions include those who are most marginalized and, consequently, often rendered invisible, by such inquiries. Balance has commonly been studied in the family therapy field as an equity issue for dual earner, white, heterosexual, couples dealing with responsibilities of work and family life. Research in this area conveys that the way most heterosexual relationships are organized day-to-day requires women to carry the bulk of both relational and household responsibilities (Berardo, Shehan, & Leslie, 1987; Blair & Lichter, 1991; Dominelli & McLeod, 1989; Hochschild, 1989; Hooyman & Gonyea, 1995; Rabin, 1994; Thompson & Walker, 1989; Zimmerman & Addison, 1997). This inequitable division of labor occurs not only in the interior of family life (e.g., housework, child, and elder care), but also in exterior contacts with the community. Women, at almost all stages of the life cycle, remain largely responsible for connecting with children's schools, recreation facilities, physicians (dentists and therapists), retirement centers, nursing homes, and social service agencies. They tend to be the managers and coordinators for individual and extended family members' needs, as well as those who purchase house and yard work (in middle- and upper-class families). Family life as is typically practiced in our society is not just, or equitable, for women (Okin, 1987). Accommodations that women make in their work lives to care for others perpetuate women's economic disadvantage relative to men for life (Friedman & Greenhaus, 2000; Ward, Dale, & Joshi, 1996; Williams, 2000).

[Heterosexual] women are made vulnerable by constructing their lives around the expectation that they will be primary parents; they become more vulnerable within marriages in which they fulfill this expectation, whether or not they also work for wages; and they are most vulnerable in the event of separation or divorce, when they usually take over responsibility for children without adequate support from their ex-husbands. (Okin, 1987, p. 170)

The intention of this article is to expand the balance discussion to broader familial and social arrangements that influence the achievement of balance and, therefore, justice in current family life. Discussions of balance that focus only on dual-earner, heterosexual, white, marriages, though important, leave out important others, for example:

1. heterosexual couples who are racially/culturally "other";
2. working women partnered with unemployed persons and the "balancing" dilemmas therein;
3. single unemployed women striving to balance caretaking in families with accountability to public institutions that financially support them (e.g., welfare, housing, medical, etc.);
4. single employed persons without children who balance householding, extended family member concerns, and work with no one with whom to share the second-shift responsibilities;
5. lesbians and gay males, partnered or not, attempting to balance work, householding, and family life in a context of homophobia and heterosexism where lifestyle and personal openness may put family members at risk;
6. undocumented citizens balancing the necessity for secrecy regarding citizenship status with need for work, schooling for children, and relationships;
7. elderly persons struggling with declining health, financial resources, and support communities living in a social context of youth worship;
8. parents of disabled children (especially mothers), who are less likely than other parents to be in paid employment because of difficulties procuring appropriate and affordable child care (Lewis, Kagan, & Heaton, 2000);
9. biracial couples facing burdens of racial socialization.

Balance (i.e., equity, fairness, and justice) is all but impossible for those who are not middle class, white, heterosexual, and/or U.S. citizens. Institutional structures created to support the power of white privileged men and women disenfranchise structural supports for others. Examples include tax breaks for the wealthy; health insurance, available only to the middle and upper classes; real-estate equity that contributes to enormous buffering of wealth and, accordingly, class status; standardized testing programs in schools that disadvantage schools and children with fewer resources; racial profiling; lack of job protection or partner recognition for homosexuals; and the wedding industry (along with state and religious marriage laws), which grant privileges to heterosexual couples and maintain rigid gender roles (Ingraham, 1999). In the U.S. today, men have more privilege than women do; white men and women have more privilege than gay men, lesbians, and people of color do; and social class matters. The convergence of social location with relative privilege creates parameters, or boundary markers, that determine certain freedoms and responsibilities: who has access to meaningful and lucrative work; who is free from racial, sexist, and homophobic slurs and discrimination; who carries more (less) of household and child/elder care responsibilities; who cuts back (increases) their work, if needed, to care for family members; who earns the most; who tends to make the major family decisions; who is responsible for socializing children into their racial, cultural heritage; and whose name is bestowed on children and partners.

If not considered inclusively, "balance" is achieved by way of women, or those with less social power, doing more (Hochschild, 1989). They often assume the "menial" (i.e., less socially valued) jobs creating the illusion of balance in relationships, families, work life, and society. On the other hand, those with more social power and privilege (e.g., men) may take on a little more of the "menial" work, and because it is more than others in their position have historically taken on (e.g., more than his father or friends)–we call this balance. Missing in this picture are all of those for whom "balance" is not even a possibility, often because their jobs are to balance life for others (Williams, 2000). For example, some middle- and upper-class families hire low-paid maids, nannies, and other workers to help bring "balance" to their lives–obscuring the contributions and sacrifices of those hired, often less educated (sometimes undocumented) women of color. Furthermore, contributions of women as teachers, nurses, social workers, and home aids are obscured by the lack of financial attribution relegated to those jobs.

Therapeutic traditions also may serve as boundary markers for male and heterosexual domination, securing the status quo through unexamined practices. For example, conceptualizations of "therapeutic neutrality" or "client self-determination" can result in therapists not focusing on issues of power, privilege, and control between partners. Current inequitable power arrangements may be fortified because they are not examined. "Neutrality," in fact, is not neutral at all. And, "self-determination" (or America's obsession with the rugged individual) is available to the extent of one's social education. People cannot envision realities they have never conceived. Most therapies still bolster, versus change, the status quo, despite the significant contribution feminist family therapists have made in terms of current thought concerning family process, patterns, and structure therapists (e.g., Bograd, 1991, 1999; McGoldrick, 1998; Walters, Carter, Papp, & Silverstein, 1988; Hare-Mustin, 1997; Goldner, 1988; Goodrich, 1991; Rabin, 1996). The "marriage movement" discourse among family therapists provides a current example. Heterosexual privilege is underscored, and alternative family forms are marginalized (Peterson, Blackman, Gallager, Markman, & Miller, 2000). While accrediting bodies such as the Association for Marital and Family Therapy and the Council on Social Work Education require that some portion of graduate level curricular content be devoted to gender, race, culture, and sexual orientation, most programs have limited content and readings infused into practice content, which tends to rely on dominant discourses of family process and structure. Furthermore, the practice of feminist family therapy is not standardized nor a requirement of graduate internships or placements. Content inclusion tends to depend on the "interest" of the field supervisor.

Before we can consider balance between work and family, we must attend first to issues of privilege, power, equity, and liberation for all people. Our inquiry must include the variety of family situations, and the individuals within families, attempting an equitable balance. We suggest below three broadly defined steps that feminist family therapists can take to begin to redress issues of equity in family life and more broadly in society. First, our therapeutic focus must rest on the process of unraveling privilege, power, and oppression. Second, we must enact measures that will provide accountability for men and others in power to make changes in the distribution of power and privilege. Third, we must shift social consciousness to build an inclusive ethic of caring. These steps require that feminist family therapists encourage action and advocacy by clients on individual, relational, community, and societal levels.

EQUITY THAT EXCLUDES NO ONE REQUIRES THAT WE DISMANTLE PRIVILEGE, POWER, AND OPPRESSION

The non-poor have created political, educational, and social institutions that further the interests of those with means. Accordingly, imbalance or injustice is stratified socially. Equity is not just a personal, family issue but is also socially determined. Consequently, feminist work needs to occur on both the public social level as well as on the personal private level. For the issue of balance to be more than a private, middle upper-class concern of women who both earn money and care for homes and families, changes must occur on the social and political levels. Williams (2000) points to entrenched American norms of the "ideal worker," who now "works full time and overtime and takes little or no time off for childbearing or childrearing" (p. 3), and "domesticity" (p. 3), and "the system of providing for caregiving by marginalizing the caregivers, thereby cutting them off from most of the social roles that offer responsibility and authority" (p. 3). Williams challenges us to "persuade women [and men] to think about their own lives in a different way, not as expressions of personal priorities [choices] that occur within their heads but as a clash between the way a society tells women [and men] that children should be raised and the way it chooses to organize market work" (p. 271). The current worker ideal discriminates against women. Changes are, therefore, needed in the language we use (e.g., from "choice rhetoric" to discrimination), the work force, and social policy (Williams, 2000, p. 14). We must work to establish protective measures and legislation regarding discrimination and harassment due to race, gender, social class, sexual orientation, age, or physical ability. Meaningful equity requires redistribution of resources, removal of poverty, and illumination and redemption of violence towards women and vulnerable others. It requires providing financial and social support to those (mostly women) raising families alone. And, access to money, jobs, resources, good schools, and a supportive community must be examined and rectified.

Feminist family therapists must be broadly situated in social and political examinations and remedies. Then they must translate the social concerns and the inequities thereof to the more private and personal issues that clients present for therapy. Treatment focus needs to be broadened from the emotional and interpersonal dimensions of clients' lives to also uncovering socially mandated hierarchies of power. To do that, therapists must themselves recognize issues of power, privilege, and oppression. They must employ a contextual lens sufficiently broad to discover the multiple, interacting social locations of family members to discern how power and privilege operate in those relationships. Once discovered, therapists need methods for getting the issues on the table with clients. Here the therapist's task is to induce partners to begin thinking about their dilemmas as having a basis in power relations. This is critical if political and social dimensions of couples' dilemmas are to be introduced into family members' awareness, then into therapeutic conversation. Raising the issues of power, privilege, and oppression, then, is *the* challenge: to raise the issues and not lose the clients, particularly the ones with more power who are not so anxious to give it up; to make what has been invisible, visible, what has been comfortable, less comfortable, what has been absent, present. Raising difficult issues for scrutiny is, of course, not unique to feminist family therapy. What is unique is the object: issues of power and privilege, which structure inequities (Goodrich, 1991; Parker, 1997).

The way a session is initially organized sets the feminist (or non-feminist) course. Session structure conveys what issues are relevant by which ones are addressed, not addressed, and how. Consequently, feminist therapists intentionally ask questions and sequence events so that a connection is made between family members' concerns and the distribution of power, privilege, and oppression in relationships and society. A first session may be structured by way of assessment questions that raise power arenas for discussion and analysis. Examples are questions that surface such data as how much money each earns, how resources are allocated, who makes decisions, who accommodates, how household and people-care responsibilities are distributed, how sexual needs are negotiated, and who maintains the family's connections to family, friends, and other community support and social service systems. The specifics of these arrangements help family members begin to move beyond what is likely a denial of power disparities in their relationships (see Almeida, 1998b; Bograd, 1999; Carter & Peters, 1996; McGoldrick, 1998; Parker, 1997, 1998a & b). Haddock, Zimmerman, and MacPhee (2000) provide therapists a practical "Power Equity Guide," a tool that helps practitioners generate specific feminist interventions in relevant areas to feminist practice.

If one or more members of the family are people of color, it is important to explore the impact of racism–both outside and within the family system. Similarly, if partners or family members are gay, lesbian, bisexual, transgendered, transsexual, or questioning, impacts of societal homophobia and heterosexism need to be discussed. Yet, this is not enough. Issues of racism, sexism, and homophobia ought to be explored with *all* clients to change the fabric of discrimination throughout community life. Questions are warranted that enlighten all families regarding their social location–their perceptions and experiences of race, social class, and relative privilege. Some good examples of questions from Killian (2001) include:

> Which aspects of your racial/ethic [cultural] heritage are important to you/are a source of pride? Which have you rejected/are a source of shame? Did you or your family experience racism or stereotyping as a member of a racial group? Do you have ancestors who were persecuted or who persecuted others? How has your family dealt with these painful memories? Whom could you "bring home to dinner" and whom could you not? . . .What parts of your heritage and history do you want to pass on to your children? (p. 40)

In a sense, the organization of sessions can provide a power-issues literacy training for clients. This can occur by way of specific, concrete questions that raise issues of power, privilege, and oppression, like those suggested above (see Bepko & Johnson, 2000; Bernstein, 2000; Laird & Green, 1996). Issues of power, privilege, and oppression can also be uncovered in genogram work (McGoldrick & Gerson, 1985), where therapists examine with family members the transmission of those issues down the generations. Hardy and Laszloffy's (1995) cultural genogram and Halevy's (1998) "genogram with an attitude" provide the reader with other good examples of this process. Pinderhughes (1998) and Colon (1998) provide illustrations of each author's own multigenerational explorations.

Therapists can also inquire into the consequences (both positive and negative) to the way relationships are organized and decisions are made. For example, what are the consequences (to the relationship and to the deemed caregiver) of decisions that put one partner's career on hold to be primary caregiver to children or elders? Are there interventions that can be implemented within families that will impact all (not just female) family members' ethics regarding caring? Can we enlighten families of privilege regarding the disparate access they enjoy to upward mobility and their ability to respond to family crises and illness compared to their less privileged counterparts–often working under or for them? Are there community resources or advocates that might be available to provide needed support (e.g., tutoring, mentoring, coaching, case work) to family members?

Equity requires that both women and men take responsibility for providing financially and assuming house and people care activities. Balance achieved by one person (usually a woman) carrying more of the house and people care responsibilities disadvantages that person. People who have been outside of the job market have less ability to support themselves and their children. They also lack ability to leave a relationship if partnered, especially important in relationships where there is violence. At the very least, all people must have financial means to exit battering relationships. Consequently, it is imperative that every adult become economically autonomous or, at the least, economically viable (Goodin, 1985; Okin, 1989; Scanzoni, 1989). As mentioned before, some of these changes require changes in norms regarding ideal workers and domesticity as well as policy. However, family members' consciousness can be raised around ethics of caring, giving, and sharing. All family members can be encouraged by therapists to look at how they contribute–to earning money, to caregiving and householding tasks, to relationship building and maintenance, and to maintaining contact with community (e.g., agencies, friends, recreation). Additionally, they might be invited to look at how they contribute to community life. Carter (1995) and others (Putnam, 2000) have written about the missing mediating element for families in today's American society, the loss of connection to community.

THE LIBERATION OF THOSE WITH LESS POWER (E.G., WOMEN) IS INTRINSICALLY TIED TO THE ACCOUNTABILITY OF THOSE WITH MORE POWER (E.G., WHITE MEN)

Traditional forms of therapy (individual, couples, or even family therapy) often limit experiences of change to the interior boundary of family/individual life. These traditional therapeutic structures often serve to maintain the status quo (of privilege and lack of privilege) because reliance on individual action as the impetus for change lacks the accountability necessary for change–particularly for persons with more power and privilege who are often reluctant to relinquish it. Accordingly, therapies that employ collective means for change emphasize the notion of family as an open unit. Change here is viewed as being community-driven politically as opposed to only occurring at a personal and private level. Examples include group approaches to therapy, community sponsors (e.g., Almeida, 1998a & b, 1999), witness groups, and reflecting teams (e.g., White, 1999). Connecting people to communities of helping (versus private psychotherapies) mentors clients into a process of building critical consciousness–committed communities of action, responsibility, accountability, and empowerment (Freire, 1971, 1978).

Therapists must realize that when we work "privately" (e.g., one therapist and a family, couple, or individual), we are working at a handicap. Accountability is much harder to provide both for therapists and clients (Bograd, 1991, 1999). Dominant cultural norms, in which we have all been raised, are more likely to remain invisible, and thus be augmented. Though this structure is how most practitioners typically operate, it contains risks:

1. It may reinforce the very power issues we are trying to unravel.
2. It contains danger of replicating a patriarchal system.
3. It isolates family from resources, asking family members to turn to each other, often within unequal power relationships, without feedback, significant others, or community to hold family members accountable for making changes.
4. It elevates the therapist as resource or expert.
5. It keeps attention focused on the interior of individual and family life. Social analysis is often missing.

Feminist family therapists must be aware of these potential pitfalls and challenge themselves to creatively meet these structural constraints. For example, therapists need to think broadly about resource people and extended family members they might include in sessions to act as cultural consultants, supports, and to provide accountability for change (e.g., Almeida, Woods, Messineo, & Font, 1998; McGoldrick, 1998; Tamasese & Waldegrave, 1994; White, 1999).

IN ORDER TO ACHIEVE BALANCE, EQUITY, AND JUSTICE, WE MUST BUILD AN INCLUSIVE ETHIC OF CARING

Consciousness raising is vital in order to achieve meaningful equity. A process of re-socialization is needed to combat the education most of us receive, which obscures (even reinforces) issues of power, privilege, and oppression and, therefore, renders balance impossible. Providing clients with social education begins to shift social awareness.

Masculinities scholarship (e.g., Connell, 1995; Dolan-Del Vecchio, 1996; Font, Dolan-Del Vecchio, & Almeida, 1998) provides family therapists tools for thinking through patterns of difference and dominance. It examines the specifics of how men and others in positions of power can be challenged while being simultaneously empowered within their specific social locations. Font, Dolan-Del Vecchio, and Almeida (1998) have developed a conceptualization of "Expanded Norms of the Male Role" (p. 96). The expanded norms build on Green's (1998, p. 83) "traditional norms of masculinity" to create new possible definitions for men by "describing accountability-based and nurturant relational patterns for men to work toward" (Font et al., 1998, p. 87).

Research conducted by Parker (1997, 2001) details the impact of consciousness raising on a diverse client population at the Institute for Family Services (IFS) in Somerset, New Jersey. Consciousness raising is a central component of the program there, focusing on norms that maintain patterns of domination and subordination in families and society. It is similar to Freire's (1971, 1978) notion of critical consciousness, the process of personal and social transformation as people begin to decode mechanisms of power, privilege, oppression, and dehumanization. Didactic materials (e.g., video clips, books, articles, and music lyrics) are presented to clients at IFS to illuminate dominant social prescriptions and prohibitions regarding gender, race, culture, and sexual orientation. Clients and therapeutic teams together develop a conceptual framework and language for understanding and describing daily experiences of power and domination. For example, traditional gender roles are deconstructed (see Green, 1998; Dolan-Del Vecchio, 1997) in the social-education component, including women's sanctioned role as "culture bearer" (Almeida & Durkin, 1999, p. 313). In this prescribed role, women are responsible for the survival of the family as well as the culture. Their job is to translate traditional masculine norms into more palatable legacies for their children and others. For example, a mother might reframe a father's scary and aggressive behavior as toughness and leadership in the face of adversity. Rationalizations such as "Men are just aggressive," or "Dad's had a bad day" excuse potentially abusive behavior toward family members. "Men will be men" can excuse affairs or use of pornography. We encourage readers to bring to mind professional sports team members in their own communities who have been charged with domestic abuse, whose partners later recanted their charges. Protection of patriarchy lives deeply in each of us, even at our own risk. For equity to be realized, traditional gender roles that privilege males and disadvantage (even demean) females must be considered and reformed as well as cultural practices that disadvantage women. Cultural legacies that reinforce male control over women and children need to be discerned from those that engender community and expand roles for both women and men.

Power and control wheels are other tools whereby clients can delineate, at both the private, couple, and family level and the public and community level, the ways that differences of gender, race, and sexual orientation contribute to predictable and patterned differences in access to power and privileges, including safety (Font et al., 1998). The wheels provide social education to help clients decipher what are power and control issues and how they manifest in both public and private life. The "Public Context" wheels (pp. 90-91) provide a framework and language that describe institutional and social prejudice and discrimination toward marginalized groups (e.g., unsafe schools, lack of job protection, disparate access to judicial and law enforcement systems, the objectification of women, etc.). Clients examine disparate unequal access to minimal standards of well-being and legitimized forms of abuse toward people of color, gay men, and lesbians. On the private level, clients examine various forms of abuse and intimidation they have experienced or perpetrated with family, friends, fellow workers, and others (e.g., psychological, physical, sexual, economic, etc.). The wheels help clients to locate and understand their problems not only within individual personalities and relational exchanges but also within a societal context.

> As the frame is enlarged such that it begins to survey the role prescriptions and power dynamics connected to differences such as gender, race, sexual orientation and class, an entirely different kind of therapeutic conversation emerges. Within this new conversation the focus moves away from the search for pathology and toward the search for justice. (Font et al., 1998, p. 92)

CONCLUSION

In this article we endeavored to expand discussions of balance, equity, and justice beyond middle class, heterosexual, dual career, couples to include those often marginalized in such discussions. To impact "balance" so that the ones with less power and privilege are not disadvantaged economically and socially requires that we carefully unpack and dismantle powerful social prescriptions that privilege some and oppress others. Those who hold more power and privilege must be held accountable for making and maintaining changes in the distribution of power, opportunity, wealth, and responsibility. And, for this to occur, a re-socialization process, optimally in collectives, is required to counter the patriarchal, capitalistic system in which we live, which requires imbalance and inequity.

How do we achieve true balance in a society where privilege is guarded, where more (and bigger) is better, and where private well-being is regarded above public well-being? In such a society privilege will be guarded and the consequences of that privilege will be obscured. We will say we are achieving balance when we are not. To seek balance, equity, or (better) liberation for all requires that we recognize where each of us is still committed to maintaining the status quo–maintaining our own or others' privilege and still others' lack of power and control over their own lives. We must be willing to give up our privilege.

REFERENCES

Almeida, R. (1998a). The dislocation of women's experience in family therapy. *Journal of Feminist Family Therapy, 10*(1), 1-22.

Almeida, R. (Ed.) (1998b). *Transformations of gender and race: Family and developmental perspectives.* New York: The Haworth Press, Inc.

Almeida, R. & Durkin, T. (1999). The cultural context model: Therapy for couples with domestic violence. *Journal of Marital and Family Therapy, 25*(3), 313-324.

Almeida, R., Woods, R., Messineo, T., & Font, R. (1998). The cultural context model: An overview. In M. McGoldrick (Ed.), *Revisioning family therapy: Race, culture, and gender in clinical practice* (pp. 414-431). New York: Guilford.

American Heritage Dictionary (Second College Edition). Boston: Houghton Mifflin.

Bepko, C. & Johnson, T. (2000). Gay and lesbian couples in therapy: Perspectives for the contemporary therapist. *Journal of Marital and Family Therapy, 26*(4), 409-420.

Berardo, D. H., Shehan. C. L., & Leslie, G. R. (1987). A residue of tradition: Jobs, careers, and spouses' time in housework. *Journal of Marriage and the Family, 49*(2), 381-390.

Bernstein, A. C. (2000). Straight therapists working with lesbians and gays in family therapy. *Journal of Marital and Family Therapy, 26*(4), 443-454.

Blair, S. & Lichter, D. (1991). Measuring the division of household labor. *Journal of Family Issues, 12*(1), 91-113.

Bograd, M. (1999). Strengthening domestic violence theories: Intersection of race, class, sexual orientation, and gender. *Journal of Marital and Family Therapy, 25*, 291-312.

Bograd, M. (Ed.) (1991). *Feminist approaches for men in family therapy*. New York: Harrington Park Press.

Carter, B. (1995). Focusing your wide-angle lens. *Family Therapy Networker, 19*(6), 31-35.

Carter, B. & Peters, J. (1996). *Love, honor, and negotiate: Making your marriage work*. New York: Simon & Schuster.

Colon, F. (1998). The discovery of my multicultural identity. In M. McGoldrick (Ed.), *Revisioning family therapy: Race, class, gender* (pp. 200-214). New York: Guilford.

Connell, R. W. (1995). *Masculinities*. Berkeley: University of California Press.

Dolan-Del Vecchio, K. (1996). Dismantling white male privilege within family therapy. In M. McGoldrick (Ed.), *Revisioning family therapy: Race, culture, and gender* (pp. 159-175). New York: Guilford.

Dominelli, L. & McLeod, E. (1989). *Feminist social work*. London: Macmillan.

Font, R., Dolan-Del Vecchio, K., & Almeida, R. (1998). Finding the words: Instruments for a therapy of liberation. *Journal of Feminist Family Therapy, 10*, 85-97.

Freire, P. (1971). *Pedagogy of the oppressed*. New York: Herder and Herder.

Freire, P. (1978). *Education for a critical consciousness*. New York: Seabury Press.

Friedman, S. & Greenhaus, S. (2000). *Work and family: Allies or enemies?* New York: Oxford.

Goldner, V. (1988). Generation and gender: Normative and covert hierarchies. *Family Process, 27*, 17-31.

Goodin, R. E. (1985). *Protecting the vulnerable: A reanalysis of our social responsibilities*. Chicago: University of Chicago Press.

Goodrich, T. J. (Ed.) (1991). *Women and power: Perspectives for family therapy*. New York: W.W. Norton & Co.

Green, R. J. (1998). Traditional norms of masculinity. *Journal of Feminist Family Therapy, 10*, 82-84.

Haddock, S. A., Zimmerman, T. S., & MacPhee, D. (2001). The power equity guide: Attending to gender in family therapy. *Journal of Marital and Family Therapy, 26*, 153-170.

Halevy, J. (1998). A genogram with an attitude. *Journal of Marital and Family Therapy, 24*, 233-242.

Hardy, K. & Laszloffy, T. A. (1995). The cultural genogram: Key to training culturally competent family therapists. *Journal of Marital and Family Therapy, 21*, 227-237.

Hare-Mustin, R. (1987). The problem of gender in family therapy theory. *Family Process, 26*, 15-27.

Hochschild, A. (1989). *The second shift: Working parents and the revolution at home*. New York: Viking Penguin.

Hooyman, N. R. & Gonyea, J. (1995). *Feminist perspectives on family care*. Thousand Oaks, CA: Sage.

Ingraham, C. (1999). *White weddings: Romancing heterosexuality in popular culture*. New York; Routledge.

Killian, K. D. (2001). Reconstituting racial histories and identities. *Journal of Marital and Family Therapy, 27*(1), 27-42.

Laird, J. & Green, R. J. (Eds.) (1996). *Lesbians and gays in couples and families: A handbook for therapists.* San Francisco: Jossey-Bass.

Lewis, S., Kagan, C., & Heaton, P. (2000). Dual-earner parents with disabled children: Family patterns for working and caring. *Journal of Family Issues, 21,* 1031-1060.

McGoldrick, M. (Ed.) (1998). *Revisioning family therapy: Race, class, gender.* New York: Guilford.

McGoldrick, M. & Gerson, R. (1985). *Why genograms? Genograms in family assessment.* New York: W.W. Norton.

Okin, S. M. (1989). *Justice, gender, and the family.* Basic Books.

Parker, L. (2001). *Addressing oppression, power, and privilege in family therapy: A case study.* Manuscript submitted for publication.

Parker, L. (1998a). The unequal bargain: Power issues in couples therapy. *Journal of Feminist Family Therapy, 10,* 17-38.

Parker, L. (1998b). Keeping power on the table in couples therapy. *Journal of Feminist Family Therapy, 10,* 1-24.

Parker, L. (1997). Unraveling power issues in couples therapy. *Journal of Feminist Family Therapy, 9,* 3-20.

Peterson, K., Blackman, L., Gallager, M., Markman, H., & Miller, M. (Speakers). (2000). *Death do us part? Family therapy and the marriage movement* (Cassette Recording No. AAMFT/oo108/G3). Denver, CO: 58th Annual Conference, American Association for Marital and Family Therapy.

Pinderhughes, E. (1998). Black genealogy revisited: Restoring an African American family. In M. McGoldrick (Ed.), *Revisioning family therapy: Race, class, gender* (pp. 179-199). New York: Guilford.

Putnam, R. D. (2000). *Bowling alone.* New York: Simon & Schuster.

Rabin, C. (1996). *Equal partners, good friends: Empowering couples through therapy.* New York: Routledge.

Rabin, C. (1994). Towards fairness in marriage. *Journal of Feminist Family Therapy, 6,* 41-71.

Scanzoni, J. (1989). Alternative images for public policy: Family structure versus families struggling. *Policy Studies Review, 8* (3), 599-609.

Tamasese, K. & Waldegrave, C. (1994). Culture and gender accountability in the "just therapy" approach. *Dulwich Center Newsletter, 2 & 3,* 55-67.

Thompson, L. & Walker, A. (1989). Gender in families: Women and men in marriage, work, and parenthood. *Journal of Marriage and the Family, 51,* 845-871.

Walters, M., Carter, B., Papp, P., & Silverstein, O. (1988). *The invisible web.* New York: The Guilford Press.

Ward, C., Dale, A., & Joshi, H. (1996). Combining employment with childcare: An escape from dependence. *Journal of Social Policy, 25,* 223-247.

White, M. (1999). Reflecting-team work as definitional ceremony revisited. *Gecko, 2,* 55-82.

Williams, J. (2000). *Unbending gender: Why family and work conflict and what to do about it*. New York: Oxford University Press.

Zimmerman, T. & Addison, C. (1997). Division of labor and child care among dual-career couples: A qualitative analysis. *Journal of Feminist Family Therapy, 9*(1), 47-72.

We've Come a Long Way?
An Overview of Research
of Dual-Career Couples'
Stressors and Strengths

Dawn Viers
Anne M. Prouty

SUMMARY. As dual-career couples have become an increasingly prevalent couple type, it is important for therapists to know and understand the research on these couples. This article reviews research from the 1960s to the present and presents relevant findings on the strengths and stressors of dual-career couples. These domains include work overload, social networks, work and family roles, identity conflicts and power, personal and societal views, marital distress levels, division of household tasks, and communication. Implications for therapists based on this research and suggestions for future research are also presented. *[Article copies available for a fee from The Haworth Document Delivery Service: 1-800-HAWORTH. E-mail address: <getinfo@haworthpressinc.com> Website: <http://www.HaworthPress.com> © 2001 by The Haworth Press, Inc. All rights reserved.]*

Dawn Viers, MS, is a doctoral candidate in the Marriage and Family Therapy Program, Department of Human Development at Virginia Polytechnic Institute and State University, Mail Code 0515, Blacksburg, VA 24061. Anne M. Prouty, PhD, is Assistant Professor within the Marriage and Family Therapy Program, Department of Human Development and Family Studies at the University of Rhode Island, Kingston, RI.

All correspondence should be directed to the first author.

[Haworth co-indexing entry note]: "We've Come a Long Way? An Overview of Research of Dual-Career Couples' Stressors and Strengths." Viers, Dawn, and Anne M. Prouty. Co-published simultaneously in *Journal of Feminist Family Therapy* (The Haworth Press, Inc.) Vol. 13, No. 2/3, 2001, pp. 169-190; and: *Balancing Family and Work: Special Considerations in Feminist Therapy* (ed: Toni Schindler Zimmerman) The Haworth Press, Inc., 2001, pp. 169-190. Single or multiple copies of this article are available for a fee from The Haworth Document Delivery Service [1-800-HAWORTH, 9:00 a.m. - 5:00 p.m. (EST). E-mail address: getinfo@haworthpressinc.com].

KEYWORDS. Couple, dual-career, research, work

The emergence of middle- and upper-class women into the labor and career force is considered one of the fundamental changes in social structure in the twentieth century (Bachelor, 1994; Hare-Mustin, 1978). The number of women working in paid labor rose from 50% of the eligible population of American women in 1988 to 62% presently (Mishra & Bose, 1997). The "traditional" heterosexual, nuclear family of the husband as the breadwinner and wife as the homemaker is becoming exceedingly rare as differing family types, such as blended families, single parenthood, and homosexual couples, have become more prevalent and less mysterious (Hare-Mustin, 1978; Yogev & Brett, 1985). Currently, only 7% of American families are considered to be a traditional nuclear family (Bachelor, 1994). However, while dual-career couples are becoming more typical, there does not seem to be much contemporary marital and family therapy (MFT) research specifically focusing on how women and men experience life within these couples. While this may be a reflection that women and men rearing a family while maintaining both of their careers has become more of the norm, these couples continue to face stressors, strains, and strengths that may be different than one-career couples and single persons.

HISTORICAL CONTEXT OF WOMEN AND WAGE EARNING

Women's Work Is Work

Although heralded as a new phenomenon, women (and often children) have worked as part of the paid labor force since pre-industrial times (Hare-Mustin, 1978, 1986; Goodrich, Rampage, Ellman, & Halstead, 1988). With the American industrial revolution, women were urged to embrace domesticity as their responsibility and destiny, whether or not they were forced to work outside the home to provide for themselves and their dependents. Many women were encouraged to leave paid jobs and work instead inside their homes, likely as part of a deliberate attempt to have women vacate factory jobs they held during World War II in favor of returning veterans (Goldner, 1988). The family progressively became separated into a private sphere, designated for women, and a public sphere, dominated by men, usually white men. Culturally and socially, the American society, from churches to schools to doctors, supported this strict division of labor (Goldner, 1985; Goodrich et al., 1988).

More recently, middle-class American women have returned to the paid labor force, frequently out of economic necessity, but also due to other motivations, such as increased need for resources or higher self-esteem, and to alleviate boredom (Walter, Carter, Papp, & Silverstein, 1988; Goldenberg & Goldenberg, 1984). However, while women are increasingly counted within the workforce, this has not excused women from their responsibility for the family and home. Further, women often work in low-paying jobs with decreased power and prestige as compared to their male counterparts (Hare-Mustin, 1978; Yogev & Brett, 1985). With these discrepancies, it becomes critical to examine and understand existing research on dual-career couples to assess if these stresses are potential problem areas.

Early research on dual-career couples and women in the workforce was predominately negative (Yogev, 1982). Women with careers did not fit the stereotypical norms and values associated with the white, heterosexual, middle-class female role popularized in the burgeoning mass-media of the 1950s and were, therefore, seen as the "antithesis of the feminine woman" (Yogev, 1982, p. 594). Both men and fellow women denounced employed women, even if only in whispers, as failures, or even as women tending towards personality disturbances. In terms of the martial relationship, husbands of working women rated their marriage less positively then husbands of non-working women. Divorce and separation were found to be more prevalent in dual-career households, thus, women's participation in the workforce was seen as a potential threat to the family. Further, this public reintroduction of a previously-seen-as privileged class of women into the labor force increased a blurring of post-world war demarcating of masculine and feminine roles at home, and was professed as a threat to marital happiness (Yogev, 1982).

Although these views are changing, negative stereotypes about working women and dual-career couples remain. In 1997, Douglas reported the results of a study in *U. S. News & World Report* that found that mothers who worked outside of the home had higher blood-levels of cortisol, a stress hormone which puts these women at higher risk for heart attacks and a weakened immune system. The article continued:

So is having kids bad for your health? Not at all, says Betty Dooley of the Women's Research and Education Institute. Studies show that mothers are happier late in life than childless women, she notes. And women who have never given birth may have a higher risk of developing breast and ovarian cancer. For mothers thinking about returning to work, the study offers no conclusive guidance. Parents can think that over for themselves, while awaiting future comparisons of working and non-working mothers. (Douglas, 1997, http://www.usnews.com/usnews/issue/4out1.htm)

Douglas implied that while women should fulfill the mothering role, they might want to think twice about continuing to work outside of the home once they become mothers. Although this story specifically related to working mothers, it typifies continuing negative impressions of working women, dual-career couples, and gendered parental responsibilities.

Dual-Career vs. Dual-Earner

The terms dual-earner and dual-career are often used synonymously in researching working couples (Yogev & Brett, 1985). However, some authors note important differences between the two terms (Aryee, Luk, Leung, & Lo, 1999; Rapoport & Rapoport, 1969; Yogev & Brett, 1985). Dual-career couples differ from dual-earner couples in that a career requires higher educational levels, high levels of personal commitment, and has a series of promotional cycles (Rapoport & Rapoport, 1971; Potucheck, 1997). Viewing work as a career also implies a psychological involvement or commitment to work (Yogev & Brett, 1985). Dual-career couples often share a philosophy of equality at the home and in the career, although this philosophy isn't always practiced (Goldenberg & Goldenberg, 1985). In contrast, dual-earner couples are more loosely defined in that each partner is part of the general workforce and shares a common residence (Aryee et al., 1999).

Although the terms dual-career and dual-earner are used interchangeably, there seems to be important economic, employment, and marital differences between the two. Dual-earner couples tend to have fewer resources, decreased power of negotiation with employers, and suffer more severe economic consequences when the woman is not working (Aryee et al., 1999). There are also significant differences in couples where a woman works by choice versus couples in which she works by necessity (Orden & Bradburn, 1969). As dual-career couples often have more financial and educational resources than dual-earner couples, women in dual-earner couples would be more likely to work out of necessity (Aryee et al., 1999). Couples in which a woman worked out of necessity reported high levels of tension and low levels of dyadic satisfaction whereas couples where a woman worked by choice reported greater marital and job satisfaction (Orden & Bradburn, 1969).

THE RESEARCH REVIEW

The purpose of reviewing this specific research area is twofold. First, research since the 1960s on dual-career couples is summarized to get an idea of the stressors and strengths of dual-career couples. It is important to review the research after the 1950s, because, as we have mentioned previously, the popular culture has often stigmatized working women. Second, several clinical implications based on the results from this research are discussed. We believe that focusing on relevant research can not only help family therapists to understand the needs of dual-career and tailor treatment, but influence family researchers to conduct more meaningful research in this important and yet under-investigated area of work and family.

Selection of Research Articles

The databases of Psyc-Info and Women's Lit were searched for research articles and descriptions of research. Resources included academic journals, books, book chapters, and dissertations on dual-career or dual-earner couples that were part of married and non-married heterosexual and homosexual couples. Hundreds of potential articles were found.

The data were then narrowed based on the following criteria. First, the research must have focused on the influence of the dual-career lifestyle on the couple. This includes strengths and stressors of dual-career couples and the impact of this relationship choice on interpersonal and career related relationships. Choosing to focus on research of dual-career couples also limited the population to those whose financial resources were of a higher income bracket with all of the choices and resources that accompany that privilege.

Second, articles were only selected if the research focused on the influence of the dual-career lifestyle on the marital dyad or couple relationship versus the influence of the dual-career lifestyle on parenting. During this sampling, it was decided that the inclusion of parenting stress could confound the investigation of other stresses faced by dual-career couples. While research on dual-career families is important, both from a family studies and clinical perspective, including literature on dual-career families entails different clinical and academic implications and deserves a separate stage. (For a good review of dual-career families, please see Rapoport & Rapoport, 1969, 1971).

Third, only articles that studied the perspective of both partners in the couple were reviewed. Focusing on both members of the couple was important for several reasons. Women traditionally have been the only respondents in research on relationships. This can lead to a bias in understanding and reporting information on couplehood as only one person in the dyad is being studied. It can also lead to blaming the female for relational problems and familial distress. As Rachlin and Hansen (1985, p. 160) note, "differences between husbands and wives point to the importance of studying both spouses in dual-career marriages rather than just one partner (typically the woman)." Many studies do not control for gender differences or analyze responses from males and females separately, which precludes examining the effect of gender (Barnett & Brennan, 1997). Studying both members of a couple allows the researcher to compare differential stressors and coping strategies of each member of the relationship (Mishra & Bose, 1997). Thus, to summarize, this is a review of research since 1960 that focused on both members' experiences of the effects of their dual-career relationship, how both of them working impacted their dyadic relationship (but not their parenting), and/or their work relationships.

After this narrowing of the sample of research, 21 studies remained. All were of heterosexual couples and most were of white, middle-class couples, mostly Americans. Although we believe these studies' results will provide pertinent information about dual-career couples in general, this narrow focus points to the pressing need for studies of diverse dual-career and dual-earner couples (e.g., of different races, sexual orientations, ages, religions) and for researchers to identify these important variables in the descriptions of their research.

For this review, the results of the 21 available studies' results were examined for themes and have been divided into five categories. The first category is stress domains, under which fell: work overload, social networks, work and family roles, individual identity conflicts and power, personal and societal views. The second domain is marital distress, the third is a second shift for women, the fourth is communication, and the fifth is strength and resiliency factors under which were marital satisfaction and couples' coping mechanisms. After these themes are reviewed, several implications for therapy are discussed.

Stress Domains in Dual-Career Couples

Rapoport and Rapoport (1969), pioneers of research and literature on dual-career families, identified five stress domains for the dual-career family: work overload, decreased social networks, balancing work and family roles, individual identity conflicts, and discrepancies between personal and social norms. Based upon the research reviewed for this article, these domains affect dual-career couples differently than dual-career families. Work overload, work distress, and balancing work and family roles are problematic for dual-career couples. However, while dual-career couples experience decreased social networks and individual identity conflicts, researchers discovered that these areas did not necessarily cause increased distress. Finally, discrepancies between personal and social norms did not seem to be as problematic in the couples studied.

Work Overload. Dual-career couples experience work overload which can lead to psychological distress. Women and men both reported that work experiences, positive and negative, influenced mental health and distress. For example, working under the pressure of time and conflicting demands, engaging in dull, monotonous jobs, and feeling underutilized at work related to high distress levels in dual-career couples (Barnett & Brennan, 1997). Barnett, Brennan, Raudenbush, and Marshall (1994) found that women experienced significantly higher overall distress levels at work and home than did men. Barnett et al. proposed two reasons to account for the sex difference in distress levels. First, they did not control for division of household tasks or sex-role attitudes within their research, two variables thought to influence distress. Second, women may face unique stressors at work, such as sexual harassment, which may affect their level of distress.

The studies by Barnett and Brennan (1997) and Barnett and her associates (1994) indicate that job conditions and experiences affect women's distress levels as much or more than men's. This research contradicts identity theory which suggests that the worker role is more natural for males and thereby changes in this role would create more distress in men than for women, whose "natural" role is in the home (Simon, 1992). Perhaps this also points out a basic flaw in such sexist and bourgeois theories that researchers studying dual-career couples have come to know: that home is always work and work is often home (Hochschild, 1989).

In a study by Jones and Fletcher, in 1993, women in working couples were likely to perceive their work as less intellectually stimulating than were men's and women also reported that they were less able to see positive results from their work. Men felt that their jobs were more formal, involved, and were subject to more conflicting demands and instructions than did women. One year later, Barnett et al. (1994) extended our understanding of women's experiences when they reported that as job quality improves, distress declines for single, childless women, but not for married women and further stated that part-time employment was as likely as full-time employment to be associated with higher distress levels for women. In 1997, Barnett and Shen expanded the picture of women working part-time outside the home by reporting that, along with decreased salary and benefits, these women take on more daily household tasks, such as cooking and cleaning, which positively correlated with increased psychological distress.

This body of research shows that work pressures and strains spill over into couples' experiences of home. Jones and Fletcher (1996) found that work stressors determined a significant amount of the variation of mood at home for both men and women. Men were likely to be negatively influenced by both work and domestic pressures, while women were more likely to be negatively influenced mainly by domestic pressures. Being in a good or bad mood was also related to the quality of interpersonal relationships at work, especially for women (Jones & Fletcher, 1996).

Although alluded to by Barnett et al. (1994) as a reason for why women were more distressed at work and home than were men, there was little research on effect of on-the-job harassment on the couple relationship. Occupational harassment, such as sexual harassment and discrimination, is thought to have more of an effect on women than men. Researching potential correlations and causal relationships between harassment and marital satisfaction would be important, as occupational harassment and other job-related stresses are thought to be chronic in nature (Mishra & Bose, 1997).

Social Networks. Maintaining two careers is associated with a decreased network of family and friends. Men in dual-career couples were more likely to have jobs that restricted their social life and that caused them to travel or move from home. This led to decreased time for interacting with friends and family (Jones & Fletcher, 1993). Dual-career couples thought that they were unable to maintain strong social networks due to time constraints and work overload. These couples also reported less time to spend with extended family and increased inability to meet social obligations and expectations with family, with males perceiving the loss of extended family support as more severe than women (St. John-Parsons, 1978).

Tobey (1981) also found that dual-career lifestyle decreased the amount of time the couple spent with extended family members. However, these couples did not necessarily report that this decrease in time had a negative impact on their distress levels and marital satisfaction. Rather, they felt able to manage their time with friends and family so that time spent together was viewed as quality time.

Work and Couple Roles. Researchers have found that family and work were intertwined in dual-career couples' lives, as couples reported that they were more likely to allow work to interfere with couplehood responsibilities than their relationship responsibilities to interfere with work. The intrusion of work into family life negatively correlated with dyadic and job satisfaction (Aryee et al., 1999). Furthermore, work and relational attitudes and behaviors of one member of a couple were systematically related to attitudes and behaviors of their mate for dual-career but not single-career couples, indicating that the job problems and successes of one partner affected the other. To counteract this effect, dual-career couples reported that they developed routines and divided up tasks in order to manage the demands of work and home. They were also likely to modify or change roles during transitions, such as getting a new job or shift at work (Yogev & Brett, 1985).

While previously the marital role was thought to be more important for women, researchers of heterosexual, dual-career marriages were finding in the 1990s that marital and family roles were also salient for men (Barnett et al., 1993; Barnett et al., 1994). Barnett and her colleagues (1994) have found that men's marital roles have as great an impact on their psychological well-being and happiness as their job role. In fact, marital role quality, defined as sum of marital rewards and lack of marital concerns, was nearly identical for men and women. Furthermore, couples who divided household responsibilities more equally were both more strongly committed to the marriage.

Individual Identity Conflicts and Power. Males and females seem to experience identity conflicts regarding consolidation of their preferred roles with stereotypical gender roles. However, females in dual-career couples experience more identity role concerns, as having a career outside the home strays from the "traditional" female gender role. St. John-Parsons (1978) suggested that women may attempt to consolidate their discrepant roles by acting out stereotypical gender roles, such as cooking, cleaning, and child care, after their paid work hours. Mishra and Bose (1997) found that women experienced more stress than men in relation to juggling multiple roles. Women were more likely to experience role overburden, role ambiguity, role stagnation, and distance within gender roles. Increased role stress was related to decreased job satisfaction. However, Sekaran (1985) found that both men and women in dual-career couples experienced the burden of multiple role stress, which was related to decreased life and job satisfaction. In terms of relational identity, couples experienced more stress if they failed to establish themselves in their career before starting a family. Couples who were more established professionally experienced fewer role and identity dilemmas (St. John-Parsons).

With a slightly different twist on the construction of the issue of power, St. John-Parsons (1978) found that household tasks were performed or contracted by the partner who decided the tasks needed to be completed, which was most often the wife. Whether this is a test of wills, a measure of who had the most patience with chaos, or a reflection of internalized gender roles was uncertain. St. John-Parsons found that although the wives in the study would often hire outside help for child care and housework, this help was often not considered satisfactory and this would lead to her increased workload stress. These findings seem to suggest blaming the victim by attacking her character, instead of placing the responsibility on the dyadic power dynamics and society's gendered expectations of domestic cleanliness and efficiency.

In contrast, Haas (1980) suggested that the dual-career lifestyle may help women achieve more power in the marital relationship. Haas interviewed 30 couples concerning their motives for choosing the dual-career lifestyle and the effects of career and monetary contribution on the distribution of marital power. Wives in this sample reported decreased resentment of their husband's power as a result of their own career. They also felt that they positively contributed to their economic status and hence, this gave them more marital power. Men reported that they benefited because their partner was able to share in the provider role (Haas).

Personal and Societal Views. Society seems to continue to uphold one traditional family structure while subtly degrading the dual-career lifestyle and working women, as evidenced by both major parties' presidential campaign platforms throughout the 1990s and a plethora of popular press stories. Dual-career couples have always had to be pioneers for alternative types of relationships. This could create increased stress as couples may have lacked role models or support from others for their relationship and work choices. As O'Neil, Fishman, and Kinsella-Shaw (1987, p. 51) note, "dual-career behavior deviates significantly from established norms in careers, marriage, family, and gender roles." However, dual-career couples seem to be able to integrate personal and societal views. Tobey (1981) found that dual-career couples are less likely to internalize negative attributions by family and society, and instead felt their own views about the dual-career lifestyle were more important than societal views.

Marital Distress

Dual-career couples continue to experience marital stress and women experience more distress than men do. Negative marital experiences are significantly associated with psychological distress for both men and women. Further, positive and negative experiences in marriages have similar effects on health of both males and females (Barnett et al., 1994). However, females continue to report higher levels of psychological distress than do men (Barnett et al., 1993). A female is likely to feel that her partner resents her work and the time she takes for herself, and is more likely to hold an internalized sense of blame for problems within both her intimate and general relationships (Bachelor, 1994).

While these studies suggest that marital distress is high in dual-career couples, they did not control for perceived equity, or relatively balanced costs and benefits, within the relationship. Women who perceived their dual-career relationship as equitable reported significantly higher levels of individual well-being and marital adjustment than women who did not perceive their relationship as equitable (Rachlin & Hansen, 1985). Therefore, if career women feel that their relationship is fair and egalitarian, they may experience less distress than women who do not work outside the home.

Second Shift for Women?

Overall, women still seem to be completing most of the household and care duties, although men perceive that they do their share or more than their share of housework (Bachelor, 1994; Barnett & Shen, 1997). Hochschild (1997) found in her longitudinal study that one in five men did as much work in their home as did their wives. Barnett and Shen (1997) reported that while wives agreed that their husbands were sharing child care responsibilities, they were not sharing equally in housework. Husbands tended to take on more family responsibilities only when the wife's job involved working overtime, long work hours, travel, or when the partners lived apart from each other (Bachelor, 1994; Barnett & Shen, 1997). Tobey (1981) also found that couples philosophically believed household and child care tasks should be shared equally. However, in reality, over half of these couples reported that the wife completed 75%-100% of household tasks and one-third reported that the wife was responsible for 75%-100% of child care. Husbands and wives more equally shared child care, but not household management, in only half of the couples. Respondents experienced significant work overload in relation to the time available to perform household management and child care duties (Tobey, 1981).

Assessing who completes certain household tasks may be a better barometer for sharing housework than looking at mean time spent working at home. Certain tasks such as cooking, cleaning, and grocery shopping are completed on a daily basis whereas other tasks such as repairing a car and mowing the lawn can be performed less frequently and with more discretion. Women in dual-career heterosexual couples reported spending significantly more time completing daily household tasks than their spouses, which was correlated with greater levels of psychological distress. Time spent in irregular activities, such as making house and car repairs, was not associated with psychological distress (Barnett & Shen, 1997).

One way to look at whether or not women and men experience a second-shift is to compare their out-of-home and at-home work schedules. Weingarten (1978) found that when males and females both continuously worked full-time, they more equally distributed housework with the exception of child care. When women worked part-time or discontinuously outside the home, the husband completed even fewer household tasks. Hochschild (1997) found that women work about a month per year more in their home than do their male partners. Based on this view of time, women are more likely than their male partners to have a daily second shift. Similarly, Barnett and Shen (1997) found that men worked more hours as paid labor in the workforce while women worked more hours in unpaid labor in the home, resulting in similar number of hours of work. Among couples employed full-time, husbands and wives each spent about 65 hours per week in paid and/or unpaid work. Even though obtaining similar results as Weingarten and Hochschild, Barnett and Shen concluded that because women and men were both working a similar amount of total hours, there was not a second shift for women.

However, Barnett and Shen (1997) failed to recognize that women's work, in addition to being unpaid, is unappreciated and unending. Domestic work is undervalued within our society, as indicated by the low wages and lack of benefits earned by those that complete this work. This societal depreciation lessens the likelihood that men will engage in domestic work while allowing them the power to assert that they need to earn money while women need to take care of the house (Hirsch & Newman, 1995). This ignores the fact that it is because women complete the unpaid labor of cooking, cleaning, and caretaking that men can work in paid positions. Further, men can leave their career duties behind at the end of the day while women live in their second job; thus this work is never completed. Finally, as housework does not provide a pension and can decrease Social Security benefits due to more zero-earning years, this unpaid labor contributes to the feminization of poverty in later life (Harrington Meyer, 1990). Thus, due to these factors and the results of the research on the completion of household duties in dual-career couples, it seems that there is a second shift for working women.

Communication

Overall, dual-career couples report positive communication with their partner. Working couples were likely to discuss work with their partners, especially interesting or entertaining events at work (Jones & Fletcher, 1993, 1996). Dual-career couples reported that they felt heard by their partner and had stimulating conversations with partner. Further, they were more likely to report greater communication, better listening skills, and better conflict resolution skills than traditional couples. Conversely, one career couples had more trouble communicating feelings. They felt less able to express themselves and felt that they were not listened to by their partner (Bachelor, 1994). Interestingly, bringing work home more frequently correlated with better communication for both males and females. Respondents reported that this was due to the partner being physically available while working at home (Litterest, 1983).

Couples reported that it was more difficult to discuss problems in their relationship when one or both partners were fatigued or when both partners were in poor health (Litterest, 1983). Fatigue was defined as a psychological and physical exhaustion that could come from a number of sources, including poor health, work overload, and family conflict. Litterest stated, "fatigue affects numerous communication-related functions such as social behavior, perception, reaction time, and information processing" (1983, p. 204). In relation to gender differences in communication, men experienced a significantly greater negative impact on communication skills when fatigued, meaning that they were less able to communicate when fatigued. Women's ability to communicate and problem solve was not affected by fatigue or they were more able to compensate for fatigue (Litterest, 1983). Men also thought that their wives did not want to hear about their feelings or want to listen when the men were upset (Bachelor, 1994). Both of these findings seem to indicate that males experience more distress in the realm of communication.

Communication also suffers when one member of the couple is in a negative mood or distressed from work. When a partner is in a bad mood, he or she is perceived by the other partner to be detached, preoccupied, and seeking to dump worries and frustration (Jones & Fletcher, 1996). Distress levels in the couple are also influenced by the type and amount of work related communication. Depressed men and women who discussed their work on a routine basis positively correlated with higher depression and anxiety levels in their partners (Jones & Fletcher, 1993). In a later study, Jones and Fletcher (1996) did not find this effect.

Strength and Resiliency Factors

Marital Satisfaction. Contrary to findings of early research, dual-career couples are as satisfied or more satisfied than traditional couples with both their careers and the quality of their marriage (Bachelor, 1994; Barnett et al., 1994; St. John-Parsons, 1978; Yogev, 1982). Dual-career couples, especially wives, reported more happiness than couples in which only one partner works (Yogev, 1982). Further, these couples reported a greater amount of intimacy and closeness in the marriage (Bachelor, 1994). While dual-career couples face overload, they feel that the intellectual and psychological benefits of the dual-career lifestyle outweigh these negative aspects (St. John-Parsons, 1978). Couples felt the dual-career lifestyle positively impacted their identity as an individual, marital partner, and parent (Tobey, 1981). Wives in single career marriages felt their husbands did not value their ability to contribute monetary resources while dual-career wives felt more valued in this aspect. One-career couples also perceived that their spouse was less likely to recognize or acknowledge their actions (Bachelor, 1994).

Dual-career couples were more differentiated than single career couples as they were more likely to "separate thought and feelings of self from other, to distinguish responsibility for self from the other, make independent choices, accept differences, and accept disagreement" (Bachelor, 1994, p. 146). These couples reported a strong sense of bonding and connection and reported having more fun together. They were also more likely than traditional couples to make financial and emotional resources available and negotiate to meet each other's needs (Bachelor).

Coping Mechanisms. Although coping mechanisms were not a focus of the research on dual-career couples, a few coping mechanisms were noted in this population. Jones and Fletcher (1993) looked at support as a coping mechanism and found that women had more sources of support from work, family, and friends, than men. Lack of social support for men was important, as men who were in demanding jobs with fewer sources of support transmitted this stress to their wives. Lower levels of support for men also correlated with greater levels of anxiety and depression in their wives (Jones & Fletcher).

Mishra and Bose (1997) found that older Indian men were more likely than younger Indian men to appraise experiences as less stressful and seek out information to change a behavior or problem. Coping mechanisms used by working women in India were not included in the study. In her longitudinal study, Hochschild (1997) found that couples constructed family myths, like who was naturally better at what, as a reason to choose to unequally divide labor by gender. Most recently, Zimmerman, Haddock, Current, Rust, and Ziemba (2000) derived a list of ten philosophies based on in-depth interviews of couples who described themselves as balancing family and work well. What was most striking about these complex and diverse philosophies was how committed and purposeful successful couples were about the importance of both their relationship and their careers.

IMPLICATIONS OF RESEARCH FOR THERAPISTS

The Need to Integrate Research into Therapy

As dual-career couples are becoming more prevalent, it is likely that marriage and family therapists will increasingly see these couples in treatment. The field of MFT began to address treatment issues in the early 1980s and 1990s. For example, Goldenberg and Goldenberg (1984) briefly outlined common strains dual-career couples face and present stress reduction strategies based upon the couple's communication and adaptation styles. Hoffman and Hoffman (1985) looked at husband-wife co-therapy teams and used their personal experience to highlight developmental tasks of dual-career couples. Sperry (1993) presented a clinically-based protocol for treating these couples. And feminist family therapists have been highlighting the connection between money and power in relationships for decades (e.g., Carter, 1988; Goodrich et al., 1988; McGoldrick, 1991; Walsh, 1989; Wheeler, Avis, Miller, & Chaney, 1986). Yet, while many clinician authors presented ideas for treating dual-career couples, they either neglected to cite the research of dual-career couples, or only tangentially referenced this body of research. Therefore, it is unclear how these treatment strategies match the actual strengths and stressors these couples face. One notable early exception was Holdner and Anderson's (1989) review in which they briefly talked about dual-career couple research that had been done and its implications for therapy. However, a majority of the research of the dyadic perspectives of dual-career couples and resulting implications for therapy have not yet been integrated into the professional discourse.

Looking at treatment research outside of MFT may also be invaluable for marriage and family therapy clinicians. Supplementing articles from social work and counseling provides a different perspective from the traditional systems literature. O'Neil, Fishman, and Shaw (1987) present some of the normative dilemmas and developmental issues, such as career development and gender role issues, that dual-career couples face. They suggest conjoint career counseling would help these couples negotiate these issues. Wilcox-Matthew and Minor (1989) highlight intrapersonal, societal, and organizational level issues for dual-career couples and counseling implications based upon these three areas. Finally, Jordan, Cobb, and McCully (1989) summarize career, household, and personal issues that dual-career couples face. They also give intervention suggestions for working with these couples, such as goal and value clarification, communication and skills training, and time management techniques. Each of these articles helps the therapist broaden the scope of treatment beyond just the family and here and now concerns to be more systemic in nature.

Integrating Research and Practice

Based upon the research on dual-career couples, there are a number of areas for intervention for both modifying stressors and facilitating strengths and coping mechanisms. As one primary assessment and intervention measure, therapists should identify and discuss household tasks. This should be done for a number of reasons. First, as shown in the research, women continue to complete disproportionately more housework and child care tasks than men. Second, time spent in household tasks is positively correlated with greater distress levels. This is especially true with ceaseless tasks such as cooking and cleaning. Third, household tasks become another work role; therefore, these tasks may interfere with both work and family roles and contribute to work overload. Finally, who decides the allocation of household tasks and who actually completes these tasks can be illuminating of power issues within the couple. Although the allocation and completion of household tasks has been extensively researched, this research has been neglected in therapeutic discussions of working with these couples. Therapists should instead consider the intersections of work and home as one of the first areas of assessment and discussion.

Therapists should also look for ways to encourage strengths and coping mechanisms within these couples. Dual-career couples "have few established guidelines to help them manage their multiple and sometimes conflicting roles and responsibilities" (O'Neil, Fishman, & Kinsella-Shaw, 1987, p. 51). They may face pressure from their family, friends, colleagues, and society in general regarding their career and family choices. As much of the research continues to focus on the stressors and distress levels of these couples, they may be discouraged about their relationship choice. Therapists can help counteract these negative images by presenting information on the strengths of dual-career couples, such as good communication skills, greater intimacy, increased resources, and the ability to ignore negative societal views. Therapists can also help dual-career couples discover their unique coping mechanisms. For example, as shown by research, these couples may be more adept at seeking out information to problem solve or finding alternate sources of support. These coping mechanisms can be built upon to help the dual-career couple manage daily stresses.

RESEARCH GAPS AND SUGGESTIONS
FOR FURTHER RESEARCH

While there is considerable research on these couples, there are gaps that need to be addressed in order for therapists to fully understand couples' needs. As we touched on earlier, there is a definite lack of research focusing on non-Caucasian dual-career couples and couples from different cultures. The majority of research included in this article was conducted on white, middle-class, American couples. Only two research articles focused on couples from different cultures (Aryee et al., 1999; Mishra & Bose, 1997). However, couples from other cultures may have different experiences due to differing traditions and norms. Aryee and associates (1999, p. 261) state, "it is critical to examine (conflict) within cultures other than that of the United States." Second, there is also a lack of research on cohabiting couples and gay and lesbian couples. Many of the studies limited the sample to married, heterosexual couples. Other studies that included non-married couples had such a small sample of these couples that the authors grouped them with married couples (Barnett et al., 1993; Barnett et al., 1994). Homosexual and non-married couples may face different dilemmas, such as societal and family pressures. Third, much of this research was conducted from the late 1970s to the mid 1990s. It would be interesting to see if the findings have changed over time as society has changed.

Research continues to focus on problems and stressors faced by dual-career couples versus the resiliency factors, coping mechanisms, and sources of support used by these couples. Focusing on these areas would be important as research seems to indicate that the use of coping mechanisms reduce the perception of work overload and stress in working couples (Jones & Fletcher, 1993; Mishra & Bose, 1997). Further, the lack of coping mechanisms and social support leads to transmission of stress and distress to the partner (Jones & Fletcher, 1993). Clearly, more research needs to focus not only on studying coping mechanisms and resiliency factors, but also on actively building these mechanisms and social supports.

CONCLUSION

As evidenced by the research, dual-career couples experience a myriad of unique stressors and strengths. Dual-career couples seem to face normative concerns in the realms of work overload, balancing work and family roles, including housework, mobilizing social supports, and integrating individual identity concerns. These couples are able to balance power differentials in their relationships, likely as a result of the wage-earning power of the women, and are also able to balance societal norms with their own personal views. Dual-career couples also seem to have good communication patterns, except when fatigued or distressed. Finally, these couples report greater marital satisfaction and differentiation and are likely to use social support and information seeking as coping mechanisms.

As therapists will likely work with dual-career couples, it becomes necessary to understand the research on these couples in order to treat within their scope of practice. Rather than provide a treatment plan or interventions for these couples, this article summarizes research in order to inform clinical practice. Marriage and family therapists should then use this information to create their own treatment plan tailored to the individual couple.

REFERENCES

Aryee, S., Luk, V., Leung, A., & Lo, S. (1999). Role stressors, interrole conflict, and well-being: The moderating influence of spousal support and coping behaviors among employed parents in Hong Kong. *Journal of Vocational Behavior, 54,* 259-278.

Bachelor, J. R. (1994). *A comparative study of gender differences in the interactions of traditional, dual-career, and commuter marriages.* Unpublished Doctoral Dissertation, Pacific School of Psychology, Palo Alto, CA.

Barnett, R. C., & Brennan, R. T. (1997). Changes in job conditions change in psychological distress, and gender: A longitudinal study of dual-earner couples. *Journal of Organizational Behavior, 18,* 253-274.

Barnett, R. C., & Shen Y. C. (1997). Gender, high- and low-schedule-control housework tasks, and psychological distress: A study of dual-earner couples. *Journal of Family Issues, 18*(4), 403-428.

Barnett, R. C., Brennan, R. T., Raudenbush, S. W., & Marshall, N. L. (1994). Gender and the relationship between marital-role quality and psychological distress: A study of women and men in dual-earner couples. *Psychology of Women Quarterly, 18,* 105-127.

Barnett, R. C., Marshall, N. L., Raudenbush, S. W., & Brennan, R. T. (1993). Gender and the relationship between job experiences and psychological distress: A study of dual-earner couples. *Journal of Personality and Social Psychology, 64*(5), 794-806.

Carter, B. (1988). The person who has the gold makes the rules. In M. Walters, B. Carter, P. Papp, & O. Silverstein (Eds.), *The invisible web: Gender patterns in family relationships* (pp. 237-241). New York: Guilford.

Douglas, J. (1997, August 4). Cold comfort for working moms. *U.S. News & World Report [online],* Available: *http://www.usnews.com/usnews/issue/4out1.htm*

Goldner, V. (1985). Feminism and family therapy. *Family Process, 24,* 31-47.

Goodrich, T. J., Rampage, C., Ellman, B., & Halstead, K. (1988). *Feminist family therapy: A casebook.* New York: W. W. Norton.

Haas, L. (1980). Role sharing couples: A study of egalitarian marriages. *Family Relations, 29,* 289-296.

Hare-Mustin, R. T. (1978). A feminist approach to family therapy. *Family Process, 17,* 181-194.

Hare-Mustin, R. T. (1986). The problem of gender in family therapy. *Family Process, 26,* 15-27.

Harrington Meyer, M. (1990). Family status and poverty among older women: The gendered distribution of retirement income in the United States. *Social Problems, 37,* 551-563.

Hirsch, C., & Newman, J. L. (1995). Microstructural and gender role influences on male caregivers. *The Journal of Men's Studies, 3*(4), 309-333.

Hochschild, A. R. (1997). *The second shift.* New York: Avon.

Hoffman, L. W., & Hoffman, H. J. (1985). The lives and adventures of dual-career couples. *Family Therapy, 12*(2), 123-149.

Holdner, D., & Anderson, C. (1989). Women, work, and the family. In M. McGoldrick, C. M. Anderson, & F. Walsh (Eds.), *Women in families: A framework for family therapy* (pp. 357-380). New York: W. W. Norton.

Jones, F., & Fletcher, B. C. (1996). Taking work home: A study of daily fluctuations in work stressors, effects on moods, and impacts on marital partners. *Journal of Occupational and Organizational Psychology, 69*(1), 89-106.

Jones, F., & Fletcher, B. C. (1993). An empirical study of occupational stress transmission in working couples. *Human Relations, 46*(7), 881-903.

Jordan, C., Cobb, N., & McCully, R. (1989). Clinical issues of the dual-career couple. *Social Work, 34*(1), 29-32.

Litterest, J. K. (1983). *The impact of fatigue on communication: A study of the dual-career lifestyle.* Unpublished Doctoral Dissertation, University of Minnesota, Minneapolis, MN.

McGoldrick, M. (1991). For love or money. In T. J. Goodrich (Ed.), *Women and power* (pp. 239-262). New York: W. W. Norton.

Mishra, P. K., & Bose, R. (1997). A study on career couples. *Social Science Journal, 13*(1-2), 31-41.

O'Neil, J. M., Fishman, D. M., & Kinsella-Shaw, M. (1987). Dual-career couples' career transitions and normative dilemmas. *The Counseling Psychologist, 15*(1), 50-96.

Orden, S. R., & Bradburn, N. M. (1969). Working wives and marriage happiness. *American Journal of Sociology, 74*(4), 392-407.

Potucheck, J. (1997). *Who supports the family? Gender and breadwinning in dual-earner marriages.* Stanford: Stanford University.

Rachlin, V. C., & Hansen, J. C. (1985). The impact of equity or egalitarianism on dual-career couples. *Family Therapy, 12*(2), 151-164.

Rapoport, R., & Rapoport, R. N. (1971). *Dual-career families.* Harmondsworth, England: Penguin.

Rapoport, R., & Rapoport, R. (1969). The dual career family: A variant pattern and social change. *Human Relations, 22*, 3-30.

Sekaran, U. (1985). The paths to mental health: An exploratory study of husbands and wives in dual-career families. *Journal of Occupational Psychology, 58*, 129-137.

Simon, R. (1992). Parental role strains, salience of parental identity and gender differences in psychological distress. *Journal of Health and Social Behavior, 33*, 25-35.

Sperry, L. (1993). Tailoring treatment with dual-career couples. *American Journal of Family Therapy, 21*(1), 51-59.

St. John-Parsons, D. (1978). Continuous career families: A case study. In J. B. Bryson & R. Bryson (Eds.), Dual career couples. New York: Human Sciences Press.

Stanfield, J. B. (1998). Couples coping with dual careers: A description of flexible and rigid coping styles. *Social Science Journal, 35*(1), 53-64.

Tobey, C. L. (1982). *A descriptive study of dual-career couples and stress.* Unpublished Doctoral Dissertation, West Virginia University, Morgantown, WV.

Walsh, F. (1989). Reconsidering gender in the marital quid pro quo. In M. McGoldrick, C. Anderson, & F. Walsh (Eds.), *Women in families: A framework for family therapy* (pp. 267-285). New York: W. W. Norton.

Walters, M., Carter, B., Papp, P., & Silverstein, O. (1988). *The invisible web.* New York: Guilford.

Weingarten, K. (1978). The employment patterns of professional couples and their distribution of involvement in the family. In J. B. Bryson & R. Bryson (Eds.), *Dual-career couples.* New York: Human Sciences Press.

Wheeler, D., Avis, J., Miller, L., & Chaney, S. (1986). Rethinking family therapy training and supervision: A feminist model. *Journal of Psychotherapy and the Family*,
1, 53-72.

Yogev, S. (1988). Relationships between stress and marital satisfaction among dual-
earner couples. *Women & Therapy*, *5*(2-3), 313-330.

Yogev, S., & Brett, J. (1985). Patterns of work and family involvement among single
and dual earner couples. *Journal of Applied Psychology*, *70*(4), 754-768.

Zimmerman, T. S., Haddock, S., Current, L., Rust, A., & Ziemba, S. (2000, November). *Balancing family and work*. Workshop presented at the annual meeting of the
American Association for Marriage and Family Therapy, Denver, CO.

Index